17/12/2022

Please return/renew this item by the
last date shown to avoid a charge.
Books may also be renewed by phone
and Internet.  May not be renewed if
required by another reader.

**www.libraries.barnet.gov.uk**

3013

D1348664

**LONDON BOROUGH OF BARNET**

HOW WOMEN CAN SAVE THE PLA

ANNE KARPF

# How Women Can Save the Planet

HURST & COMPANY, LONDON

First published in the United Kingdom in 2021 by
C. Hurst & Co. (Publishers) Ltd.,
83 Torbay Road, London NW6 7DT
Copyright © Anne Karpf, 2021
All rights reserved.
Printed in Great Britain by Bell and Bain Ltd, Glasgow

The right of Anne Karpf to be identified as the author of
this publication is asserted by her in accordance with the
Copyright, Designs and Patents Act, 1988.

A Cataloguing-in-Publication data record for this book
is available from the British Library.

ISBN: 9781787384613

This book is printed using paper from registered sustainable
and managed sources.

www.hurstpublishers.com

*For Bianca and Lola*

# CONTENTS

PART TWO
WOMEN AND CLIMATE JUSTICE

# ACKNOWLEDGEMENTS

This book was written over a very short period of time, but its roots stretch back far. It was conversations with John Percival in the 1970s that first started me thinking about the environmental costs of unfettered economic growth. In the 1980s, the expertise of my fellow members of the Politics of Health Group, along with my postgraduate degree in the sociology of health and illness, helped develop my understanding of the social and environmental causes of ill health. I learned first-hand about collective action through joining the mass women's protests at Greenham Common (somewhere in the vaults of Granada Television, there's some archive footage of me with a dodgy haircut, presenting an edition of *What the Papers Say* in which I rage about the tabloid reporting of those protests).

In conversations over the years, Mayer Hillman drove home to me quite how urgent the climate situation was, while talking to and reading Sally Weintrobe enabled me to glimpse how and why I and others were so strongly resisting the work of facing up to it.

# ACKNOWLEDGEMENTS

This book was written during lockdown(s), when I've been teaching and supervising at London Metropolitan University remotely. While I was trying to support them, my MA and PhD students were generously encouraging me back. I also want to thank my colleagues Matthew Barac, Jenny Harding, Anna Kamyk and Gian Carlo Rossi for making things easier for me whenever they could; and Vice-Chancellor Lynn Dobbs for her personal support over the past two years.

A pool of brilliant feminist climate scholars has been working in this field for nearly two decades. I've been inspired by the pioneering research of, among others, Ulrike Röhr, Seema Arora-Jonsson, Gerd Johnsson-Latham, Joni Seager, Susan Buckingham, Irene Dankelman, Greta Gaard, Bernadette Resurrección— and in particular Sherilyn MacGregor.

Many of the ideas in this book were first articulated in articles for *The Guardian*. I want to thank the editors who commissioned them, including Katharine Viner, Becky Gardiner, Katherine Butler, Sonia Sodha and Alison Benjamin.

I'm so grateful to my interviewees for their involvement in this project. When there were already so many competing demands on their time, Jacqui Patterson, Tracy Kajumba, Adenike Oladosu, Maureen Damen, Bindu Bhandari, Kathrin Gutmann and Licypriya Kangujam battled through sometimes-temperamental Zoom connections to talk to me about their concerns and campaigns. The eight women whose stories are woven through the book worked closely with me as I greatly condensed their interviews for clarity and length. Thank you so much Aneesa Khan, Ama Francis, Scarlett Westbrook, Rosmarie Wydler-Wälti, Bridget Burns, Stella Nyambura Mbau, Annette Wallgren and Daze Aghaji for participating so enthusiastically, and for responding so uncomplainingly to my torrent of emails.

I want to thank my agent, Tracy Bohan of the Wylie Agency, several times over for her tireless support and help in finding the right home for this book. At Hurst I've been enormously fortunate to have, in Lara Weisweiller-Wu, an outstanding editor. In sympathy with the book's ideas, and working with tremendous flexibility around my scarily tight schedule, she pushed me to develop my thinking, and again and again helped me frame the argument more effectively. Her scores of smart suggestions have made this a much more robust and expansive book. Thanks, too, to Alice Clarke for brilliant fact-checking, Susan Boxall for brilliant proof-reading and to production director Daisy Leitch for turning around this book in record time.

Lockdown was made easier by the genial presence of Joshua Flack, and by Nikki Jackson's twice-weekly Pilates classes—exercising and groaning with my fellow class members, remotely but together.

My friends have been a fabulous support. Thank you, Lennie Goodings and Katina Noble, for cheering me on.

# ACKNOWLEDGEMENTS

Caroline Pick and Barbara Rosenbaum: your lovely texts and our weekly conversations played a vital role in helping me over the finishing line.

My daughters have been integral to this project. Bianca, under great work pressure herself, read the first three chapters and gave me invaluable feedback. Her constant interest and unwavering support buoyed me up more than she knows. Before I'd even started to write, Lola, a climate campaigner herself, fed me a stream of terrific suggestions. She read the entire manuscript, and her detailed comments on every page, both critical and enthusiastic, proved absolutely indispensable: she has hugely enhanced the book.

And finally, I'll never be able to thank Peter Lewis enough for the profoundly generous way he sustained me through the writing of this book, with his domestic labour and humour, his encouragement and love. He embodies, beautifully, men's capacity for care.

Anne Karpf
London, February 2021

# INTRODUCTION

The late, great American writer Audre Lorde coined the phrase the "mythical norm" to mean a person who was white, thin, male, heterosexual, Christian and financially secure (everything that Lorde wasn't).[1] For a long time, the mythical norm has hovered over the climate crisis, enlightening us about what caused it, how it affects us and how to solve it. Discussions in public, parliaments and the media have persisted in treating the environment in this gender-neutral—which is to say gender-blind—way.

Sometimes the mythical norm becomes an actual embodied man, openly leading the climate conversation. It's all about the species, he tells us, the human species—issues around gender are nothing but a distraction from the catastrophe unfolding before our eyes. Put aside your special pleading, your individual sense of grievance—there'll be time enough for them later, but this thing is bigger than all of us; it needs unity and not separatism.

On every count, this turns out to be wrong. A wealth of research, carried out over nearly two decades, shows that women are affected by the climate crisis in power-fully distinct ways. And if you don't recognise the role that gender plays in causing the climate emergency, especially when it intersects with race, you stray far from solutions that work and risk getting enticed by those that don't. For the climate emergency looks different when you view it through the lens of gender;[2] and gender looks different if you view it through the lens of the climate emergency.

Men are seen as the prototype, the reference point, the standard—able to speak on behalf of all humanity; while women are regarded as a variant who can speak purely on their own account.[3] Because of this, 'gender' has come to be used as a euphemism for 'women'—as though only women are gendered. What gender really describes, though, is how ideas about masculinity *and* femininity shape our everyday lives—our expectations of ourselves and others; the conventions, roles and practices that govern our relationships; and how we fulfil them in school and college, within the family and at work. In our identities and our institutions, gender and the climate crisis are laced together.

Let me tell you what this book isn't about. You won't be reading here about the speed with which the Arctic ice is melting, the effect of plastic on sea turtles, or the climate-linked breeding struggles of the humpback whale. Not because disasters-in-progress like these aren't important or tragic—they are, but they've already been described eloquently by others, like David Wallace-Wells,[4] or shown in ultra-high definition on television. I'm also wary of adding to the apocalypse-porn genre of climate writing—those books and articles that, when they're not sounding biblically punitive, seem almost erotic in the masochistic relish with which they portray the destruction awaiting us. I'm a 'pessoptimist' myself, and prefer a little uplift stirred into my doom. I also don't want to be terrified before breakfast.

My focus here is exclusively on human beings, who sometimes get edged out of our climate concern by polar bears and other fluffy creatures—maybe because the climate narrative is controlled by people in the global North, many of whom find it easier to empathise with cute white animals than with people who have black or brown skin.

(This brings me to terminology. I use 'global North' and 'global South' in this book, rather than talking about 'developed and developing nations'. The northern hemisphere is generally wealthier than the southern one, but the 'global North' also includes countries like Australia and New Zealand that lie in the geographic south. My chosen terms are imperfect, because they ignore differences between and within countries in the same category, but they're commonly used and widely understood, and the alternatives also come up short.)

There's also no advice in these pages about how to shop green, wear green, eat green or die green. A whole load of that already exists too, an awful lot of it targeted at women. For years now, feminist climate scholars have been describing this as the 'feminisation of responsibility'. The idea of 'everyone doing their bit' suggests that each bit is roughly equal, or equally small—another of the corporate lies that landed us in such a mess in the first place, and which I unpick here, looking at how cheery pieces of nonsense like this have been gendered and racialised.

Of course none of us should be living as if there's no tomorrow, because this will play some part in hastening such a scenario; but the enormous focus on the role of consumer choices in raising or reducing carbon emissions is frankly designed (and I don't normally subscribe to conspiracy theories) to distract us from its real causes. I've come to the conclusion that, for this reason, green shopping advice—although I've dipped into it myself now and then, and sometimes found it useful—is actively harmful.

This book also isn't about women as victims. It's striking how often the fragility of the climate gets projected onto women or appears to have been located in their bodies. Equally seductive, but wrong-headed, is the idea that womankind-as-superhero will save us all from destruction—over to you, girls!

So why the title? Well, *Gender inequality has helped cause the climate crisis and you need gender equality to help solve it* hardly trips off the tongue. Nevertheless, this book makes perfectly clear—on every page, I hope—that in no way do I task women alone with saving the planet. Indeed I actively recoil from such a stance. The question of the book's title reminds me of an American book about community radio called *Sex and Broadcasting* (1975). You reach page 351, the final page, with no hint of carnal knowledge nor even the odd flirtation having popped up along the way, only to find in the final sentence this confession: "I really wanted you to buy this book and my Great Aunt Beulah convinced me that a book with the word *Sex* in its title would double its sales, and quadruple its readership."[5]

We are living through what Jacqui Patterson, Environmental and Climate Justice Program Director at the NAACP (National Association for the Advancement of Colored People), calls a "syndemic"—not a single pandemic, but a convergence of three global emergencies at once.[6]

First came a sharp rise in awareness about the climate crisis, set off in 2019 by mass demonstrations by Extinction Rebellion and the school climate strikers, led by girls and young women. In October of that year, a survey of 2,000 of them, aged 14–22, found two thirds "very" or "extremely" anxious about the planet.[7] You could call this an appropriate reaction—realistic, even; it also fits in with other studies' findings that women are more anxious about the climate crisis than men.[8] Perhaps it's their anxiety that turns them into activists, although it's possible that their activism—temporarily, at least—might have increased their anxiety: the more they learn about global heating, the scarier it becomes, even though many young activists say that taking part in activism modifies their anxiety, rather than intensifies it.

Barely had school climate strikes got into their stride before Covid-19 arrived in early 2020. Then, in late May, the structural and racial inequalities that were causing so many black deaths from the virus were crystallised dramatically in the single, filmed event that was George Floyd's death, triggering huge Black Lives Matter demonstrations across the globe. As Patterson put it, "The great awakening on racism is really just an awakening of the rest of society, because for us [people of colour], it's not changed. It's just televised."[9]

This trio of crises didn't just randomly coincide; they were connected. "Climate change is not the problem," as a Peruvian activist put it, "but a symptom."[10] As were the pandemic and the Floyd protests. People of colour are more likely to live in areas of high air pollution,[11] which exacerbates breathing difficulties; even a small increase in exposure to air pollution is thought to heighten your risk of dying from Covid.[12] "I can't breathe," Floyd cried out, twenty times before he had no breath left—echoing not just Eric Garner, as he too lay dying six years earlier in a police chokehold, but also the Covid patient struggling for air.

The thread joining together the three emergencies of 2020–21 is inequality—racial, gender and social inequality. If you're a woman of colour, you're more likely than anyone else to have lost your job in the pandemic,[13] and more likely to die of Covid than a white woman.[14] Like black and brown men, you'll be on intimate terms with racism. And as for the climate crisis, the pages that follow here will unfurl the story of how women of colour and Indigenous women are the ones most likely to suffer the harshest effects of carbon emissions, which they have done least to cause.

When President Joe Biden appointed Gina McCarthy as the first White House National Climate Advisor, one of the first things she did was to home in on these links. "Climate change is a racial justice issue," she said, "because it exacerbates the challenges in the communities that have been left behind. It goes after the same communities that pollution has held back and racism has held back."[15]

This book is divided in two. Part One covers the problems in the relationship between women and the climate crisis. It starts by documenting the ways in which the climate emergency impacts upon women's lives, directly (Chapter 1) and indirectly (Chapter 2). Chapter 3 explores the gendered causes of global heating, and Chapter 4 some of the belief systems driving them, as well as alternative gender cultures that challenge this. Despite all of this evidence that gender is at the heart of climate breakdown, Chapter 5 shows how women have been marginalised, if not excluded, from the negotiations and summits where climate policy is thrashed out. As the economist Kate Raworth has pointed out, this risks turning what's often called the Anthropocene—the era of human impact on the eco-system—into a Manthropocene.[16]

Part Two turns to solutions, celebrating in Chapter 6 the campaigners pushing for change in the global South and North and in Chapter 7 the schemes and politicians making it happen. Chapter 8 asks what it would look like if we expanded these gender-just climate solutions into a Global New Deal for Women, and what's blocking that from happening. Finally, the conclusion explores how near or far we are from that vision today, and the causes for optimism.

Sandwiched between each chapter—the filling, if you like—are testimonies that have resulted from my extended interviews with eight women. Lawyers, scientists, campaigners, environmental project workers, even a schoolgirl, they describe in their own words how and why they became climate activists, and what they're doing to try and arrest global heating.

They speak about the hard realities of the climate emergency without flinching, but they also sing their way through the book in an inspiring aria of hope.

# PART ONE

# WOMEN AND THE CLIMATE CRISIS

# ANEESA KHAN, 25, INDIA/USA/UK

*I was born in Chennai, India, but grew up in Oman. About 80 per cent of Oman's GDP is based on the fossil fuel industry—it's cheaper to fill up your car there than to drink water.*

*I was told, "If you recycle, if you use the right light bulbs, if you do all these small individual actions, you will save the planet"—when in reality it's so much more of a collaborative thing that also involves questioning the power of the fossil fuel industry, of government.*

*[Aneesa studied at the College of the Atlantic in Maine, joining a youth climate justice collective called Earth in Brackets, "because when in the UN climate negotiations they can't decide on a word in the text, it gets put in brackets".] It was an amazing but also disheartening experience to go every year to the UN climate conferences and see the same thing—global North negotiators, saying, "Yes, we caused climate change, but now it's a shared responsibility." Not being naive, I understood that this was more a diplomatic process than anything else, but while they're negotiating the nitty-gritty details of a UN text, time is passing*

*superfast, and frontline communities are saying, "Our families are already dying."*

*I was in Paris when the Paris Agreement came out, actually in the room when it was gavelled through, and at the same time a massive hurricane hit Chennai, where my parents were living. Three hundred people died in the city, our house flooded, I lost contact with my parents for a few days—it was really scary. And I remember thinking, "I don't understand what I'm doing in this room, watching all these negotiations happen when the climate crisis is very real outside these doors."*

*After I graduated, I moved to DC and worked with the Navajo tribe on the phasing out of coal mines. How does a community that, for economic reasons, has been made dependent on a dirty energy source move away from that? How do we recreate jobs, retrain them? I also started working with SustainUS, the only organisation that sends young people from the US to the UN climate conferences—currently I'm the executive director.*

*I was selected to lead our delegation to the 2018 UN climate conference in Katowice, Poland. I said I wanted our first delegation to be mainly youth of colour and Indigenous youth: it felt very important that people who are on the frontlines of crisis are also at the forefront of change. While we were there, the Trump administration put on a panel about how fossil fuels are still part of the solution to climate change, which was kind of wild to me— that they showed up after pulling out of the Paris*

*Agreement and spending millions of dollars denying climate change. So we disrupted them, we occupied their room with 300 people and stood up, took over the stage, put up our own speakers and highlighted stories from Indigenous communities, immigrant communities and queer communities in the US and the global South instead.*

**How much do you feel your activism is connected to your position as a young woman of colour?**

*Oh, massively.*

*The level of injustice that I see, and how it impacts my family, my country, people I care about, other people who look like me—it feels like a very harsh lived reality. I was in India for seven months in 2019 and we went through a drought, we didn't have water for months. We were collecting water every day in a bucket, people were fighting over water, and it's just a small picture of what the world is going to look like when we don't have access to the things we need to live—an entire city of millions of people ran out of water. And by 2030, 40 per cent of India won't have access to drinking water. That's 40 per cent of a billion people.*

*That's not far in the future—that's in my young lifetime, I'll be in my thirties. I remember thinking, "I don't think I should bring a child into this world, no matter how much I want this." Then someone said to me, "Why are you working on climate justice if you're not working for all the things you want—families, health, safe air and safe cities? Why are you fighting for these, if you're just going to give up on what you want as well?" And that really shifted the perspective for me.*

*I'm working for another organisation called Oil Change International on exposing the true cost of fossil fuels. The climate crisis doesn't have any borders. For example, if a Green New Deal comes into being in the US, does that mean that all the non-renewable-energy materials will be mined in Jamaica or other countries in the global South, and we'll continue to exploit them while developed countries have their new green revolution?*

*Progressive welfare initiatives like the Green New Deal often end up creating policies that just sustain capitalism and injustice, because they have to pass through a political process. Market-based solutions to climate change, things like carbon trading, basically just export your difficulty somewhere else. To me, carbon trading [a scheme through which a country or company can buy the right to higher carbon emissions by purchasing additional allowance from emitters below the limit] is like paying someone to go to the gym on the other side of the world for you to lose weight.*

*That's a conversation a lot of progressive leftist groups around the world have started having: what does a Green New Deal look like globally? And what does recovery from the corona pandemic look like? Because it's a drill for what the climate crisis is going to look like. How do we come out of this with the public healthcare and welfare that we need for a green recovery?*

## ANEESA KHAN, 25, INDIA/USA/UK

*I want a Green New Deal to talk about all the unseen, unpaid work that women do, in families and outside of families, and how we are going to support them financially to do this caretaking work.*

1

# ON THE FRONTLINE

## HOW THE CLIMATE CRISIS IS HARMING WOMEN

It's dawn, but the women are already up and on the road.

Margaret Atiir, a 40-year-old mother of four from Kapua, Kenya, describes her daily trek to collect water: "I have to walk four kilometres from my home to the well just to fill a twenty litre bucket. I ... make several trips to have enough water for my children. Some days I'm too weak to go so we either borrow from our neighbors, or wait until I'm strong enough."[1]

In Afdera, north-east Ethiopia, where Fatuma lives, it's a similar story: there's no fresh water for 200 kilometres. "All my life, since I was a young girl, I walked miles every day for water. The only time I had a day off were on the days I gave birth. We would get up at dawn, and return at midday." Fatuma has carried, on her back, up to 30 kilos at a time—the equivalent of a British luggage allowance for a long-haul flight.[2] Also in Ethiopia, Aysha, 13 years old, leaves home at 6.30am every day for an 8-hour round trip to collect water, with just her camel for company.[3]

Margaret, Fatuma and Aysha are water pilgrims. They're responsible for meeting the daily drinking, cooking and washing needs of their family—a job that costs women and children around the world 200 million hours a day,[4] and which can use up nearly one third of their daily calorie intake.[5] And climate change has made the chore unimaginably harder. In southern Mozambique, for example, women and girls used to spend 2 to 5 hours a day fetching water. Now, because of drought intensified by the climate crisis, these trips often take them 10 to 12 hours.[6] The longer journeys carrying heavy pots can damage their spines, neck muscles and lower backs,[7] while also causing chronic fatigue, pelvic deformities and miscarriages. To make it back in time even though they have further to travel, they set out earlier in the morning, in the dark—leaving them open to sexual attacks.

The 'we're all in it together' slogan of some climate campaigners is curiously reassuring, as though global warming were a sort of secret socialist, bestowing its damage on everyone equally and in the same way. On first thought, it seems perverse to believe otherwise: don't men and women breathe the same air, drink the same water, eat the same food? Surely the climate can't search out one gender and select them for especially brutal treatment?

No, the climate doesn't do this; but human societies do. Rules and roles, norms and divisions of labour mean that, both in the global South but also in the global North, women's lives and experiences differ from men's in a bundle of different ways. The climate emergency then swells these differences, multiplying and amplifying inequalities already bedded in. This chapter explores some of the direct and demonstrable ways that women's lives are changed, often dramatically, by global heating and the disasters it provokes, while the next chapter shows some of its many profound, but indirect, effects on them.

The climate crisis is no abstract concept for women in the global South. The long-term changes it is bringing to their environments are reflected in long-term changes to their lifestyles, making them even more taxing. Because of the work that they do, women are the ones shouldering many of the burdens that have come with global heating.

Women, for instance, are usually responsible for collecting and burning the wood, charcoal and animal dung (sometimes called solid fuel) for cooking and heating. Burning solid fuels damages women's health: we associate air pollution with cities choking on carbon monoxide from cars, or industrial plants belching out toxic fumes—not with rural residential cooking—yet indoor air pollution prematurely kills around 3.8 million people a year,[8] and women are more exposed to household air pollution than men. They breathe in the smoke generated by burning firewood or coal, charcoal, animal dung or kerosene while preparing meals, often in small and poorly ventilated rooms.[9]

This increases women's risk of respiratory infections and of having a low-birthweight baby.[10] Nearly half a million newborn babies died in 2019 from air pollution, two thirds of them from household air pollution caused by their mothers' and their own exposure to solid fuels burnt for cooking.[11] There's a terrible postscript to this: Covid-19 is a respiratory disease, and you are more likely to contract it if you have been exposed to air pollution, or suffer from the conditions pollution often brings in its wake—diabetes, cardiovascular disease and chronic obstructive lung disease.[12]

Global heating has added to the harms women suffer in their role as keepers of the household's fuel. Collecting fuel is as time-sapping as collecting water: in South Asia, women can spend more than 20 hours a week on the task.[13] And, as with water, so with firewood: deforestation driven by heat, drought and illegal logging—all linked to the climate crisis—means that women now have to travel further just to gather the essentials they need.[14] To obtain energy for cooking and heating, women have to expend more of their own. There's an additional sting here too: burning biomass fuels contributes to deforestation, itself a major cause of climate change, and so women are bound, unavoidably, into a grim and growing cycle: because of the climate crisis, they're making longer journeys to find the fuel which, when it's burnt, aggravates the crisis, therefore making their journeys even longer...

The climate crisis changes the lives not only of women, but of girls too, since it's mostly girls and not boys who are called upon to share these essential daily tasks. Global warming makes poor women and girls time-poorer. Because of these demands, they often have to drop out of primary school, and can't go to evening classes or participate in communal activities. And so the cycles of marginalisation and exclusion are perpetuated.

## Disasters discriminate

The language around climate change can conceal as much as it reveals. As commentators like Amartya Sen have observed, there's nothing 'natural' about natural disasters: they may occur in nature, but 'nature' itself didn't cause them. For large stretches of time, these climate-induced changes to daily life are gradual—until they accelerate, and climax in catastrophe. Disasters are mostly just the tail end of creeping environmental degradation, even though they're often portrayed as something that arrived out of nowhere, something elemental and inescapable—an event in their own right, unconnected to what went before or what comes after. Of course the climate crisis isn't the sole cause of extreme weather events like tropical cyclones, heatwaves, drought or apocalyptic wildfires; but it's almost certainly made them more frequent and more intense. Floods, for example, are having increasingly catastrophic effects because of the rise in sea levels.

The impact of the climate crisis on the natural world and biodiversity is widely known now, but some of its consequences on the human, social world—and especially on women and girls—are only just becoming apparent. Until recently, it was assumed, in public debate at least, that disasters like these didn't discriminate—that this, surely, was the whole point of them: they tear through entire communities bringing random, universal destruction. Yet there's now reams of evidence to show that women are affected by disasters in different ways from men. Again, this isn't because cyclones and floods single out women in some bizarrely vengeful way, but because these catastrophic events aggravate and multiply the gender inequalities that existed before they struck: their impact falls upon real, embodied human beings, situated in communities where social roles bring unequal power.

Disasters overwhelm not just the land women live on, but also their capacity to escape and save themselves. Women and children are fourteen times more likely than men to die in climate disasters like floods and drought, especially in the global South.[15] In India, Sri Lanka and Indonesia, Oxfam found, far more men survived the

2004 Asian tsunami than women.[16] A staggering ninety per cent of the 140,000 Bangladeshis who died in the 1991 cyclone were women.[17] Nor is this phenomenon confined to the global South: of the more than 70,000 people who died over two months from the severe heatwave that hit Europe in 2003, nearly two thirds were women.[18]

The after-effects of climate change-induced disasters also fall differently on men and women. In the chaos after a hurricane, families get separated, leaving women and girls more vulnerable to offers of help that can end in their being sexually trafficked. This phenomenon, known as 'hurricane trafficking', happened after Typhoon Haiyan hit the Philippines in 2013,[19] and migration induced by climate change is predicted to ramp it up even more.[20]

And then there's child marriage. The climate emergency is creating a new generation of child brides, and that number is now predicted to increase by 2.5 million over the next five years because of the hardship resulting from Covid-19—the greatest surge in a quarter-century.[21] In countries like Malawi and Mozambique, climate disasters bring so much extra poverty that families have no choice but to arrange quick marriages for their young daughters.[22] The risk of domestic violence increases if there's a large age gap between husband and wife, but child marriage is an economic survival strategy for struggling households—there's just not enough food to go round. "This is a place affected by river erosion," Azima B's parents told her, explaining why she had to marry at 13. "If the river takes our house it will be hard for you to get married so it's better if you get married now."[23]

Ill health caused by the climate crisis is also gendered: women, young and old, are especially affected by global heating, which is having a profound effect on food security—degrading the land, leading to desertification, decreased yields and food shortages.[24] When food is in short supply, women eat least and last.[25] And, of course, cyclones, hurricanes and floods bring in their wake water-borne diseases like malaria, cholera and diarrhoea. Whenever families get sick, the responsibility of caring for them falls, inevitably, on women. The care tasks—tending to young children and old relatives; seeking out medicinal plants as well as food, fuel and water; upkeep of the home; myriad other daily invisible micro-tasks where love meets duty—are essential, but also taken for granted. And the climate crisis makes all of them harder.

If, amid all this care for others, the women themselves fall ill, they will have greater difficulty accessing medical facilities: older women in particular often can't afford to pay for medicines or visits to clinics, or they may not manage to get to a treatment centre in the first place. Mobility problems may prevent older women from travelling beyond the home, and cultural restrictions governing when and where women should move around on their own can make it hard to even contemplate undertaking such a visit.[26]

*Is that right?*

In these ways and many more, global heating has been reshaping the lives of women around the world.

But stop! Everything you've read here so far is true—but it's also not. Or rather, it's misleading: this picture flattens and thins out reality, presuming that only women in the global South are affected by the climate crisis, and portraying them purely as victims without agency. It reinforces stereotypes of these women as Other—as poor, brown-skinned, pot-carrying, suffering but mute—in a way disconcertingly similar to the recurring images itemised so wryly by Binyavanga Wainaina in his 2019 essay *How to Write About Africa*:

> Among your characters you must always include The Starving African, who wanders the refugee camp nearly naked, and waits for the benevolence of the West. Her children have flies on their eyelids and pot bellies, and her breasts are flat and empty. She must look utterly helpless. She can have no past, no history; such diversions ruin the dramatic moment. Moans are good. She must never say anything about herself in the dialogue except to speak of her (unspeakable) suffering.[27]

Look at the most common images of women and girls affected by climate change, and what stares back at you

are pictures strikingly similar to those stubbornly enduring representations of poverty in the global South that—
despite oh-so-many critiques—the major NGOs are still
disseminating. In these images it's sometimes hard to
distinguish Africans from Asians from Pacific Islanders,
since all are similarly passive, emptied of diversity and
complexity.[28] Nandita Dogra studied a year's worth of
public messages in the British press from international
NGOs. She found that they depicted women as a "homo-
geneously powerless group of innocent victims of problems that just 'happen to be'".[29] They've been recast as
generic archetypes, decontextualised and apparently
timeless women-with-problems: while the global North
transforms and whirs increasingly fast, these 'traditional'
women are placed out of time, as though history has
passed them by without laying its finger upon them.

It's important to acknowledge that images perpetuating these stereotypes have also served a real purpose:
they've been an effective tool in the struggle by campaigners to insert women into the climate crisis conversation, at least to get a hearing for the female experience
at the seminars and summits where policy is debated.
Ulrike Röhr, head of GenderCC—Women for Climate
Justice, put it this way: "seeing women as victims or most
vulnerable in society provided a 'foot in the door' in the
climate change discussions",[30] making the case for paying
special attention to the particular effects of the climate
crisis on women.

Yet stereotypes like this also closet women and girls in an old but persistent narrative where they're purely "objects of colonial concern and rescue".[31] These stereotypes have an ideological function, too, because they erase the responsibility of the global North for the vulnerabilities of the global South: women are portrayed as vulnerable because they're women, or because they're poor—that's just how these things are. Well-intentioned though the 2005 charity campaign Make Poverty History was, it skewed perceptions away from the reality of poverty's causes, as Dogra points out: "Shared world history is the central plot in the story of global inequalities. *History makes poverty.*"[32]

When we obscure the enduring historical links between the wealth of the global North and the poverty of the global South, the gendered inequalities deepened by climate change come to seem like geographical or biological facts of life that can be improved after the fact by charity or philanthropy. 'We' of the global North are nowhere to be seen in the story when it's told this way, since it's been flushed free of any sociopolitical and economic causes in which we might be implicated. Our only appearance is as a generous, well-meaning benefactor—Lady Bountiful.

Ultimately, seeing the impact of the climate crisis through this paternalistic lens prevents us from really understanding the many different ways in which global heating is scorching women's lives, and why this is happening. Even worse, it distracts us from solutions that could really make a difference.

## An alternative narrative

There's another story to be told here—a more nuanced, complex and, I think, more interesting one. For example, women don't 'just' cook food: although they're often airbrushed out of discussions about agriculture (the very term 'women farmers' assumes that 'farmers'—unmarked—must be men), they also produce food: 43% of the world's farmers are women,[33] and in India and Bangladesh they're responsible for as much as 80% of rice production.[34] The African farmer, it's been said, is primarily a woman, even though she owns under 2% of the land.[35] Global heating increases the demands and stresses on already overstretched women, in their roles as both food producers and those responsible for their family's meals—especially since, around the world, women have far fewer rights to and control over land and property than men.

Some women in sub-Saharan Africa have even been driven to 'transactional sex'—sometimes called 'survival sex'—in order to obtain more food for their families. Among the most extraordinary of such transactions is women trading sex with fishermen, who otherwise refuse to sell them their catch.[36] The idea of 'fish-for-sex' is particularly disturbing, perhaps because it values a woman's body as being of no greater worth than a piece of fish displayed on a slab, a commodity for consumption.

So, yes, women resort to many different strategies to ensure that their families can eat, but there's another climate-related food story here. Around the world, women, especially Indigenous women, are playing a key role in mitigating the climate crisis—by planting new climate-resilient crops, for example, and, as Part Two of this book shows, leading many different initiatives in adapting to the changing climate. These women are not at all passive and mute; they're just not often given the space and tools to speak and act.

The image of women as victims of climate change has not only been normalised, but naturalised too—as if there were something inevitable about it. This is especially true when women are bracketed with their off-spring as 'women-and-children'. It's as though, because women spend so much time caring for children, they become indistinguishable from them. This infantilisation also presumes—wrongly—that all women are wives and mothers, padlocked into families and with little or no life beyond them. Increasingly, not just in the global North but also the global South, this is untrue.[37] Women are marrying later or not at all, and growing numbers choose not to have children.

'Women,' anyway, is a baggy word in itself, because it obscures the differences between women. Rich white women can withstand the shocks of global heating in ways that poor black women can only dream of. The experiences of LGBTQI+ women demonstrate many different ways of living as a female or a woman. In Fiji, for example, sexual and gender minorities, already discriminated against, faced additional and specific challenges after Tropical Cyclone Winston hit in 2016: "Straight after TC Winston ... they would call out that it is 'us people' that caused TC Winston. I asked them 'what people?' And they said LGBTQ people. I told them it is climate change, not LGBTQ people."[38] This is not only a division between 'poor' and 'rich' countries.

Bushfires are a good example. These have become strikingly more frequent and intense in the last few years, with spectacular and disastrous wildfires in the US and Australia. Hot, dry weather is likely to cause bushfires, and climate change has boosted the risk of such weather by at least 30 per cent—probably more.[39] Prolonged exposure to fire smoke increases the risks of complications in pregnancy, including high blood pressure, gestational diabetes, low birthweight and premature birth. It can interfere with the placenta's development and function, increasing the foetus's risk of cerebral palsy or visual and hearing impediments. A 2018 study followed half a million women in Colorado between 2007 and 2015, when the state was exposed to smoke from wildfires in California and the Pacific Northwest: the researchers found a spike in the number of premature births during this period.[40] Any level of ultra-fine particles in the air that exceeds 25 micrograms per cubic metre is unsafe for vulnerable people, including pregnant women. In the first week of January 2020, Canberra was averaging 200 micrograms per cubic metre.[41]

But we shouldn't fall back on the idea that the climate crisis affects women differently from men purely because of biology, even though it's true that climate-caused disasters can do different things to male and female bodies. Yes, the climate crisis is inscribed into and onto the bodies of women, especially black and brown women—but not just because they were born into a female body. It's because they were born into gender-unequal societies. Think back to some of the statistics I mentioned earlier in this chapter.

In the 2004 tsunami, the greater physical strength of men undoubtedly made them more able to cling to trees or climb to safety. Yet even more significant in preventing more women and girls from surviving were the social and cultural factors—the fact that, in many parts of the world, girls are rarely taught to swim or encouraged to climb trees, for example. Or the fact that their long, loose clothing restricts their movement. Women also stopped to scoop up their children, and were often weighed down when trying to flee by the household goods they wanted to save. For all these reasons, they were less able climb to safety.[42]

Similarly, in Bangladesh's 1991 cyclone, part of the reason why nearly five times as many women as men died is that warning notices were posted in public spaces, from which women were often excluded. Even if they were able to see them, the higher illiteracy rate among women meant that they couldn't read them.[43] Warnings of cyclones are also broadcast on radio but, by 2012, more than one quarter of Bangladeshi women still weren't able to access radio, or any other media—twice the number of men.[44] Back in 1991, even if they were aware that the cyclone was coming, many women weren't allowed to leave home without their husband or a male relative, and so waited in vain for one to return and usher them to a place of safety.[45] And what of women caring for an elderly, immobile relative? They were faced with the choice of saving themselves or staying behind with the family member they were caring for.

It's gender and not sex that helped cause the death of these women—more specifically, gender inequality. The responsibilities that they shouldered; the cultural norms and restrictions they faced as women; the lack of access to resources, both social and material—together, these made them more likely to die when disaster struck. Even in the case of bushfires, you can only understand the different effects on men and women if you take account of gender rather than sex. In Australia's 'Black Saturday' in 2009, for example, more men than women died. Those women who died did so when they were trying to evacuate, which they usually prefer to do, while most men had stayed behind and died trying to defend their property and other assets—differences again shaped by gender norms.[46]

So, climate-induced disasters don't blast away existing social relationships and inequalities, as if out of the rubble comes a chance to reset. They do the opposite: what was unequal before becomes even more unequal after. The climate crisis heightens those inequalities, often dramatically, and not just directly.

# AMA FRANCIS, 31, DOMINICA/USA

*I work at Columbia Law School's Sabin Center in New York, a legal think-and-do tank on climate change law. I focus on climate migration, especially free movement agreements that make it easier for people to migrate, like the Intergovernmental Authority on Development's agreement in East Africa. It's important to acknowledge that most people would prefer to stay in place, myself included. I was born in Dominica and lived here until I was 2, then we moved to Canada for 5 years, and since then I've been in and out of Dominica and the US.*

*I think free movement agreements should be recognised and used as a solution in the climate context. After Hurricane Maria (2017), about 20 per cent of the population of Dominica left and went to neighbouring islands like Antigua or St Lucia. That was possible because of CARICOM, a group of twenty countries that make up the Caribbean Community, and OECS, the eleven countries that make up the Organization of Eastern Caribbean States. Both of these had free movement agreements that allowed people to shelter and access job markets in other islands, and sometimes permanently resettle there. This is huge for climate migrants, because of the lack of legal protection at an international level.*

*When people are displaced because of climate-related disasters, they mostly move regionally, which means that the global South is the area where most of this movement is happening. That places an immense burden on national governments. The global South is friendlier towards global Southerners than the global North is towards people from the global South, but global South governments have less capacity for taking on the burden of integrating migrants into society.*

*I've started to think about 'trapped regionalism'—people getting trapped within regions or within the global South and, as climate impacts worsen—making more and more of the world unfit for human life—I think this will become more and more of a problem. Right now sovereignty is constructed through this idea of exclusion—that countries are sovereign by excluding people; but free movement agreements demonstrate that it's possible to remain sovereign even with more liberal admission policies.*

*I migrated under very favourable circumstances and even that was an extreme loss. So, first, it's really important that there's work and resources that support people staying in place. But if climate impacts worsen, more people will be forced to move—so it's also important to provide regular migration pathways or just legal options for people to migrate, so that receiving communities and countries have a better chance of capturing the benefits of migration.*

*I've spent almost my entire life moving in one direction or the other and that has come with great privileges and pleasures—and also great losses. I recognise that the mobility that I enjoy is not the mobility that everyone does: people in the global North enjoy a lot more movement than others and so I also feel personally driven to contribute to levelling that playing field. What cemented this was Hurricane Maria, which was devastating.*

*I was in the US when the hurricane hit. My parents lived in Dominica but were travelling at the time, but most of my extended family was here on the island—my paternal grandmother, most of my aunts and uncles. My granny's house was pretty severely damaged so she moved, as did most people. Most of my family's homes were destroyed. My mom's a doctor: she works for the medical school, which had to move off-island. They moved permanently to Barbados, which was a huge economic hit to Dominica, because the school contributed about 30 per cent of GDP.*

*Some days I think we're all doomed! On those days I find some peace, because I think, "Human society will have participated in our own destruction, but the earth itself will actually be fine, although a lot of other species will also die." On other days, I keep hoping that we're moving towards a tipping-point where this stops being a speculative future that most of us are afraid to confront, and we start making real changes.*

*I need to be honest: the way that this pandemic has rolled out doesn't give me much hope for our national gov-*

*ernment's capacity to plan for disaster. But it feels really important to do the work nonetheless, because I want kids, and I do feel I'm indebted to the people who came before me and also to the people that will come after me.*

*Most of us who are in black bodies feel under threat on a number of levels all of the time, and especially right now. The disenfranchised of the world, which tends to be black and brown people, face the most severe impacts of any health crisis, environmental crisis or social crisis, and most people know that. What's different right now is that the coronavirus has created an enormous amount of pressure—most people either losing their jobs or having to go to work under very dangerous conditions. And to witness black people dying in droves in this crisis and then also being murdered by the police—I think it was just too much. What's different about this moment is this effort to speak out: it's really transformative and gives me hope for the power of collective movement.*

*Sometimes people think it's strange that I'm a black person doing climate work. A lot of people of colour care about climate but there's this view that it's a white elitist social issue that doesn't hugely matter to people of colour around the globe. But now people have started speaking about the connections between race and climate in new ways. So that's been hopeful too: the way that people are connecting different structural crises. What the young people are doing for climate, and how young girls are at the front of that—I just find that really inspiring. There are also a lot of queer and gender-nonconforming voices that are speaking up at the intersections of all of these issues, and that's really exciting.*

2

CRISIS MULTIPLIER

HOW GLOBAL HEATING HURTS WOMEN
INDIRECTLY

It's 24 April 2013. A terrifyingly loud cracking sound, and then the floors begin to collapse and the concrete pillars to crumble. Ninety seconds later and the 8-storey Rana Plaza garment factory in Dhaka, Bangladesh is in pieces, looking more like a rubbish tip for scrap, not humans. More than 1,134 garment workers, most of them women, will eventually be found dead and over 2,500 left injured and traumatised, few of them receiving any compensation. But the Rana Plaza disaster also shows the intricate tapestry that the climate crisis weaves around women's lives.

Most of the Rana workers had come to Dhaka as migrants—among the 400,000 who arrive in the city each year, fleeing floods. What reporter George Black discovered, in an article called "Your Clothes Were Made by a Bangladeshi Climate Refugee", was that many of the women working in the factory came from the same place: Barisal, which lies at the mouth of the Meghna River in south-west Bangladesh. They'd been forced to abandon their homes because of rising sea levels and the effects of cyclones. In conversation with Mahmudul Sumon, a professor of anthropology at Jahangirnagar University, Black learned that a high percentage of those who'd died in the 2012 Tazreen Garment factory fire—just a year before the Rana disaster—had similarly migrated to Dhaka from a single small district in north-western Bangladesh, an area notable for its falling water table and frequent crop failures.[1]

But casting the Rana Plaza survivors purely as victims distorts the picture. The survivors of the disaster, like those who died, worked for desperately low wages in often literally fatal conditions, and they were more vulnerable to sexual violence in the city than back home. Yet Black reported that many relished the mobility and the small shoots of independence that they'd gained as migrants, freed from some of the restrictive taboos of village life.

In other words, what drew the Rana Plaza workers to the city was environmental degradation—but not only environmental degradation. Similarly, the climate crisis alone didn't cause the factory to collapse: what fissured the building and buried its workers were cost-cutting, exploitative owners, assisted by drastic failures of oversight, exploited in turn by profit-seeking transnational companies manufacturing fast fashion for wealthy countries. Nevertheless, the climate crisis delivered these women to the doors of their exploiters, reinforcing the existing exploitative relationship between the global North and South.

To understand how women's lives are being reshaped by global heating, we need to go beyond the firewood-and-water-collecting stories; beyond the impact of air pollution on women's bodies and health. We need to stray into more complex systems and structures, where the effects of the crisis are often much more indirect, but no less powerful—and none more so than migration.

## Climate migrants

Migration and the climate crisis are closely linked: in 2019, 33 million people around the world became 'internally displaced' (within their own region). Almost three quarters of them were forced to leave their homes by weather-related disasters—like storms, heatwaves, floods and rising sea levels—caused or exacerbated by climate change.[2] Sometimes people in this situation are called 'climate refugees', although those who deal with migration prefer 'climate-displaced', since international law doesn't extend protection to people moving because of climate or disaster: to qualify as a refugee under the 1951 Refugee Convention, you have to be fleeing from persecution.[3]

Anti-migrant rhetoric has so commandeered the debate that we've focused almost exclusively on where migrants are heading or want to end up, rather than exploring what they're fleeing—to the point where it's startling to learn that international bodies concerned with the climate crisis, like the Intergovernmental Panel on Climate Change, view migration as a legitimate and valuable way of adapting to it, and of helping some people escape its worst impacts. Viewed like this, migration becomes not a problem facing the world, but a reasonable solution to the real problem: climate breakdown. It's a solution being used by the people facing the crisis, not a crisis in itself.

By 2050 there'll be at least 25 million climate migrants, possibly as many as 1 billion.[4] Most migrants, though, are displaced in their own country and don't cross international borders—not that you'd know this from the moral panic around migration, fomented cynically by populist politicians in the global North, who conjure up invading hordes of young black and brown men (sometimes women) intent on leeching off the state in the UK, or dealing drugs in the US.

When men migrate, leaving behind their families, women's lives become harder in some ways, but better in others. In Sudan, for example, drought induced by climate change has made the crops fail, degraded the soil and made water scarce, forcing growing numbers of young men to migrate to big cities like Khartoum in search of work. The women left behind, not all of whom would previously have been involved in agriculture, raise sheep and goats and grow small crops that they can sell for cash—a feminisation of agriculture that has increased their self-sufficiency and made female-headed households normal. But now that they're the sole providers, with added responsibilities, it's also greatly increased their workload—yet the balance of power still hasn't changed. Women remain marginalised politically and economically in their communities.[5]

It's especially difficult to leave home if you are responsible for the care of children and old people. But women also migrate—in 2018, half of those internally displaced were women.[6] This is a burden, too: even when you choose it, migration always brings an element of trauma—you leave behind your local culture, support network, friends and family, and often also language and food. And when it isn't chosen—when climate change has compelled you to abandon your home, the place that you've been tasked to care for—it's an 'option of last resort', and doubly traumatic.[7] Then there's the problem of where you end up. This is not just about the difficulties of cooking, washing and maintaining privacy in crowded, strange places; the risk of sexual violence facing women is even greater in evacuation, transit and refugee camps. Queer and trans women and nonbinary people, of colour particularly, face extra challenges: largely invisible and remarginalised in relief efforts, they often face homophobia or transphobia in shelters.[8]

*Climate violations*

Here, perhaps, is the most powerful evidence of the long-term gendered impact of the climate emergency: 'climate violence'. It's hard, of course, to prove a direct and simple cause-and-effect between global warming and sexual violence, although in Congo a correlation has been found: districts with higher temperatures experience greater conflict, which leads to gender-based violence, like rape, sexual assault and exploitation.[9] In Uganda, meanwhile, there are instances where prolonged dry seasons lead men to try and sell the crops grown by women for the family to eat; if the women are reluctant to hand them over, they get beaten to coerce them.[10]

We know for sure that sexual and gender-based violence escalates after climate-related disasters.[11] Women and girls in the Pacific region suffer more from violence than they do almost anywhere else in the world—in one survey of the Solomon Islands, nearly two thirds of women had experienced physical or sexual violence from a partner.[12] And domestic violence cases trebled after two tropical cyclones hit Tafe province, Vanuatu in 2011.[13] When people who already have little suddenly have even less, it's not surprising that existing tensions are ramped up, and that those with marginally more power hit out, literally, at people more abject than themselves—usually those closest to hand. As this man from north-east Uganda explained to researcher Tracy Kajumba,

Climate change has made us less of the men we used to be. We have lost our cows due to drought ... In our culture, a man's wealth [is] defined by the number of cows one owns. So we cannot even feed our families, not take care of our wives and children. So instead of staying home, we walk away in shame and stay out. However in returning, the women abuse us and call us useless as if we don't know it already. In anger we strike back and beat them to make them quiet.[14]

These are men attempting to restore their sense of masculinity and power, after it's been undermined by the collapse of institutions and social spaces that used to sustain it. What has been called 'disaster masculinity' produces disaster violence.[15]

Yet again, though, it's important not to oversimplify the issue: it's not just a case of downtrodden global Southerners abusing one another. The high levels of violence against women in the Pacific Islands also have a historical dimension and, it's been argued, are partly a legacy of colonialism and the subjugation that it brought.[16] You don't have to look to the past, to see these links between colonialism and the abuse of women: take the scandal when it was discovered that senior Oxfam officials, in Haiti after the devastating earthquake in 2010, were using sex workers. There are plenty of other recent examples of 'humanitarian' staff in charge of recovery efforts perpetuating the sexual exploitation of children, showing that practices like these continue still today.

Sexual coercion, violence, trafficking and rape—all these violations can be ways of maintaining power not only over their victims, but over land and scarce resources; and they can be seen as responses to the loss of that power, when the climate crisis reduces those resources even further.[17] Gendered violence is also used to discourage or stop environmental rights activists from seeking climate and land justice. Berta Cáceres was murdered in 2016 after she led a vocal campaign in Honduras against an internationally financed hydroelectric dam on the Gualcarque River, which is sacred to the Lenca Indigenous community.[18] Indigenous women challenging mining, agribusiness and illegal logging on their lands are especially vulnerable to intimidation, torture, rape and other kinds of violence designed to end their environmentalism.[19] So, here again, the climate crisis is written into and onto women's bodies—not by 'nature' or biology, but by society.

*Not just 'over there'*

Reading all this, it's easy to fall back on the stereotypes of suffering women in the global South, so different from their emancipated and empowered sisters in the global North. It's also wrong: climate-related violence isn't confined to poor people or the global South. In the first few weeks and months after the 2004 floods hit Whakatane, a town on New Zealand's North Island, agencies reported double and sometimes triple the number of calls for help for domestic violence—across all ethnicities, ages, incomes and educational levels.[20] Violence against women in New Orleans almost doubled in the six months after Hurricane Katrina struck, regardless of age, marital status or education.[21]

The same pattern emerges after Australian bushfires. One reason that bushfires have increased male violence against women, two women's health researchers speculated, was men's inability to live up to expectations of masculinity in the face of a climate emergency. Trying to contain fireballs and control flames over 40 metres high is beyond what any human being can do; but, because of the enduring idea that men should be invincible providers and protectors, it left them feeling inadequate. Writing in the *Australian Journal of Emergency Management*, they pointed out that "We [society] accept that violence against women increased after earthquakes in Haiti and cyclones in Bangladesh, but nobody wants to hear that men who embody the spirit of resilient and heroic Australia are violent towards their families."[22] Disaster emergency planning, the researchers argued, needs to incorporate this unwelcome reality, and should include training for dealing with domestic violence in the aftermath of a climate disaster.

*Hurting both women and the earth*

Sometimes, the link isn't as linear as climate change causing violence—A causes B—but more of an indirect consequence—A causes both B and C. For instance, the extractive forms of energy that contribute to the climate crisis also produce violence against women. That's what is happening in north-east British Columbia, Canada, where intensive energy development (oil and gas extraction, coal mining, hydroelectric dams) has had a shocking impact on Indigenous women and girls. The higher rates of violence they've experienced come from several factors, but primarily the arrival of a group of well-paid, transient workers, mostly young, male and single. These labourers have a high disposable income, are doing highly pressurised jobs in the extractive industries, and spend long stretches of times isolated in so-called 'man camps' in so-called boomtowns, places that suddenly mushroom in economy and population size. Add in drug and alcohol misuse, and misogynistic, racist attitudes to Indigenous women and girls, and violence results.[23]

One shocking situation around the Lake Chad Basin shows how climate change can multiply many different threats. In 2014, the Basin, bordered by Nigeria, Niger, Chad and Cameroon, saw the kidnap of almost 300 teenage girls by Boko Haram jihadists in Nigeria. This event, which attracted so much media attention at the time, was originally reported as a religious conflict. More recently, though, it and the other incidents of sexual violence perpetrated by Boko Haram in the area have come to be understood as climate-linked ones.

The climate crisis was implicated in this story in several ways. First of all, increased floods during the rainy season, and droughts during the dry season, affected harvests and attracted hungry young men into the arms of Boko Haram—that's how the perpetrators got recruited. But the victims were also delivered into their hands by the degradation of the environment. Instability, climate-linked hunger, violence and indeed the threat of violence from groups like Boko Haram have together internally displaced more than 2.3 million people since 2013, many of them flocking to the Basin; and, when they got there, women and girls became even more vulnerable.

Once the largest freshwater lake in the world, Lake Chad shrank by 90 per cent between the 1960s and the 1990s, partly because of failures in governance,[24] but also because of climate change. Yet more and more people are being displaced, many of them housed in refugee camps rife with sexual exploitation and violence, where women and girls are increasingly turning to 'survival sex' for food and money.[25] Today around 45 million people rely on the lake's resources, living on its shores or its 942 islands: the climate crisis helped bring them there, but their presence is also putting further pressure on the environment. And now, according to a letter leaked to *The Guardian*, the Chad government has signed agreements with extraction companies to explore oil and mining opportunities in the region.[26]

Inevitably, this will fuel climate breakdown even more—climate change begets more climate change. But you can hardly blame Chad, one of the poorest countries in the world and already a leading producer of crude oil in Africa, for wanting to enrich itself from its natural resources and raw materials, after they've been plundered and exploited so heavily by foreign companies like ExxonMobil, Chevron and Petronas.[27]

"Climate change fuels insecurity," says Nigerian climate activist Adenike Oladosu. "Climate change doesn't create insecurity but it provides an enabling environment."[28] At every stage, global heating provides a link in the chain between women, hunger, displacement and violence.

### *"Vulnerability does not just fall from the sky"*[29]

While it's urgent and overdue for us to recognise how women are hurt by the climate crisis, we need to be careful that we don't fall into a narrative where women are all equally and solely described as victims. It's more complicated than that: depicting women as vulnerable ignores the climate (and general) vulnerabilities of boys, men and trans or nonbinary people, instead homogenising everyone—equating men always with power, and women with powerlessness.[30] If men are always victimisers, there's no way to recognise that men can also become victims of other men, or to comprehend the effect on them of poverty, racism or war.[31] If women, full stop, are always victims, there's no way to see or acknowledge how different women experience climate breakdown differently. And if this is some universal rule separating men from women, that comes dangerously close to seeing it as a *natural* rule.

Over a decade ago, a group of feminist climate scholars began to challenge the characterisation of women as climate victims.[32] Vulnerability, they claimed, wasn't some intrinsic women's characteristic, but the result of unequal power relations. As Irene Dankelman put it, women "are not vulnerable—but they are *made* vulnerable by different external drivers … such as age, race, class, caste … vulnerability is dynamic and therefore can/should (be) change(d)".[33] What the now-familiar images of women as climate victims erase is who or what made them vulnerable in the first place. If you focus on women's victimhood, you not only obscure this responsibility, but also deflect attention from factors that intersect with it—the ones Dankelman mentions above, plus disability, age, sexual identities and preferences, and so on. Pooling all women together in one 'vulnerable' category depicts their identities as somehow fixed and homogenous. But gender doesn't act alone.[34]

After Hurricane Katrina in 2005, for instance, it wasn't women as a generic group who were hardest hit—it was poor African American women. The combination of race and sex discrimination and poverty did it for them; it was no more just gender than it was just water.

Fewer African American women had cars in which to evacuate from New Orleans, and then, post-Katrina, they were priced out of the city: many of the homes that had been swept away were the affordable ones, and their reduced availability in the damaged areas hugely hiked up the rents.[35]

In the European heatwave of 2003, the reasons that the majority of the fatalities were women lie not only in gender, but also in how this intersects with age and living conditions: in cities like Paris, many old women live alone on the sixth or seventh floor of old buildings, in very small apartments that were originally maids' quarters. Lacking air conditioning and often also decent ventilation, these older women quickly became dehydrated and disorientated. Many were either single, widowed or so isolated from their families that their bodies weren't discovered until days or even weeks later—this has been called 'fatal isolation',[36] and it is a feature of the way old people live in the global North. The same elderly women would have been much more likely to live with their extended family in the global South.

There's a tragic symmetry to the fact that these inadequate dwellings, built in a previous era for young women whose needs didn't matter, have become the graves of old women who were also invisible, until they turned up in the mortuary. The social and cultural conditions shaping these women's lives, alongside their age and gender, together left them particularly vulnerable to the effects of global heating.

## *Women-as-solution*

One reaction against the stereotyping of 'women-as-climate-victim' has been the creation of another stereotype: woman as 'climate saviour'. Instead of portraying women affected by the climate emergency as passive and vulnerable, this idea trumpets them as agents of change: because of their key role in caring for and managing resources like forests, as well as household dependents, they are heralded as the solution to the climate crisis. Behind this development lurks the old idea that women are supposedly innately environmentally conscious: they instinctively care not only for their families, the sick and so on, but also for the planet. Chapter 4 takes a close look at this idea, which has understandably riled activists like Ulrike Röhr:

> It is not desirable to shift from one extreme: vulnerability of women is the main gender issue, to another: women are agents of change. This leads to a romanticisation of women, based on women as individuals, rather than questioning their societal roles and responsibilities. In my view, the idea of the 'Agents of Change' is a myth. It shifts societal responsibilities, e.g. for transitioning to a low carbon society, onto *individuals*, to those having least impact on political decisions ... It is so much more important to put the underlying reasons for gender inequalities into the centre of discussion.[37]

The woman-as-saviour narrative sneakily displaces the burden of environmental care: away from those who cause environmental degradation, and onto those who suffer most from it. It becomes another task to add to the already formidable list that most women face every day: shopping or gathering food, cooking, feeding, cleaning, washing, childcare, eldercare—oh, and fixing the planet. It's a 'privatisation', and more specifically a 'feminisation', of environmental responsibility.[38] Seeing women as either victims or heroines (sometimes both at the same time) ignores the differences between them, erasing those very issues of power and inequality that have made them more vulnerable to the climate crisis in the first place.

The lives of real, embodied people are far richer and more complex than these crude stereotypes admit. Beware the single story, warned Chimamanda Ngozi Adichie,[39] yet many of the most widely circulating images and stories about climate change fall back on neat slogans and reductive narratives, as though the lives of women in the global South were made up of a single strand, rather than the braided, composite identities allowed to those in the global North. If we're to understand the multiple effects of the climate crisis, and to contest them, we need to recognise the intricate web of relationships, structures and systems of power that all of us, of all genders, inhabit; and to stop seeing gender in a simplistic way, used as just another word for 'women'.

Perhaps the most harmful effect of the women-as-victims-or-heroines narrative is the way that it severs

Them from Us, unconnected except sometimes by aid and concern. This expunges all those global imbalances of power that have devastated swathes of the planet—colonialism, imperialism and slavery, all handily magicked away. Missing too is the role of these forces in the conversion of swathes of the world away from subsistence economies, towards the intensive production of mono-crops for markets in the global North (so-called 'industrial farming'). Producers in the global South may find themselves less resilient to global heating, but the historic reasons for this often have little to do with nature, the elements, or anything else beyond the reach of humans. We can trace them back to this shift away from an agriculture based on producers' own needs, towards one revolving around meeting those of the global North.[40]

In other words, what's also missing, when women are portrayed as either heroines or victims, are the neo-colonial patterns of trade that still structure the world right now.

## Exporting climate change

Let's start in London—or Paris, or New York. Wealthy nations, concerned about greenhouse gases and searching for technological solutions, have come up with the electric car. An essential ingredient in the car batteries that power them is lithium, so now fly (but only in your mind) to Bolivia, which has the world's second-largest lithium deposits, at Salar de Uyuni. Just as well, you might say, since our demand for the stuff seems infinite—lithium-ion batteries are also used in mobile phones, laptops and solar energy panels; lithium is a critical component in low-carbon technologies. Not for nothing is it known as 'white oil'.

In Bolivia, you see only too clearly how mining lithium disfigures the landscape, diverting enormous quantities of water from agriculture like quinoa farming, and yet producing only limited local labour, and almost none of it for women.[41] Lithium extraction has also been linked with the lowering of groundwater levels and the spread of deserts, and no one knows yet what large-scale extraction will do to the natural ecosystem, or whether it will contaminate the reserves of clean water, as protesting Indigenous groups in Chile have argued.[42]

You don't need to head south, though, to find lithium—Portugal is also rich in it. Hurrah! It's in Europe: for European producers, it doesn't bring with it transport-linked emissions. They haven't, however, factored in local opposition to open-pit lithium mines. "So much destruction," says 43-year-old Maria Carmo, who lives near the planned site of a mine. "And for what? So eco-minded urbanites in Paris and Berlin can feel good about driving around in zero-emissions cars."[43]

The other end of electric cars' life cycle is also problematic. Batteries don't last for ever and aren't biodegradable. They can be recycled—that's why battery collection points have become so common. Many of the UK's spent batteries end up in a reprocessing plant in Belgium that can extract some of the metals (copper and cobalt), but now a Finnish company has developed an innovative process that can recycle 80 per cent of the materials in a lithium-ion battery. Great, except for the fact that it costs more to recycle a lithium battery (by extracting the lithium) than it does to mine more lithium for a brand-new one—up to five times more. This is probably why less than 5 per cent of lithium-ion batteries in the UK and US are currently recycled.[44]

The rest are sent to landfill, where their toxic elements can leak into the groundwater and soil and enter the food chain; or they are incinerated, releasing toxins into the air; or they are dispatched elsewhere, largely to poorer countries where the wealthy nations prefer to dump their toxic electronic waste—because it's cheaper and far away. The UK is the world's second-largest producer of this waste, known as e-waste or WEEE (waste electrical and electronic equipment); only Norway produces more. Officially, the UK has signed the 1992 Basel Convention, which reduces the amount of hazardous waste that a 'developed' country can transfer to a 'less developed' one, supposedly for recycling—but in reality it's hard to know how far the guidelines are followed, since a lot of the waste is exported illegally under the guise of being re-used.[45]

In 2017 the Basel Action Network (BAN), a global environmental watchdog, decided to investigate whether the rules were being adhered to. In the first study of its kind in Europe, which reads like a detective story, they secretly installed GPS trackers into 314 old computers, printers and monitors, then dropped them at recycling depots set up by governments in ten EU countries. All the equipment qualified as hazardous under the Basel Convention.

Two years after their drop, BAN revealed where the equipment had fetched up. Six per cent had been exported, probably illegally. Perhaps unsurprisingly, as it consistently misses its recycling targets, the UK was the worst violator, sending e-waste illegally to Nigeria and other countries.[46] Fourteen years earlier, BAN had discovered that three quarters of what was exported to Africa for supposed re-use was in fact unusable, and instead had been dumped by the side of the road and then burned, "creating far more toxicity than the original material". Presumably, a similar fate awaited BAN's 2017 haul. The so-called circular economy (the re-use alternative to take, make, dispose) doesn't resemble any circle that most of us have ever seen.

Meanwhile the US, the single largest exporter of hazardous material in the world, hasn't ratified the Basel Convention, and so doesn't have to even pretend to abide by the rules: it blithely dispatches the e-waste that it doesn't recycle to Africa, China, Latin America, India and other digital dumping grounds. There, e-waste workers risk their health using low-tech tools like acid baths to extract valuable precious metals and sell them for processing,

We know that this cycle of exploitation is endemic to the extractive industries, but it's also just becoming apparent that it's equally rampant in seemingly 'green' technologies like solar panels and other supposedly decarbonising solutions, such as hydrogen, recently pioneered in the running of trains. Our appetite and demand for such minerals is soaring, and looks to be almost infinite. In such ways are we outsourcing the toxins produced by our shiny new 'green' panaceas onto women's (and men's) bodies in distant places. Helpfully, they don't show up in the global North's carbon footprint—in the case of that lithium, these emissions would 'belong to' Bolivia or Chile, where it was extracted. Nor do they appear in our illness statistics—over to you, India. We are exporting our toxic emissions.

And we are not only exporting them to impoverished countries in general; we are exporting them to impoverished women, specifically. E-waste work is stigmatised and poorly paid so it's often lower-caste women's work, carried out in India by Dalit women, for example. While they appreciate the stable, flexible employment, it also exposes them to hazardous chemicals and environmental toxins that make them sick—with anaemia, autoimmune disorders and cancers of the reproductive system.[47] Lucy

McAllister, a researcher into women and American e-waste, calls it 'toxic colonialism'.[48]

Ma Jian's powerful novel, *The Dark Road*, brings this process vividly to life. We're in China, at the time of the one-child policy, when Meili, a poor young peasant woman who already has a daughter, gets pregnant. The family become fugitives on the Yangtze River and, searching for a place to live and work in peace, finally reach Heaven township (actually modelled on Guiyu, the largest e-waste site in the world, whose economy is built on the dumped e-waste of Western countries). The author, who went undercover as a scrap worker himself to research the book, shows what it's like to rummage through mounds of discarded TVs, mobile phones, computers and batteries, and to sort and disassemble them to recover the reusable materials, in an area where the air, water, land and eventually the workers themselves are polluted, poisoned by toxic chemicals. Tragically, there's nothing 'sustainable' about the human life here.[49]

Because of the complicated supply chain, however, we consumers never get to see the first and last stages of this cycle. We can comfort ourselves with the thought that assorted new products and processes, instruments and devices, will 'solve' the climate crisis, even though these do nothing to disturb the global inequities out of which the climate crisis was born, and which sustain it—the 'enabling environment' identified by Adenike Oladosu.[50] Nor do we have to think about the sweeping changes that are needed to really transform the system. The right not to see is a valuable one—and this, too, is unequally distributed.

## Out of min(e)d

To pose this purely as a 'North vs South' problem, though, is misleading—you only have to look at the situation facing BIPOC (Black, Indigenous, People of Colour) in North America. Jacqui Patterson, Environmental and Climate Justice Program Director at the NAACP, put it this way: "We are the global South in the global North."[51] Or, in the words of Stokely Carmichael and Charles Hamilton back in 1967, people of African descent in the USA "stand as colonial subjects in relation to the white society".[52]

In a rich country like the USA, the harm from technologies that belch out carbon isn't equally distributed; it targets BIPOC, as the environmental justice movement has tirelessly pointed out. More than 1,000 uranium mines, which once produced uranium weapons and later nuclear energy, are situated on Native American lands. The Navajo men working in those now-abandoned mines would bring radiation back home with them on their clothes, compromising their own health and their family's.[53] Years later, the exposure to water and soil contaminated by the waste from these nuclear plants is still having chronic effects on Native Americans' health.[54]

Then there's coal: America is still in love with coal mining, even though it's one of the most environmentally dirty industries, emitting not only carbon dioxide and methane—the top drivers of the climate crisis—but also mercury, arsenic, lead and other contaminants. And they're going into the lungs of African Americans. Coal-fired plants are disproportionately situated in communities of colour—over 78 per cent of African Americans live within a 30-mile radius of one, even though they're linked with chronic asthma, inflammation of the lung, bronchitis and birth defects. No wonder these areas are nicknamed 'sacrifice zones'.[55]

This proximity to toxic pollution among communities of colour isn't new: when sociologist Robert Bullard, often called the father of the environmental justice movement, got his students to investigate, they discovered that five out of five landfills in Houston and six out of eight incinerators were sited in black neighbourhoods. "We calculated that 82% of all solid waste dumped in Houston from the 1930s to 1978 was dumped on black communities, when black people were only 25% of the city's population." Little has changed since then.[56] Except, that is, for Covid-19. Add that to police violence and it's clear that, for African Americans and other BIPOC, breathing freely can't be taken for granted. An extra insult is that, much of the time, residents don't even benefit from the polluting industries on their doorstep. In a horrible irony, 70 per cent of people on a Navajo Nation reservation where a coal plant is sited don't have access to the electricity being generated by that very plant.[57]

Women, of course, are part of these communities; but they also suffer specific effects through exposure, at work, at home or both, to endocrine-disrupting chemicals used in the plastic and pesticide industries. These can affect their menstruation, ovulation and fertility.[58] Men are also impacted by pesticides—they've been linked with sterility and prostate cancer—but women of colour are disproportionately affected.[59] Yet again, the pollutants that poison the air are doing the same to those who help manufacture them—black and brown women, in particular.

## SCARLETT WESTBROOK, 16, UK

*We had an amazing science teacher in my primary school: even though we were little 6- and 7-year-olds, we had our first lesson on climate change—not only about animals, but also the humanitarian impact of it, where you're taught about refugees and displacement. After that, Ed Miliband became leader of the Labour Party and was advocating for a decarbonisation date, so I started canvassing for them. I was 10 and one of my parents would follow behind me when I'd go knocking on people's doors saying, "Please can you move to Labour so we can abide by the Paris agreement and decarbonise?" And my main selling point was the climate.*

*In December 2018, the UK Student Climate Network was formed; I was involved in starting it up. And then we had the climate strikes: our biggest one was in September that year, we had 100,000 people in London, 20,000 in Edinburgh, 15,000 in Glasgow, 3,000 in Birmingham.*

*Climate activism didn't start with Extinction Rebellion, it started with Indigenous people protecting their land and their communities. When we dissociate climate activism from its true roots, that's when we get whitewashing and making climate activism into a conservation issue, although we know it's also a humanitarian crisis. We need to remember that conservation and social justice are completely interlinked.*

*In the Birmingham group I joined, I don't think they really understood colonialism. They thought countries in the global South were underdeveloped, and that we just need to have fewer cars in the city centre and recycle more, when that's not quite how it works.*

*With a few other student activists I helped set up Teach the Future, a student-led campaign to decarbonise the education sector and reform the education system to entrench climate justice education at its core. Now I'm employed there, for around 12 hours a week, depending on how much schoolwork I've got. We want to decarbonise education buildings, to ensure that all new education establishments—from nurseries to universities—are built to be carbon-zero by 2022, and to retrofit existing buildings to be carbon-zero.*

*But the campaign's main focus is on changing the education system—so that the climate crisis is centred in every subject and in every stream of education. We need to ensure that future generations are equipped with the skills and knowledge necessary to build a resilient society, to cope with the effects whilst we try and mitigate them.*

*I'm asking the Department of Education to conduct a review into the teaching of climate education because, from* research we've done, 75 per cent of teachers don't feel like they've got enough knowledge to teach about the climate crisis, and only 4 per cent of students think they know enough about it. So we need to ensure that teachers are taught about how to teach the climate crisis adequately. I helped write a Climate Emergency Bill that would mean all students learned about the climate crisis, whatever subjects they choose. We're hoping that an MP will sponsor it.

I think that being a person of colour, with the intergenerational trauma I get from climate change, natural disasters and colonisation, means I have more of a stake in this—although I'm also a middle-class Westerner who goes to a grammar school. I have Kashmiri and Dutch heritage. The Netherlands is projected to be completely submerged under water by 2100.

Black Lives Matter and the climate crisis are obviously linked, because we know people of colour are disproportionately impacted by both—in the so-called global South, it's because their countries have been economically stunted by colonisation. Even in the UK and other Western countries, people of colour tend to be less well off, living in inner-city areas where they experience more air pollution; and then looking at the Covid crisis, people of colour have been dying disproportionately. That comes from environmental racism—unless we dismantle the systemic racism that's upholding this unfair oppression, it's just going to be exacerbated.

The protests surrounding George Floyd's death [in May 2020] were incredibly important. I knew things were bad for *black people because of things like misogynoir—the intersection of colourism and women being disproportionately discriminated against. But obviously, as someone who's fairly light-skinned and from a quite privileged background, I didn't truly understand. Hearing people's stories and the collective grief of the black community really hit me.*

*I spoke at International Women's Day this year [2020], about the link between gender inequality and the climate crisis. We know that, throughout history, women are the people who pick up the pieces after natural disasters and have to rebuild communities and their families. And I think that that has carried on here too, because women are going to be the ones probably picking up the pieces [with climate breakdown].*

*Doing live TV was terrifying at the start, but now it comes a lot more naturally. I still go to parties, and like to go shopping with my friends and go see musicals; a lot of music. But I had to cut down a bit, because I had to write a bill or go to the EU Parliament in Brussels to talk about climate policy. My parents make sure that I'm still having a childhood. I also have to prepare for my exams, because I want to study medicine.*

*Greta Thunberg is the face of this movement. She's done some great things but, because the media latched on to her so much, it really commercialised the notion of climate activism and isolated it from its roots in Indigenous activism. The movement itself has been liberalised and turned into something that's trendy.*

*I'm all up for a good selfie, but it shouldn't be a hashtag, you know—we need decisive policymaking. I've met Greta and I think she's fabulous, but she's never advocated for any policy except 'decarbonise'—she's never put concrete stuff out there, she just says something like "Protect the planet." And that's what millions of her followers will say. They don't understand that people are dying and their lives are at stake right now, not just in 10 or 20 years' time—they don't understand the link between inequality and the climate crisis. Social media are a really powerful tool when it comes to connecting with young people, but it doesn't have to be in such a shallow way. We can have thoughtful captions that aren't just meaningless hashtags that don't have any substance to them.*

# 3

# MAN-MADE

## THE ORIGINS OF THE CLIMATE CRISIS

Beware the climate 'we'. This is the one so often used by climate campaigners to warn of the peril we face, as in David Attenborough's "We've not just ruined the planet, we've destroyed it."[1] It points its finger at the entire human species.

Well, yes: we are all members of the human species. But not all members of the human species are to blame, or equally to blame, for causing climate breakdown. As well as being members of the human race, we're also members of different races (or have been racialised differently)—and then there's class, gender and the many other ways that we're positioned in our daily lives, all of which shape our carbon emissions. There is no question that those experiencing the greatest ill effects of the climate crisis are those who've done the least to cause it.

The climate 'we' erases these differences: it's an appeal to stop harming the planet that invokes not just a comforting universal humanity, but also a global human sameness. We humans have a shared responsibility for degrading the environment, it suggests, and a common vulnerability to its effects; we're all in it together. It slips almost imperceptibly from the idea that we need to unite to stop global warming to the idea that, unitedly, we produced it.

This ideological trick cleverly obscures a different 'we': those who benefit from the products and processes that cause global warming—the elite high-emitters among countries, classes, races and genders, who can also buy their way out of experiencing its worst effects. When it comes to the climate crisis, there is no 'we'.

In this chapter, we unpick who that 'we' really is—the parties that have brought us to the brink. Who are the climate guilty? Is it countries, companies, financial institutions or individuals? And how does gender fit into the story?

*Emitting nations*

Our starting point needs to be with countries. The world's richer half of nation-states emits 86% of global $CO_2$ emissions, while the poorer half is responsible for just 14%.[2] More specifically, North America—home to only 5% of the world's population—emits a whopping 18% of the world's $CO_2$. Compare this with the entire continent of Africa, whose 16% of the world's population is responsible for just 4% of global $CO_2$ emissions.[3] What neat reverse symmetry: the USA emitting more than three times the very maximum than it fairly should, and Africa producing just one quarter of what would be representative.

Britain comes off shamefully in such comparisons too. Staggeringly, the average Briton emitted more carbon in the first two weeks of 2020 than a citizen of Uganda, Malawi or Rwanda does in an entire year.[4] According to calculations by *The Guardian*, "even a short-haul return flight from London to Edinburgh contribut[es] more $CO_2$ than the mean annual emissions of a person in Uganda or Somalia". And London–New York? This produces more carbon dioxide than the average annual emissions of someone from any one of fifty-six different countries across the world, from Burundi to Paraguay.[5] When Greta Thunberg roared at world climate leaders, "Our house is on fire," The Wretched of the Earth—a grassroots collective of Indigenous, black, brown and diaspora groups demanding climate justice in the UK and global South—responded, "For many of us, the house has been on fire for a long time."[6]

China famously tops the list of countries that emitted most carbon dioxide in 2018. But there are almost 1.5 billion people in China. When you factor in the population of each country (its per capita emissions), the People's Republic drops well down the chart, to number thirteen. The USA, on the other hand, weighs in at number four.[7]

Even then, however, China's per-capita ranking is still misleading, because of the way that emissions are measured and attributed. All those Made-in-China toys, clothes and bits of plastic strewn around our homes are included in China's carbon emissions, even though we (that's another 'we' I'll return to) are the ones who created the demand for this pollution by buying the products. As Yang Ailun of Greenpeace China has argued, "All the West has done is export a great slice of its carbon footprint to China and make China the world's factory."[8] We have 'offshored' our carbon-heavy production, which is why the global North owes a 'climate debt' to the global South: we are responsible for the climate crisis, in both its ecological and social forms.

But isn't Chinese pollution linked somehow with that country's disregard for human rights and the rule of law, its political repression? Can't it pump out whatever it likes with impunity because its citizens are so controlled and unfree that they can do little to protest or campaign for change?

Well, welcome to London, more than 2 million of whose residents live in areas that exceed legal limits for air pollution—among them, 400,000 children.[9] When a Greater London Authority report showed that the capital's toxic air disproportionately affected deprived schools, the then mayor Boris Johnson held back its negative findings, only publicising the positive ones.[10] ClientEarth, a charity made up of international environment lawyers, has won three cases against the British government over the country's illegal and harmful levels of air pollution.[11] Difficult, in these circumstances, to make out who are the good guys.

## The company we keep

While we've begun to get used to North–South/rich–poor comparisons of carbon emissions, there's a newer way of discovering who's caused climate breakdown: by looking at it not by country, but by company. The results here are even more disturbing: they tell a story of reckless, unfettered extractivism, and a complete indifference to its impact on human beings and the environment.

Most shocking of all is how recent this practice is. In his powerful book *The Uninhabitable Earth*, David Wallace-Wells noted how much climate change had taken place since the birth of his mother in 1945. What threw me was realising how much had occurred in a much shorter period of time, since the birth of my first child in 1989. In the first 28 years after the Intergovernmental Panel on Climate Change was established in 1988, the fossil fuel industry emitted as much greenhouse gas as in the preceding 237 years (from the start of the Industrial Revolution).[12] Between 1965 and 2017, twenty companies collectively emitted 480 billion tons of carbon dioxide and methane from the combustion of their products—equivalent to 35 per cent of all fossil fuel and cement emissions in that period.[13]

It's not as if they didn't know. A report by Elmer Robinson and R.C. Robbins of the Stanford Research Institute, prepared for the American Petroleum Institute in 1968, warned that growing $CO_2$ emissions from fossil fuels would "lead to melting ice caps, rising seas and potentially serious environmental damage worldwide".[14] The Union of Concerned Scientists has published a 'Climate Deception Dossier', based on internal fossil fuel industry memos that, they say, reveal decades of corporate disinformation.[15] Yet also for decades, the fossil fuel companies have been lobbying furiously and expensively to block any legislation that would have curbed their right to emit.

Where are the women in all this? Interestingly, gender isn't mentioned by either of the two groups monitoring corporations' carbon emissions; but Catalyst, a non-profit organisation promoting research on women in the workplace, found that there are fewer women in the oil and gas industry worldwide than in almost every other major industry—17 per cent at senior or executive level, and only 1 per cent of CEOs.[16] Perhaps, for a variety of reasons, women are reluctant to apply for jobs or promotions in such male-dominated industries. But whatever the case may be, I couldn't find any of those twenty ultra-emitting companies in the list of US female CEOs since 2000.[17] Nor could I find data on the numbers of women of colour in prominent positions in those companies.

This doesn't mean that simply swapping male CEOs with female ones would be somehow transformative— that kind of 'lean in' mantra just wants elite women to share some of the corporate spoils of extraction currently enjoyed by elite men. In itself, a change of gender does nothing to change a fossil fuel company's objectives. But given the disproportionate and specific impacts of the climate crisis on women, it's certainly interesting to note that, in the relatively short history of catastrophic carbon emissions, women seem to have had little role to play in its leadership.

*The money men*

If you track back a little from the extractive companies themselves, you'll find yourself looking at those financial management firms that fund them. As economist Ann Pettifor shows in her illuminating book, *The Case for the Green New Deal*, the international monetary system itself is implicated, to an almost unimaginable extent, in supporting the industries that have caused the climate crisis.[18] Yet even at the corporate level, the portfolios held by the world's fifteen largest asset management groups are significantly out of line with the Paris Agreement.[19] These companies, investing money from individuals' private savings and pension contributions, seem to have abdicated any responsibility for financing the transition to clean energy.

And then there are the banks. Global banks and investors are knowingly financing agribusiness giants, which in turn are fuelling fires in rainforests so that the land can be cleared for commodity production. In the four years after the Paris Agreement was signed (2016–20), global banks funnelled almost $154 billion in loans or guarantees to companies producing or trading in commodities that are driving deforestation and land degradation in South-East Asia, Brazil and Central and West Africa. You know those fires, often illegal, that we've seen blazing in the Amazon on the news? This is the money trail that has funded them, scorching Indigenous lands and Indigenous rights in the process. Worst still, some of those very banks are signatories to the UN's Principles for Responsible Banking, according to which they're supposed to align their operations with the Paris Agreement.[20]

Climate campaigners, though, are on to them, and have started to ramp up the pressure on banks and other financial bodies. They include organisations like Climate Action 100+, a group of powerful investors trying to push the largest fossil fuel producers to show how they'll meet targets to reduce carbon dioxide; ShareAction, a charity that ranks the world's largest asset managers according to their approach to responsible, climate-friendly investment; Fossil Banks, No Thanks!, trying to persuade banks to stop financing new fossil fuel projects and phase out finance for existing ones; Insure Our Future, lobbying to hold US insurance companies responsible for their role in the climate crisis; Reclaim Finance, which pressures financial institutions to work for the climate; and Make My Money Matter, which campaigns to stop pension funds being invested in fossil fuels, tobacco or arms.

Both men and women are involved in these campaigns. In ShareAction, women seem to outnumber men by two to one, whereas Make My Money Matter was founded by the writer-director Richard Curtis. So why focus on gender? Well, as it happens, those banks and financial institutions that lend so readily to the extractive industries are gendered: as in the emitting corporations themselves, men are largely responsible for the decision-making. By the end of 2019, women made up only 14 per cent of asset managers,[21] and were found on only 20 per cent of the executive committees in major financial services firms.[22]

Again, parachuting women into these finance companies won't automatically whoosh funds away from fossil fuels and into green energy. The point is this: keep reminding yourself of these crucial, primarily male drivers of the climate emergency when the blame starts getting gendered—as we're about to see.

## Individualising emissions

Is looking at individual emissions always a distraction from corporate responsibility, or can it nonetheless tell us something useful about who consumes and emits most? Oxfam thinks it can. Matching individual wealth with global warming, it found that, between 1990 and 2015, the carbon emissions of the richest 1% of people in the world were double those of the 3 billion people who made up the poorest half of humanity.[23] As Winnie Byanyima, former executive director of Oxfam International, remarked, "It would take my aunt—a farmer in rural Uganda—175 years to produce the same emissions as one of the 1%."[24] Indeed carbon inequality is so stark that the emissions of just the richest 10% in the world would trigger catastrophic climate change by 2033, even if everyone else's emissions were cut to zero.[25]

Another study found that just 1% of the world's population are responsible for half of the carbon emissions from passenger air travel—the so-called 'super-emitters', who take at least three long-haul flights a year, or one short-haul flight a month, or a combination of the two. Because neither these individuals nor the aviation industry pay for the damage that they cause, these very wealthy frequent flyers enjoy the benefits of what is essentially "a major subsidy to the most affluent".[26] Among them is Bill Gates, gloriously unperturbed to have written a book called *How to Avoid a Climate*

*Disaster* at the same time as taking fifty-nine journeys by private jet in a single year.[27]

Dario Kenner decided to research the "unequal ability to pollute" enjoyed by the richest Americans and Britons. These high-net-worth individuals—the 'polluter elite'—enjoy extraordinary hypermobility in the form of luxury cars, yachts and private jets, moving between countries and continents. They also choose to invest in fossil-fuel companies; Kenner argues that this makes them complicit in the climate crisis. They don't just (literally) drive environmental degradation—their wealth derives from it. Based on their shareholdings, Kenner tried admirably to work out the metric tons of $CO_2$ 'investment emissions' that we can reasonably judge to be the responsibility of individuals like Rex Tillerson: former CEO of ExxonMobil, the world's largest oil company (2006–17), and appointed by Donald Trump to run the US State Department. The answer? An awful lot of metric tons.

But there's a gendered truth that dare not speak its name here. Tillerson is a bloke, as are most of the other individuals singled out by Kenner—and yet gender is mentioned nowhere in his research.[28] While we're on the super-emitters, let's not forget that these folks also lavish some of their enormous wealth on politicians who are certain to block any emissions-curtailing legislation. Koch Industries, majority-owned by Charles and David Koch, is notorious in this regard, and unstinting:

Greenpeace has alleged that, between 1997 and 2018, Koch Family Foundations have spent over $145 million directly funding "90 groups that have attacked climate change science and policy solutions."[29] Emily Atkin, who writes the excellent HEATED newsletter exposing the forces behind the climate crisis, has listed seven 'stealth climate villains of 2020': billionaires donating to the two climate-denying senators who were seeking re-election in Georgia, USA. All of these donors were white. (African Americans produce 20% less carbon dioxide than white Americans.)[30] They were also all men.[31]

I could pipe up here again to point out that only 11.9 per cent of the world's billionaires are women.[32] (So, what, now we're arguing for women's equal right to become billionaires?)[33] Perhaps, then, we shouldn't be surprised by Oxfam America's finding that the twenty-two richest men in the world have more wealth than all the women in Africa: I haven't been able to find any research comparing the emissions of American women of colour versus American white men, but this research clearly factors in global inequalities based not only on gender, but also on race and ethnicity, nationality and class—all of which helped make those twenty-two men so rich, enabling them to notch up such vast carbon emissions, at the expense of black and brown women.[34]

If we dip below the ultra-rich, though, focusing on an individual's carbon footprint raises all kinds of difficulties, as we'll see. Of course we should each try and cut our emissions as much as we can—the idea that we're just helpless pawns entirely controlled by corporate power isn't just defeatist, but wrong: most of us have some degree of individual power, however limited. Yet, for much of the time, it is severely limited.

In 2008, MIT professor of mechanical engineering Timothy Gutowski got his students to study the carbon emissions of Americans. They estimated that, whether they jetted around the world or were a sedentary vegetarian, anyone who lived in the US contributed more than twice as much greenhouse gas to the atmosphere as the average citizen of the world (4 tons). Whatever their energy choices, and "Regardless of income, there is a certain floor below which the individual carbon footprint of a person in the U.S. will not drop," explained Gutowski. That floor turned out to be 8.5 tons—the emissions calculated for a homeless American who eats in soup kitchens and sleeps in homeless shelters.[35]

This is backed by a piece of research from New Delhi's Centre for Science and Environment. Environmentalist Chandran Bushan, tired of hearing people ask, "But what about rich people in India, why don't you point a critical finger at them for their emissions?", decided to do a comparative analysis. He discovered that the carbon emissions of the richest 10% of Indians were similar to those of the *poorest* 20% of Americans; as for a comparison with the richest Americans, those same Indians were emitting less than one twelfth the emissions of America's top 10%. "If the rich of India can live 'luxuriously' with annual per capita emissions of less than five tonnes of $CO_2$," he asked, "why can't the rich of the developed world? How much consumption is enough?"[36]

*Engendering emissions*

Sticking with the idea of individuals, to what extent are personal carbon emissions gendered?

That's hard to answer, because gender is rarely included in climate statistics, forcing researchers to use a variety of sources plus a dose of speculation. What we know for sure is that, around the world, women travel less often and less far than men, especially in private cars. A Swedish study found that men owned three quarters of the country's cars and that one tenth of the population, mostly men, were responsible for 60 per cent of the emissions from driving them. The study's author, Gerd Johnsson-Latham, concluded that men accounted for the bulk of Sweden's $CO_2$ emissions, air pollution and climate change.[37] There's a similar pattern in Canada, where women—on the face of it—are responsible for just over one tenth of all road vehicle emissions, although they fly a little more. Canadian men, a researcher claimed, are responsible for more than three quarters of all greenhouse gases emitted in the country.[38]

Transport also figured prominently in a study comparing the consumption patterns of men and women in four European countries: Germany, Norway, Greece and

Sweden. Again, it found that women made shorter trips, tended to use public rather than private transport, and made more trips to serve someone else's travel needs. In all four countries, single men ate out more, smoked and drank more, and ate more meat—all of which affected their carbon dioxide emissions. The difference between genders was especially marked in Greece, where men emitted 39 per cent more than women, and Sweden (22 per cent more).[39]

There are problems, though, in divvying up emissions like this—partly because they're often based on surveys of household consumption and income that obscure an important reality: that the benefits from products and services might not be distributed equally within a house-hold.[40] Or what about household purchases that are clearly shared, like a sofa? Whose balance sheet does that go on, men's or women's? The way we attribute carbon dioxide emissions is shaped by ideas about the world that are rarely articulated or made explicit. Why, for example, asks Ulrike Röhr, are emissions resulting from care linked to the people dispensing it (usually women) and not those receiving it (both genders)?[41] And, if you're trying to calculate who pollutes more, what do you do about 'dirty industries' in oil and gas, say, where men dominate the workforce? You can't simply lump these jobs in with a decision to buy an SUV; one of those is a free choice, but your work might not be yours to choose.

On the other hand, how do we define a 'choice'—a 'voluntary' versus an unavoidable carbon emission? Driving some kind of car might be the only way a man can get to work.

In the US, for example, men are more likely to drive long distances to reach their workplace: around 3.5 million Americans have a daily travel time of 4 hours a day, and two thirds of them are men.[42] Four hours? What a poignant symmetry: the water pilgrims we met in Chapter 1 walk for at least 4 hours a day to fetch water because of the global heating that has exacerbated drought, while an American man—let's call him John Doe—spends almost the same amount of time in his car emitting the carbon dioxide that drives global heating.

We can agree that the women carrying water shouldn't be the ones paying the price for this pollution. But who exactly is the polluter here? Is it John Doe, or the manufacturer of the car he drives to work, or the system that positions his workplace so far from his home, or the failure to provide reliable, regular and cheap public transport as an alternative route to work? Rather than blaming John Doe, we could see his lengthy daily car trip as actually disadvantaging him—a less physically demanding daily 'commute' than that of the water pilgrims, to be sure, but pretty tiring all the same.

In any case, we shouldn't frame this as a story about bad men and good women, as though one gender has more selfish genes than the other—this is about cultural and social norms, not biology. The gendered imbalance of carbon emissions isn't the result of the choices made by each of us individually, nor does women's small carbon footprint make them intrinsically more virtuous. As feminist scholars have argued, women aren't necessarily more 'climate-friendly'—often they just lack the opportunity to generate a large carbon footprint.[43] What's more, efforts to reduce individual emissions often focus on our purchase power and the choices we make with it, but it doesn't make sense to artificially separate consumption from production: the goods that we consume need to have been produced before we can consume them.

Focusing on individual emissions can be very useful, though—to corporations.

## *The emergence of the 'carbon footprint'*

In the early 2000s, a new idea began to enter popular parlance: the personal 'carbon footprint'. It was a genius concept, in that it seemed to engage ordinary people in the climate crisis, drawing them away from seeing global warming as some distant, abstract catastrophe too big to grasp, and encouraging personal responsibility and action. Mark Kaufman, who has traced the origins of the 'carbon footprint', summarises the idea this way: "No ordinary person can slash 1 billion tons of carbon dioxide emissions. But we can toss a plastic bottle into a recycling bin, carpool to work, or eat fewer cheeseburgers."[44]

The idea of the carbon footprint rapidly caught on—for a while you couldn't escape it, whether on websites or in newspapers and magazines. The nifty 'carbon footprint calculator' let you work out how much your daily activities—shopping, cooking, going to work—were heating the globe. You could then tot up the amount of the world's energy that you had consumed, just like you can add up your calories; instead of a low-carb diet, you could then switch to a low-carbon lifestyle. But it turned out to have been part of a brilliant but mendacious propaganda campaign for British Petroleum (or, as it began to style itself, Beyond Petroleum), dreamt up for them in 2004 by the advertising agency Ogilvy & Mather. "Calculate the size of your household carbon footprint, learn how to reduce it, and how we're reducing ours," trumpeted the ads for a company whose sole purpose was the extraction and sale of crude oil.

In this way, as researcher Julie Doyle pointed out, BP appropriated social concern for the environment, to suggest—misleadingly—that the company was part of the solution to climate change, and not its cause.[45] Indeed, with its verdant hues and sunburst logo, BP has spent decades trying to rebrand itself as a 'green' oil company, despite a record of noncompliance with environmental regulations and safety violations,[46] a failure to adhere to human rights standards, and a habit of partnering with repressive regimes.[47] Go to BP's website today and, if you didn't know anything about it, you'd be forgiven for assuming that the company's sole purpose was to green the planet. Its declared purpose is "reimagining energy for people and our planet. We want to help the world reach net zero and improve people's lives."[48] BP, you would assume, has become one of the good guys—or indeed gals: its board of twelve now includes five women.

In reality, in 2018 BP spent $10.5 billion on its biggest acquisition in twenty years, in the form of new oil and gas reserves in Texas and Louisiana, increasing the company's crude oil reserves tenfold.[49] In that same year, BP invested just 2.3 per cent of its budget in renewable energy. When InfluenceMap, a UK think tank, examined the 'corporate carbon policy footprint' of the fifty companies with the most influence over the global climate agenda, it found that BP (along with Chevron and ExxonMobil) topped the list of companies spending millions every year on opposing climate policy: splashing out on sophisticated messaging strategies to capture the public narrative, while lobbying to control, delay or block regulation globally.[50]

The purpose of BP's carbon footprint calculator, it transpires, wasn't to help it slash its own carbon footprint; just to get us to slash ours. What has this to do with women? Read on.

## Blame the dame

When business succeeds in moving the focus of climate breakdown discourse away from their own practices and onto the role of individual consumption, something else also comes into play—something insidious. Pulsing through many of the pleas to shop sustainably lies what's been called the 'feminisation of environmental responsibility'.[51]

Though such pleas may be well-intentioned and rest on real concern about the environment, they differ from what Ines Weller calls 'political consumerism', where citizens and groups campaign for greener facilities (like renewable energy) or against polluting ones (for instance, boycotting genetically modified food). When you instead place the emphasis on rooting out individual green products for your household, you privatise environmental responsibility and inflate the influence of consumers.[52] And, because women still have most responsibility for household shopping, this burdens women with the task of making sustainable choices.[53] Natalie Isaacs, an Australian campaigner on climate change who founded the women's climate action organisation 1 Million Women, points out that "women make between 70 and 80% of all the purchasing decisions that affect a household's footprint ... In fact, by 2028, women will be responsible for about two-thirds of consumer spending worldwide."[54]

But here's where Isaacs, a can-do evangelist for sustainable consumption, takes a well-meaning but wrong turn. After an epiphany led her to turn off appliances instead of leaving them on standby, her household electricity bill came down by 20%, which set her off on the path to reducing her household's food waste by 80%. Admirable though these actions and outcomes are, they ended with her proclaiming that "Our spending (or non-spending) choices have a major impact: they can make or break businesses, change store policies, drive consumer trends—and help save the world."

Buying our way to a sustainable planet? Not only does this hugely exaggerate consumer power, it also places the responsibility for saving the planet squarely on the shoulders of women—no inkling within this approach that it might be a good idea for men to share in purchasing decisions, for instance. Isaacs, to be sure, is also critical of overconsumption and advocates a sharing economy; but, while her female 'empowerment' agenda urges you to "ditch the guilt", some of the advice is at best dubious (for example, carbon offsetting to 'reduce' your emissions from flying has been widely discredited).[55] Isaacs's other suggestions include making your own worm farm, growing your own lemon tree, making your own aloe vera gel mask or coconut and lemon lip balm, boycotting any cosmetic products containing microbeads—oh and don't forget to install ceiling insulation as well as solar panels, and to make sure that your pension fund invests in renewable energy.

This is a green variant of the advice long meted out to the careful housewife to 'shop around'. It turns up again in the urgings of eco-friendly fashion campaigners to "take the initiative to research the delivery methods of your favourite brands and email them about their packaging habits" (yeah, right),[56] and to look for materials with low environmental impacts like natural bamboo— only, hang on, "note that the process to turn bamboo into a fabric can be impactful, so it's important to understand how the fabric was made".[57] But all I wanted was a pair of socks...

Such so-called behavioural changes are often described as lifestyle changes—although, as Jane Fonda is reputed to have said, "I don't have a lifestyle, I have a life." They seem to magic away any impediments to or problems with individual self-greening. But this overlooks some obvious limitations. Rosemary Randall is the co-founder of Carbon Conversations, a project addressing the practicalities of carbon reduction, while recognising the social and emotional pressures that can make this difficult for women. She argues: "If using less energy means using fewer labour-saving devices then it isn't hard to predict who is likely to be providing that labour ... If the conditions that make behavioural change flow easily are not there we should not expect women to compensate for these lacks."[58]

Indeed, the hidden seam running beneath so many discussions about 'greening' your life is time. Women's time is probably the single most invisible resource in the economy: like any other natural resource, it's finite, even though it's often treated as infinite. Neoliberal policies that have slashed public services have already ramped up the demands on women as carers and household managers,[59] and yet, again and again, the advice dished out to women is to conduct their own mini-research project— because surely they understand petrochemicals, can read a balance sheet and have the spare hours to ensure that whatever they need to buy is environmentally and ethically untainted.

Of course, it's rarely that simple or pure. Want milk in your tea? Lay off the cow's milk—it's bad for your health,[60] as well as the planet's. Okay, we'll switch to soya. But what about its oestrogenic properties? And are you sure it's not genetically engineered? All right, we'll go for almond milk—except that each almond nut apparently takes a gallon of water to produce and so has helped create California's drought.[61] We're safe with oat milk, surely? It's low-fat, takes much less water to produce and is responsible for far fewer greenhouse gas emissions than soya or dairy milk.[62] Whoops: one of the most popular brands, Oatly, is facing a consumer boycott after it was bought in 2020 by Blackstone, a private equity consortium allegedly involved in Amazon deforestation.[63] Oh, forget it: I'll take my tea black.

The absurdity of assuming that consumers can ferret out food that's sustainable was evident when, in 2020, it was revealed that supermarkets such as Tesco and Lidl and fast food outlets like McDonald's and Nando's were inadvertently contributing to environmental destruction by selling chicken fed on imported soya that was linked to thousands of forest fires and mass clearance in the Brazilian Cerrado—an important savanna eco-region. As the campaigner Chris Packham put it, "Most people would be incredulous [if they realised] they're buying a piece of chicken in Tesco's which has been fed on a crop responsible for one of the largest wholesale tropical forest destructions in recent times."[64]

Advice about changing our consumption habits rarely mentions money, either. What of those individuals who'd dearly love to buy green, but can't afford to? Ultra-processed or 'junk' food may be bad for our health and the environment, but in the finely-balanced time–money continuum where so many women live, their choices are few. This is especially true for women of colour, who are more likely than white women to be poor—nearly half of all UK families whose head of household is black are living in poverty, for example.[65] For them, the challenge is simply buying enough food, not buying organic, local or plastic-free. And 'shopping green' will be particularly hard for women who live in a 'food desert' area, where it's hard to find food that's both affordable and healthy, or even fresh.

The young climate activist Mikaela Loach nailed the problem when she suggested that, "if you're spending more time having to go to maybe many different shops to try and get plastic-free stuff, when you could use that same time to join an activism group ... or start lobbying against these bigger corporations, then ... we need to think about where our time is best spent".[66]

Maybe *this* is the way climate-conscious women should shop around.

## *Birthing the climate crisis?*

Whenever an assumption is made that women have unlimited power to stop climate breakdown, and then it turns out that they don't or can't, you can be sure that those twin evils of shame and blame aren't far behind.

A few years into the twenty-first century, one old idea proved this when it was dressed up in some shiny, recycled clothes: population control. In the 1700s, Thomas Malthus, an English cleric, had warned that food production wouldn't be able to keep up with runaway population growth, which therefore needed to be controlled by family planning. This idea, revived by Paul Ehrlich in his 1968 book *The Population Bomb*, resurfaced again in 2010 with the argument that "reduced population growth could make a significant contribution to global emissions reductions" of at least 37 per cent by the end of the century.[67] Research like this usually pays lip service to the birth rate in the US and to the role played by consumption in the global North, sometimes noting that this is a 'sensitive subject',[68] but then moves swiftly on to its real focus: sub-Saharan Africa and South Asia.

The population–environment link has gained extra legitimacy from the Intergovernmental Panel on Climate Change (IPCC), whose 2014 report fused together economic growth and population growth, claiming that "Globally, economic and population growth [have] continued to be the most important drivers of increases in $CO_2$ emissions from fossil fuel combustion."[69] It also backed the idea of slowing population growth by lowering fertility.[70] By the time it produced its 2018 report, the IPCC was identifying high population growth as a key impediment to limiting global warming to 1.5°C above pre-industrial levels.[71]

Project Drawdown, a climate mitigation project, had already ranked family planning as number seven of 100 potential solutions to global warming,[72] and the media were quick to follow in articles and columns with titles like "Want to save the planet? Invest in family planning."[73] But what's really blasted the subject into the heart of public debate has been the intervention of David Attenborough in autumn 2020. In an interview on *BBC Breakfast*, the broadcaster and patron of the charity Population Matters thundered, "We have overrun [the planet] and now we're realising what appalling damage we've done."[74] There's that climate 'we' again.

In reality, the seductive and reductive equation that the climate crisis has been caused by population growth is seriously misleading; we've seen in this chapter who and what has or hasn't brought us to this point. Yet when marketing company Jarrow Insights analysed tweets following the interview and release of the Netflix documentary *David Attenborough: A Life on Our Planet*, they found huge numbers discussing Attenborough's comments on overpopulation, most of them supportively, and spreading them by a factor of millions.[75] The 'population vs environment' debate was back on the international agenda, as a panacea for the climate emergency.

This time around, though, it has been reframed as an issue of 'women's empowerment'.[76] Repudiating coercion and using instead the language of women's rights, today's campaigns for population control emphasise an individual woman's right to (voluntarily) choose the size of her family. Black and brown women in the global South are depicted as being haplessly controlled by their fertility, denied the choices available to their wealthier, self-improving sisters in the neoliberal global North—handily skating over the despair of many women in the global North who also lack access to contraception and abortion, or feel that they can't afford to have a child, or decide not to have one because of the climate crisis itself.[77]

In reality, 'women's reproductive rights' often turn out to be a euphemism for the right to control women's reproduction, pathologising poor women of colour for their supposed excess fertility. (Strikingly, women's fertility is always spoken about as if it happened by partheno-genesis—virgin birth—or as if women had inseminated themselves, so missing are the men from these debates and campaigns.)

We should see this latest argument for population control as part of the history of forcible sterilisation—not only in countries like Bangladesh, where food aid was denied flood victims who refused to be sterilised in 1983,[78] but also, for instance, in the US, where around one quarter of all Native American women of child-bearing age were sterilised in the 1970s, often without their consent.[79] The practice continues today in Canada, where Indigenous women are still being sterilised with-out their consent,[80] while, according to reports in *The New York Times*, immigrant women detained in centres run on behalf of US Immigration and Customs Enforcement have had their uteruses removed, once again without consent.[81]

Of course, at a time when reproductive rights are at risk all over the world, in particular the right to abor-tion, and when birth control is either inaccessible or unaffordable for millions of women who want it in both hemispheres, we need to campaign for women's sexual and reproductive health rights, and access to freely avail-able contraception—but not because of the climate cri-sis. Jade Sasser, who has documented how population control has been repackaged under the banner of wom-en's rights, points out that none of the countries in sub-

Saharan Africa with high fertility rates (like Nigeria, Tanzania and Ethiopia) figure in the world's top seventy-five greenhouse gas-emitting nations.[82]

Promoting family planning as the solution to the climate crisis is often smuggled in under the umbrella of another unimpeachable feminist idea, that of educating women and girls. A Brookings Institution study even calculated the amount by which a country's resilience to climate change would improve for each additional year of schooling for girls.[83] Cue countless more articles along the lines of "Want to stop climate change? Put more girls in school."[84]

Who, except for Taliban ideologues, could possibly object? Sounding somewhat like the enlightened Malala project of extending a boy's right to an education to girls, the beauty of this particular pathway to population control is that it leapfrogs all the problems around the 'sensitivity' of the issue, and any hint of eugenics: as the Brookings researchers put it, "efforts focused solely on reducing fertility rates and stabilizing population growth are wrought with ethical issues. Instead, the global community must approach women's reproductive health from a gender justice and rights-based perspective delivered through quality girls' education programming."[85]

There's something deeply disconcerting about the education of girls being used as a Trojan horse for the acceptability of reducing women's fertility. Of course girls and women should have access to free, good-quality education at primary, secondary and tertiary levels, and to adult education too; but for its own sake, not as an indirect way of making sure that they limit their families to the size that Western countries and NGOs think is suitable. It's also hugely oversimplifying: the number of children a woman has will be shaped by a great number of different variables, whereas the assumption often underlying this debate is that an educated woman is inevitably a contracepting one who chooses a small family.

Eugenics is no new phenomenon, but, when environmentalism meets white supremacism, it takes a sinister new turn. Certain groups of women, for instance Muslim women, are identified as 'hyper-fertile'; there are warnings of 'climate conflict'.[86] The fear of a 'great replacement' of white Europeans by non-European, sub-Saharan Muslims, as alleged by French conspiracy theorist Renaud Camus, was taken up by far-right marchers in Charlottesville in 2017, who chanted, "You [or sometimes: Jews] shall not replace us!"

Camus's theory has now been invoked to justify mass murder. Just before he massacred fifty people in a mosque in Christchurch, New Zealand in 2019, the killer released a document that began "It's the birth-rates".[87] The 21-year-old responsible for the El Paso Walmart shooting of Mexicans called himself an "eco-fascist" and labelled immigration "environmental warfare".[88] These men bewail not just that immigrants reproduce too much, but that white women reproduce too little (no lip service to female reproductive rights here). In this way, argues Betsy Hartmann, longstanding colonial and neo-Nazi ideologies have been repurposed as anti-Muslim ones, and thus "eliminating [the wrong kind of] births becomes the goal instead of eliminating the fossil fuel industry".[89]

So here we are. The climate crisis has been caused essentially by wealthy countries, fossil fuel companies and enabling financial institutions, and helped along by the overconsumption of wealthy individuals—all categories dominated by men. And yet women are held responsible for it, both as consumers who could solve the problem and as bearers of children supposedly contributing to it. This responsibility is especially imposed on mothers of colour, for the 'population vs environment' argument is also clearly an example of whitesplaining. As the environmental campaigner and writer George Monbiot put it,

> I can't help noticing that at least nine out of ten of [those people going on about population growth] are post-reproductive, middle-class white men. They come from a group which is, in other words, more responsible for environmental destruction than any other class in history. Their consumption of just about every known resource outweighs that of most of the world's people put together. There's just one major issue for which they aren't to blame: current increases in population. And—

wouldya believe it?—this is the one they want to talk about.[90]

They call climate change anthropogenic—caused by humans. But isn't it more accurate to call it androgenic, literally man-made? A group of black South African women summed it up succinctly: "The white man stole the weather."[91]

# ROSMARIE WYDLER-WÄLTI,
## 70, SWITZERLAND

*We started KlimaSeniorinnen (Senior Women for Climate Protection Switzerland) in 2016. Greenpeace, along with an experienced environment lawyer, was looking for older women to take the Swiss government to court, because 70,000 people had died in the heatwave in Europe in 2003—the majority of them old women. Urgenda [a Dutch NGO] had already taken the Dutch government to court [in 2019 the Dutch Supreme Court ruled that the Dutch government had to immediately reduce emissions, in line with its human rights obligations] and Greenpeace decided to try and do the same in Switzerland.*

*Some of us were part of a group called the Grandmother Revolution. Not all of us are grandmothers but we're the age of grandmothers. We used to demonstrate about issues around care, because care work is mostly done by women and is either unpaid or very badly paid. So we were used to going on demos. They asked me to be the German-speaking co-president of KlimaSeniorinnen (KS)—we also have a co-president for the French-speaking part of our country.*

*I've always been involved in environment issues, although we didn't call it $CO_2$ then. I used to be a kindergarten teacher, and in the 1970s I demonstrated against a proposed nuclear energy plant quite near here—it ended up not being built. Later, we handed out non-plastic bags on the street, tried to start discussions about the effects of growing bananas on tropical countries, campaigned to keep streets car-free and other environmental issues. My family didn't have a car or eat much meat; we tried to eat organically and live sustainably. Then in 1986 there was a fire in a chemical factory near Basel, where I live. We woke up to a terrible smell—we didn't know if it was toxic—and what looked like red rain. Pesticide was discharged into the Rhine; fish died and we were told to stay indoors. I had four small children and so this made a deep impression on me. After Chernobyl I forbade my children from playing on the grass in the garden.*

*We invited lots of women to join us in KS. We now have more than 1,800 members. In summer 2016, we chose four private citizens who had respiratory illnesses caused by heatwaves, according to their doctors. And in October 2016, about 450 members and four private citizens sued the government for violating the Swiss constitution that enshrines our human rights and the right to life, arguing that older women were particularly susceptible to the effects of intense and frequent heatwaves. At the beginning of our press conference, the media didn't take us seriously—they only took notice of the most famous women on board.*

*The government didn't agree to our demands, so we turned to the Swiss Federal Administration Court. They too ruled against us: they said that everyone was in the same boat and older women weren't affected more than anyone else. We then took our case to the Swiss Federal Supreme Court: in May 2020 they said that global heating wasn't yet intense enough to prove our case—that we could claim again when the Paris Agreement's long-term temperature goal had been exceeded and the climate had heated up by 2 degrees or more!*

*We were very disappointed and decided to go to the European Court of Human Rights in Strasbourg. In October 2020 we started a big campaign with a demonstration in Basel. Then, early on a Sunday morning, my co-president and I took the Greenpeace boat Beluga down the Rhine, from Basel to Strasbourg. We brought with us a chain, more than 300 metres long, of flags made by our members and other concerned people, who we felt were accompanying us—symbolically at least. In Strasbourg we paraded our flags in front of the Court. Because this is a court of human rights, we hope they will take our demands seriously.*

*We know that older men, children and other groups also suffer the ill effects of heatwaves and climate change, but in Switzerland you can only win a case like this if you can prove that you're suffering in some special, distinctive way; so we have to say that we're doing this for the health of old women. Some people say that we're selfish—thinking only about ourselves—and that we all have to die sometime: we explain to them that legally we have to take this route, to make it easier for our lawsuit to succeed, but actually we're doing it for the next generation—it doesn't matter if you yourself have children or not.*

**And women aren't allowed to do anything just for themselves?**

*Yes, yes that also. Lots of newspapers emphasise the fact that we're mothers and 'grannies'—some of our members hate that, they say, "No, we're old women."*

*Here in Basel things are going on quite well. I was one of a group of people who helped create Basel 2030, a citizens' initiative to put pressure on our city government to reduce greenhouse gas emissions to net zero by 2030. It is called a climate justice initiative, as it's the rich countries which are creating such high $CO_2$ emissions while the poor countries in the South don't have the money to help protect themselves: they can only migrate, and then we say, "No, you can't come to us for asylum." It will be very hard.*

*This is my heart's mission—it's what I want to do with the rest of my life, and what I can do; the most important thing and the most urgent.*

4

# CULTURAL CREEDS

## ECO-FEMINISM AND PETRO-MASCULINITY

The United Nations often designates special days to promote awareness and action: there's an International Day of Forests, for example, and an International Civil Aviation Day (bit of a contradiction there?). In 2009 it named 22 April International Mother Earth Day, the General Assembly acknowledging that "the Earth and its ecosystems are our home" and adding, a tad defensively, that "Mother Earth is a common expression for the planet earth [sic] in a number of countries and regions, which reflects the interdependence that exists among human beings, other living species and the planet we all inhabit".[1]

Curious that the UN didn't just call it International Earth Day, although it's no surprise that they didn't plump for International Father Earth Day, given the way that fathering is understood in Western cultures: you need only compare the dictionary definitions of the verb 'to father'—cause a pregnancy resulting in the birth of a child—and 'to mother': bringing up a child with care and affection. The first a brief act, the second the job of a lifetime. And if, as the UN suggests, Earth is our home—well, we all know which gender is supposed to take care of that.

The gendering of the planet and its nurturing is the bedrock upon which so much debate, campaigning and policy around climate change is based, whether explicitly or implicitly. It helps explain why women are so often appealed to as caretakers of the planet, tasked with mitigating and adapting to the climate crisis they have done least to cause.

To understand how we got here, we need first to untangle some longstanding and deeply held ideas about the natural world and the place of men and women in it.

*Nature, dead or alive*

"Is female to male as nature is to culture?" asked Sherry Ortner, in an influential 1972 essay that explored some of the ways in which nature has been gendered.[2] Trying to understand the reasons for women's "second-class status", Ortner suggested that, for various reasons, women have come to be identified with nature and seen as closer to it. Men, by contrast, are associated with culture and human consciousness. Since the role of culture in our society is to transcend nature, it's therefore not surprising, she claimed, that women are considered inferior to men, devalued in the same way that our culture devalues nature.

It wasn't always thus. In her 1980 book *The Death of Nature*, environmental historian Carolyn Merchant argues that, up until the Scientific Revolution of the sixteenth and seventeenth centuries, there was no split between nature and nurture, or nature and culture. Nature *was* nurture—it was characterised as female (a nourishing mother) and therefore deserving of respect:

> One does not readily slay a mother, dig into her entrails for gold or mutilate her body, although commercial mining would soon require that. As long as the earth was considered to be alive and sensitive, it could be considered a breach of human ethical behavior to carry out destructive acts against it.[3]

The Scientific Revolution, though, brought about a radical shift in thinking: "the image of an organic cosmos with a living female earth at its center gave way to a mechanistic world view in which nature was reconstructed as dead and passive, to be dominated and controlled by humans".[4]

No one exemplified this more, Merchant argues, than Francis Bacon, the seventeenth-century English philosopher and politician, often seen as one of the founders of modern science. To Bacon, nature wasn't some kindly, caring mother dispensing her largesse: he insisted instead that "nature takes orders from man and works under his authority".[5] Under his gaze, one shared by the philosophers Descartes and Hobbes, nature, society and the human body were no longer a living organism but were instead composed of discrete parts. If they malfunctioned, they could be replaced through what we now call a 'technological fix'. Nature was now a different kind of woman: one to be controlled and exploited, by men; submissive and ripe for exploitation.[6]

Nearly four centuries later, eco-feminism homed in on this idea. Eco-feminists (a term coined by Françoise d'Eaubonne in 1974) saw clear parallels in the ways women and nature were treated: the same power structure that oppresses and exploits girls, women and non-binary people also wreaks destruction on the natural world.[7] And if you follow the path of these debates, it takes you into the heart of the climate crisis and gender.

## M/Othering the earth

In one corner are feminists who don't have a problem with the idea of women as instinctive carers of children and caretakers of the earth. The real problem, they believe, lies with those men and women who devalue 'the feminine'. Like men, they'd say, such 'equality feminists' overvalue production—implicitly male in this view—and undervalue reproduction—implicitly female—and so ally themselves with male institutions, turning their backs on the 'feminine principle'.[8]

In the other corner, we find those who rail against the way that the feminine has been identified with nature, as if women were a kind of noble savage, existing in some place untouched by culture. In this view, the very idea of Mother Earth (together with its cousin concept, the Earth Mother) stereotypes women—firstly, by comparing the earth's fertility with women's (at a stroke dismissing those women who either choose not to have children or can't), and secondly, by implying that, simply by virtue of their biology, women possess an innate capacity to care.

This supposed innate empathy romanticises women as well as nature, casting them—in the words of Australian philosopher, Val Plumwood—as the "angel in the ecosystem". But "Women do not necessarily treat other women as sisters or the earth as a mother," Plumwood points out, "women are capable of conflict, of domination and even, in the right circumstances, of violence."[9] I offer as proof two words: Margaret Thatcher. The first British woman prime minister neither promoted women nor introduced women-friendly policies—indeed her own mother was famously missing from her 862-page memoir, while her entry in the biographical reference book *Who's Who* mentioned only her idolised father, as if he'd "conceived and given birth to [her] by himself", as *The Independent* put it.[10]

Particularly troublesome in the idea of Mother Earth is its idealisation of motherhood as some kind of magically self-replenishing reservoir of care that never runs out. This fantasy isn't an accurate description of how most of us mother, could mother or indeed have been mothered; it also handily ignores the challenging circumstances in which the majority of the world's women have to bring up their children. Critics in this camp argue that the caring carried out by women—whether for the children, the home or the earth—doesn't flow from innate selflessness, but rather from social arrangements that exploit women and take their labour for granted while rendering it invisible.

"The very idea of a feminine connection with nature," writes Plumwood, "seems to many to be regressive and insulting, summoning up images of women as earth mothers, as passive, reproductive animals, contented cows immersed in the body and in the unreflective experiencing of life."[11]

Those who think women have a special affinity with nature often justify their opinion by quoting the beliefs and practices of Indigenous people. In the global South, they say, the earth is regarded "as a living being which guarantees their own and all their fellow creatures' survival. They respect and celebrate Earth's sacredness and resist its transformation into dead, raw material for industrialism and commodity production."[12]

Undeniably, Indigenous people have a very different relationship with the natural world. Indigenous women often describe themselves as caretakers and defenders of the earth, and nature as their larder. At the same time, there's something unsettling about these selective borrowings from Native American, Eastern and Aboriginal cultures: writer Greta Gaard calls them "cultural cannibalism". "[T]he image of Mother Earth," she warns, "cannot be stolen from Native American cultures and used in Western culture while retaining the same meaning. This notion [of the earth as sacred] grows out of a constellation of values, and deprived of that cultural context, assumes meanings from our own culture instead."[13]

The very idea of 'the natural' as a fixed entity in Western culture also doesn't stand up to historical scrutiny. And, all too often, it's roped in to prop up dubious ideas: how often has homosexuality been labelled 'unnatural'? And where does this appeal to 'nature' leave queer, lesbian and trans women? Ethnicity, too, is deeply embedded in our ideas of the natural: nature and the environment have often been racialised as white,[14] as the next chapter shows. If you're black and you venture outside the city, you risk being seen as threatening. J. Drew Lanham and other birdwatchers have described the scary experience of 'birding while black'.[15] Binary ideas about nature and culture turn out to be close relatives of binary ideas about and within gender and race.

Another problem with this view of women and nature is that caring tasks aren't treated as work. As Selma James, the American writer and co-founder of the International Wages for Housework Campaign, wryly observed, "the woman who cleans a house is not 'working', but the military man who bombs it, is ... the work of the same woman, if hired by her husband [to do it formally] ... would pop into GNP".[16] This reminds me of a cartoon that shows one woman on a plinth and another nearby in overalls. The caption reads: "First you put us on a pedestal and then you expect us to dust it."

As the critics in this corner point out, the idea of Mother Earth also treats women as a single, undifferentiated group: it doesn't distinguish those who've benefited from the fossil fuel industry (including wealthy women in high-income countries, most of them white) from those whose lives and livelihoods are being destroyed by it. Indeed, in many circumstances, white women stand in the same colonial relationship to Indigenous women as white men do (or as men stand in relation to women).[17] What's more, the image of infinite bounty evoked by the idea of Mother Earth is especially inappropriate today, when the earth has been so despoiled, degraded and contaminated by a fossil fuel industry indifferent to its limits.

In short, this is the idea: there aren't any intrinsic links between women and nature; nor are there innate differences between men and women. Both men and women are in and of nature—the difference is that, in our current culture, masculine identity depends on disavowing dependence on nature, while feminine identity has been shaped around the opposite idea. The manufactured woman–nature link is used to keep women in their place and exclude them from other spheres with higher social value.[18]

But there are limits to choosing one corner or the other, in an argument over whether women's association with the earth is natural or cultural. If you simply repudiate the idea of women's special affinity with nature and duty to care for it, you risk fitting in with an 'alternative master model', where nature is there to be transcended and dominated—where women are simply claiming the right to abuse nature the way that men do. It's not a case of either valuing nature or demanding equal rights: instead, Val Plumwood proposes, we need to move beyond the dualism of nature versus culture and integrate them. Both women and men need to position themselves "*with* nature", in a caring role, "against a destructive and dualising form of culture" that harms both people and the planet.[19] In other words, we don't have to choose between nature and culture; we need to change our culture toward nature, together. Never has this been truer than today.

## Petro-masculinity

In all the debate about climate and gender, it's striking just how absent men have been: as I've said, all too often 'gender' turns out to be a euphemism for 'women'.[20] Yet "When gender is uncritically equated with women," as one scholar remarked, "power relations are made invisible."[21] At last, though, the question of men and the environment is emerging as an object of study and debate. As with women's relationship to nature, this has nothing to do with chromosomes.[22] It's about masculinity, or rather a particular, powerful and inescapable version of it: hyper- or petro-masculinity.

Coined by Cara Daggett, 'petro-masculinity' describes the "entanglement of masculinity and fossil fuels". Here climate anxiety meets gender anxiety, boosted by the 'petro-nostalgia' of some white American men for 1950s suburban life, which was based on the nuclear family, traditional gender roles, cars and a continuing supply of cheap energy. The loss of these structures and the anxieties provoked by it, she argues, have fired "a violent compensating practice": a "disastrous convergence" between fossil fuels, masculinity and authoritarianism that manifests itself in climate change denial and misogyny.[23]

Petro-masculinity is almost cartoonishly embodied by Donald Trump, who took the US out of the Paris Agreement, vowed to restore coal-mining jobs in the Appalachians and has been accused of multiple sexual assaults against women. It's also a good description of the Brazilian president, Jair Bolsonaro. A self-declared homophobe, Bolsonaro ordered school textbooks to remove references to violence against women, while at the same time sanctioning the ruthless exploitation of

Indigenous lands and deforestation of the Amazon rainforest, one of the most important carbon sinks in the world: "For Bolsonaro, the Amazon is a woman whose body belongs to him, for him to do as he pleases with."[24]

This form of machismo valorises physical strength: the dirtier the industry, the more phallic the technology it uses, the better. Drills, oil rigs, earth movers, crushers—it's as if the metallic hardness of this machinery bestows similar qualities on its users, while the move away from extraction risks enfeebling or, worse, effeminising them. No industry sums this up better than mining.

## Rollin' coal

Generations of Zack Rearick's Pennsylvania family worked in fossil fuels—first coal, then fracking. In a 2020 column for *The Philadelphia Inquirer*, he insisted that you can't understand Trump's Rust Belt popularity without understanding the gendered idea of work.

> Deindustrialization emasculates. It hits at men's pride and devalues a kind of blue-collar physicality that has traditionally been revered ... and rewarded ... As 'good' jobs increasingly move to the knowledge and caregiving economies, long-held notions of masculine and feminine work shift under our feet. This threatens long-standing masculine ideals of labor—'getting dirty' and 'working with your hands'—that have deep roots in the

Rust Belt. A *New York Times* headline was blunt: "Men don't want to be nurses."[25]

Trump, Rearick goes on to argue, used fracking as a proxy for masculine labour at large, aligning the Democrats with the feminisation of the workforce and hinting that the Green New Deal threatened patriarchal power. The young Democrat congresswoman Alexandria Ocasio-Cortez has been subjected to so much vitriol, Rearick suggests, because she speaks proudly of her days as a waitress and bartender.

> By assigning dignity to those jobs, she challenges foundational and gendered ideas about the types of work that deserve value and power ... Economically, fracking and coal are competing industries. Culturally and psychologically, they stand together as the last vestiges of lionized masculine labor. A clean energy future is as much about liberation from gendered ideas of work as environmental policy.[26]

Try telling that to those who enjoy nothing more than 'rollin' coal', the practice of retro-fitting diesel trucks so that their engines get flooded with gas and, in a protest against environmentalism, belch out thick plumes of black smoke at those symbols of green consumerism: cyclists and drivers of hybrid Prius cars.[27] Tough guys, eh? One of them helpfully made the link between gender anxiety and climate anxiety explicit, in a meme picturing a Prius above a line of trucks. The caption read: "You keep your fuel mileage. We'll keep our manhood."[28]

## *Macho and meaty/weak and wimpy*

If you can't extol coal or oil as proof of your manliness, you can still wolf down a whopping 16-ounce ribeye steak. As the sayings went, real men don't eat quiche, and salad is for wimps (quinoa would clearly put you beyond the pale). In her exploration of the sexual politics of meat, Carol J. Adams argues that vegetarianism challenges an essential part of the masculine role. (She also rebuts the myth that Hitler was a vegetarian.) Among the images Adams has explored is a beer brand poster that seems to suggest tofu has the power to threaten masculinity: "As a sign of male dominance, meat eating must be anxiously reiterated ... Apparently you have to keep participating in the construction of maleness by eating animals..."[29]

Adams's argument, first advanced in 1990, was borne out nearly twenty-five years later by a study finding that meat-eaters were regarded as more masculine than vegetable-eaters.[30] We know that industrial meat is terrible for the planet: it often entails deforestation, it's a shockingly inefficient use of land, and its production involves enormous greenhouse gas emissions.[31] And yet, possibly because of its associations with killing, "To the strong, traditional, macho, bicep-flexing, All-American male, red meat is a strong, traditional, macho, bicep-flexing, All-American food. Soy is not. To eat it, they would have to give up a food they saw as strong and powerful like themselves for a food they saw as weak and wimpy."[32]

Eco-friendly products in general, it turns out, bring with them a high risk of being seen as unmanly: seven experiments involving over 1,700 American and Chinese participants found that consumers who engaged in green behaviour—even something as small as taking your own canvas shopping bag to the grocery store instead of getting a plastic one—were stereotyped as more feminine, by both other people and the users themselves, so associated is green behaviour with femininity, thus framing it as a threat to a man's masculinity.[33]

Reflecting on their study in *Scientific American*, two of the authors later concluded that:

> Men may eschew green products and behaviors to avoid feeling feminine ... emasculated men [may] try to reassert their masculinity through non-environmentally-friendly choices ... one could harm the environment merely by making men feel feminine. Ironically, although men are often considered to be less sensitive than women, they seem to be particularly sensitive when it comes to perceptions of their gender identity.[34]

Maybe harping on about Mother Earth and women as the planet's caretakers brings even more negative, long-term consequences than we have imagined.

## The climate sceptic

After all this, perhaps we shouldn't be surprised to learn that, despite the nearly unanimous scientific consensus around anthropogenic climate change (caused by humans), conservative white American men are more likely to deny the climate crisis than any other group. This phenomenon of gender norms and racial privilege shaping individuals' perceptions of risk has been dubbed the 'White Male Effect', and those studying the climate crisis are starting to apply it to their analysis too.[35]

Is it that white men will actually be less vulnerable to the effects of catastrophic climate breakdown than women and people of colour? This isn't the case. Instead, researchers have suggested a more likely explanation: these men benefit from the economic system on which fossil fuels are based. Climate change denial serves to protect their interests. But, beyond this, it nourishes their sense of identity: the study also found that, among these male climate deniers, a higher proportion than in any other adult group thought that they had a good understanding of global warming.

So, the climate denial of these white conservative men goes hand-in-hand with (misplaced) confidence in their (inaccurate) knowledge. Who'd have guessed?

The conclusions of this study were echoed by a Swedish one—here again most of those denying that anthropogenic climate change was real were men: "for these climate sceptics it was not the environment that was threatened, it was a certain kind of modern industrial society built and dominated by their form of masculinity".[36]

Were this purely an individual quirk, it might be little more than an interesting but trivial fact. Together, though, these elderly white men make up a powerful and well-funded 'denialist' movement.[37] They occupy prominent positions, enjoying status and influence, and yet view themselves as marginalised, banned and oppressed dissidents—a phenomenon I've described elsewhere as 'victim envy', and which bears out the saying that 'to the privileged, equality is oppression'.[38]

What's surprising is how stubbornly these individuals remain attached to fossil fuels—what Joni Seager calls their 'petro-bromance'. Even as the banks and big money were abandoning fossil fuels and heading in droves towards renewables, politicians like Trump and Australia's Scott Morrison vowed never to give up their oil, gas and coal. Their irrational affection for these increasingly uneconomic industries can only be described as a form of identity politics centred on masculinity.[39]

## Grief

Wealthy, white, elderly male climate deniers, pumped up on their own pomp and power, are easily mocked (we must take our pleasures where we can); but we shouldn't confuse them with those men who, because of the slow decline in fossil fuels, now have even less privilege than they once did. Visit any ex-mining community, or former ship-building or steel town, and you see a place where the buildings themselves seem to be in mourning and the very air emits despair. The fossil fuel industry extracts whatever it can, not only from the earth but also from those who work for it, literally at the coal-face. When neither pits nor workers can be mined further, they're abandoned, without any transitional plan to develop sustainable jobs instead.

The Lucas Aerospace Plan, developed in Britain in the 1970s, offered a pioneering vision of an alternative route. When redundancy threatened one fifth of the workforce at Lucas Aerospace—a major designer and manufacturer of combat aircraft and missile systems—the trades union representatives, along with outside experts, drew up an alternative corporate plan for "socially useful and environmentally desirable production", using the existing machinery. Although for political reasons the Plan was never realised, a number of its proposed products were prescient and have been produced in the years since, while others remain innovative even today. Both the process and the products showed how the imagination of the workers could be mobilised collectively to transform swords into ploughshares.[40]

Nearly forty years on, we can see the Plan as another way of doing masculinity—flexibly. The Lucas workers didn't react to the threat of redundancy simply defensively, to save their existing jobs; or angrily, with misogynistic contempt for all things environmental; or even by falling back (understandably) on alcohol or drugs.

Instead they responded creatively, looking to see how their work could be adapted to new circumstances or even improved. Contrast this with some of the methods that have been suggested to lure men by stealth into acting more greenly, through 'masculine branding', for example. One researcher even proposed that, because men see soy as feminine and steak as masculine, soy patties should be designed to look like cuts of meat, replete with artificial grill marks.[41]

Do Not Disturb: Traditional Masculinity at Work.

## *Endgame*

This isn't the only masculinity in town, though—as the Australian sociologist Raewyn Connell pointed out more than twenty-five years ago, there are multiple masculinities, and they change over time.[42] While the petrobromancers resist any attempt to prise them from their love objects, other men have been exploring new forms of manhood, based on a less exploitative relationship with the natural world: 'ecological masculinities' deeply sympathetic to eco-feminism.[43] This is critical, because—as we know—women shouldn't be expected to clean up the planet alone, especially since they played a much smaller role in messing it up in the first place.

Polarised positions are obstacles in tackling the climate crisis—not just those between men and women, but also, as we've seen, those between different varieties of feminism, between nature and culture, and indeed between human beings and the natural world. (Donna Haraway refuses to place her dogs in a different category to humans: she playfully claims that they're a "companion species" and "significant others".)[44]

Instead of these unhelpful binaries, campaigners and researchers alike now argue for the Plumwood third position: that we need to disrupt the opposition between nature and culture and "abandon the dualism" that asks women to choose between participating uncritically in male-developed ways of dominating the natural world, in the name of equality, and accepting oppressive ideas of women as earth mothers, living outside culture.[45] Men and women are both part of culture and nature—but, asks environmental scholar Bob Pease, "How do we build a world in which men are no longer in control of women and the environment? How do we explore a way of men being in the world where they no longer have to deny their emotional and physical vulnerability?"[46]

Debates about the nature of masculinity might seem a long way from the immediate realities of soaring $CO_2$ emissions or the amount of particulate matter in the air—why are we obsessing about how women and men are labelled when the planet is burning? But these aren't abstract or peripheral issues: this is how gendered inequality is lived, every day; and gender inequality is fundamental to the climate emergency.

Reams of research have shown that we can't solve this crisis with 'cosmetic' technological fixes that make no change to the existing social and gender relations underpinning it. You won't stop the climate crisis using the very mechanisms and power imbalances that caused it in the first place, just some tinkering with cars here and finessing of building regulations there. In the words of writer Audre Lorde, "The master's tools will never dismantle the master's house."[47]

## BRIDGET BURNS, 35, USA

*My journey into this world started as a graduate student at the London School of Economics, majoring in gender, development and globalisation. Coming from a rather conservative working class background in the Bronx, NY, the exploration of sex and gender and their distinctions was really an awakening for me.*

*I've been with the Women's Environment & Development Organization (WEDO) around eleven years, now as its director. WEDO is a global advocacy organisation asking, "How do we create spaces where women in all their diversity, including grassroots and Indigenous women, are leading the conversation of what global climate and environmental policy should look like?" The organisation was founded in the early 1990s around the first Earth Summit, by visionary women leaders like US Congresswoman Bella Abzug, Dr Wangarī Maathai, Vandana Shiva, Thais Corral and many others.*

*When we started working in earnest with the UNFCCC (United Nations Framework Convention on Climate Change), about 2007, it was completely gender-*

*blind—I'd say even human-blind. There was this idea that we were going to technologically fix the amount of carbon and greenhouse gases in the atmosphere and humans had nothing to do with it.*

*In terms of gender equality and social issues, we've seen some measurable progress in the Convention's outcomes, as well as women's leadership, with more women in negotiating positions. But the pace of change is slow, and we often find that women are gaining power in spaces with less power— with less representation in decision-making spaces like the annual Conference of the Parties (COP), as well as boards and bodies related to finance, science and technology.*

*Since the beginning, WEDO has tracked progress on gender equality issues under the UNFCCC, whether that's a reference to women or gender in a decision text, or the number of women in country delegations. At first this involved manually counting each Ms or Mme on the official participant list, but now this data is tracked by several sources, and WEDO shares it open-source via its Gender Climate Tracker, for anyone to use.*

*The Women and Gender Constituency, which has observer status under the UNFCCC, was first formed around 2008. Since then, we've grown from five gender/ women's rights organisations to about thirty. We make statements collectively and, during a COP, deliver thirty to forty interventions in the negotiations. WEDO also runs a project called the Women Delegates Fund, providing training, capacity-building and travel support to women from the global South, to help them join their national delegations.*

*I've always tried not to fall into the trap of assuming that there's a particular innate leadership style in women, or that we're going to add women and suddenly the problem will go away and you'll get a more gender-responsive policy. But I've found that, when large groups of people with particular experiences—whether by gender or race or class—are missing, you're going to end up with policy that's ineffective. When women leverage power, they push forward issues around gender equality and social justice because, when they enter a space that's been male-dominated for many years, they prioritise issues in a different way.*

*At the same time, our work to create an evidence-based policy agenda—to ensure gender equality cuts across all areas, including adaptation, technology, finance and mitigation—requires consistent advocacy. After decades doing this work, I've often wondered why we keep having to reiterate this language across all decisions: is there a golden policy ticket, an action plan that will mean gender is taken care of, so that we don't have to be at every table? And, certainly, instruments like the Gender Action Plan and having gender equality as a guiding principle of the Paris Agreement have made the work to integrate language a bit easier; although real action and accountability—and effective advocacy—requires you to be in the game for the long haul.*

*In 2019, when the Markey/Ocasio-Cortez Green New Deal came out, the easy thing to do would have been a* quick gender analysis of what was missing, because gender analysis was essentially missing. Instead, with a coalition, we created a set of principles for a Feminist Green New Deal, with a strong global justice perspective, racial justice analysis, and analysis of US militarism and trade as well.

I think, in many ways, the current pandemic has revealed the fault lines in our society—and in ourselves—of systems that just aren't working. In March 2020, the Commission on the Status of Women, which we'd been preparing for with our global partners, was the first UN conference cancelled because of the pandemic. We—global feminist friends and allies—really turned toward each other in that moment. We started with a Zoom check-in, seventy-five feminists from around the world, and we all just cried together and breathed together. That ended up being something we did every Monday for the rest of the year. It was and remains a deeply honest space for talking about experiences and self-care. I tweeted at the end of November, saying, "I think I'm officially burnt out," and got a lot of support from my colleagues. In 2019, I travelled for 6 months of the year, going from country to country, conference to conference. I was determined not to travel as much in 2020, and then coronavirus happened—I hope I didn't accidently cast a spell.

But I think that in the pandemic, we find openings for revolutionary thinking. For years we'd been sitting in rooms, saying things that people couldn't connect with. And now with Covid, as well as uprisings around white *supremacy, I can talk about the care economy in relation to climate policy, and have folks understand—because they see this complete failure of a care infrastructure in responding to the pandemic. It gives this entry point to understanding multiple forms of injustice.*

*As a student of history, you have to recognise that these things take generations as opposed to 4 or 5 years, so there could be tough times ahead; but in the US we're seeing climate movement folks in the new Biden administration in a way we never did under Obama, and we're able to reach out to them because we have those connections.*

*We call ourselves WEDO Fierce: Feminists, Intersectionalists, Environmentalists, Revolutionists, Climate activists and Eternal optimists. As many have said, hope is a political act. We feel it's a choice as opposed to a feeling, because the alternative is... there is no alternative.*

# 5

# WHERE ARE ALL THE WOMEN?

2019: *TIME* magazine names Greta Thunberg, the young Swedish climate activist, Person of the Year—the youngest ever.

2019: The *Collins English Dictionary* chooses 'climate strike' as its word of the year, after more than 4 million young people gather in demonstrations across the globe on 20 September, demanding action to address climate change. Prominent among them are Hilda Nakabuye, Isra Hirsi, Vanessa Nakate, Jamie Margolin, Artemisa Xakriabá, Mikaela Loach, Luisa Neubauer, Holly Gillibrand, Leah Namugerwa, Alexandria Villaseñor and Anna Taylor—new names that quickly become familiar names.

Images of the protesters, with their megaphones and homemade placards and banners, are all over television, print and social media. Reporters and commentators remark upon their youthfulness, but few draw attention to their gender—even though an international survey of the March 2019 Fridays for Future climate strike in thirteen countries found, to the researchers' surprise, that the protests were dominated by women and girls, representing two thirds of participating school students under 20.[1]

It would be easy to imagine, then, that women have taken over as prime movers in the climate emergency. Well, on the streets, maybe—but in the chambers and halls where policy is thrashed out and action decided, it's a very different story. The world has been stuffed full of climate conventions, declarations and resolutions, but until very recently women have been present only on the fringes, their concerns simply a last-minute 'add-on'. The top table is a male table.

*Absent women*

Consider the facts.

The United Nations organises yearly international climate summits, the Conferences of the Parties (COPs). The 2015 COP saw the signing of the Paris Agreement—a landmark event that produced a global commitment to address the climate crisis. It was brokered by Christiana Figueres, UN executive secretary for climate change, and yet women comprised just 9% of heads of delegation to the Paris COP21, down from an already-paltry 24% the year before.[2]

Immediately after this, it looked like change was afoot. By 2016, delegations headed by women had doubled to 18%; and by 2018, in the session that took place between COPs, the figure had grown to 34%. But six months later at COP24 in Katowice (December 2018), the stats had plummeted once more to 22%. At COP25 the following year, the figure fell again, to 21%.[3] In other words, over a period of just four years, women's high-level participation in our international climate summits seesawed disturbingly. At this rate of change, gender parity for heads of delegation will be achieved in 2068.[4]

To see the full dismal picture, you need to step with me into bureaucratic hell.

The UNFCCC (the United Nations Framework Convention on Climate Change) is the body that runs the COPs, and is charged with 'stabilising' greenhouse gas concentrations. It's a vast job, and so the Convention is awash with committees. In the single year between 2018 and 2019, women's representation on its Consultative Group of Experts diminished by 15%, on the Standing Committee on Finance by 8%, and on the Technology Executive Committee by 10%.[5] Since these committees are relatively small, these percentages sometimes amount to the loss of just one or two women from each committee—but equally, this can also mean a single woman left in the room.

There's more. The executive board of the Clean Development Mechanism "has only 10% women members and has never had a woman chair". The following bodies were one-third women or fewer in 2020: the

Compliance Committee Enforcement Branch, the Compliance Committee Facilitative Branch, the Facilitative Committee Executive Branch, the Joint Implementation Supervisory Committee, the Climate Technology Centre & Network Advisory Board, the Technology Executive Committee and the Least Developed Countries Expert Group. The Green Climate Fund has never had more than seven women board members, out of a total of twenty-four.[6] With so many different bodies under the umbrella of the UNFCCC, and so many of them failing to achieve anything close to gender parity, it is hard not to see this as a systemic problem, embedded in the institution's culture.

The Intergovernmental Panel on Climate Change (IPCC), one of the most important international forums for climate science, has improved the number of women who are lead authors on its reports—but from a pitiful 5% in 1990 to still only 20% in 2018.[7]

Don't flag! We're not quite done. At the last count, among the major international environmental and climate conferences and conventions, six of nine had women decision-makers representing at most a third of the total. Of ninety-two nations that send national committees to the World Energy Council, a mere 4% have female chairs, and in only 18% do women occupy the secretary position. Across the 881 national environmental-sector ministries from the 193 UN member states, guess how many are headed by women? Just 12%.[8] As for the number of female agriculture or transport ministers across the globe, nobody seems to have totted these up, but if you bet some money on 'very few', you'd be unlikely to lose it.

The prize-winner in the tone-deaf, gender-stupid category goes—as it so often does—to the British government. Although the numbers of British women participating in climate diplomacy are impressively high,[9] when it comes to hosting COP26 in Glasgow in 2021, the British government has chosen a team of climate ministers, energy ministers, lead negotiators and civil servants, plus a climate champion, in which the number of women was: precisely zero.

It's not hard to see why climate conferences have been dubbed male, pale and stale.[10]

## Why?

Well, the old faithfuls are still with us: women have to juggle childcare and family responsibilities, leaving them less time for work; when they are at work, they continue to face discrimination, bias and unequal pay. Authoring an IPCC report, for instance, is unpaid—many women, especially single parents, can't afford to take on such a commitment.

One, in a survey of the IPCC's women members, described a meeting in which "The leadership ... [was] rather arrogant and not very inclusive. He only seemed to be interested in your opinion if you were an Ivy League–tenured, white male professor. In particular, researchers from developing countries felt excluded by him."[11] Those women who were older and not white had a particularly hard time being listened to and heard. Confidence may have come into this marginalisation. A 2019 study found that highly educated women were less confident of their knowledge about climate change than highly educated men, with people from ethnic minorities (of any gender and level of schooling) least confident of all.[12] That backs up the findings of earlier research that women know more about climate change than men, but underestimate their knowledge more.[13] This isn't just some entrenched female tendency to self-doubt regardless of 'reality'—it's what happens to many scientifically minded women after a lifetime of being negatively stereotyped and underestimated by their male peers.[14]

The idea that science is a male sphere and the scientist most likely a man is so hard to shift that, although women make up half of America's college-educated workforce, they represent less than one third of its scientists and engineers; people of colour make up just one tenth.[15] In the UK, it is even worse: more women are starting to join the STEM sectors (science, technology, engineering and mathematics), but they are still less than a quarter of the core workforce in those fields.[16] The energy sector, in particular, is one of the most gender-imbalanced sectors in the economy globally—and this is true of renewable energy, too.[17]

This leads us to a related, but specific reason for men's over-representation in environmental policymaking: climate change is still framed largely as a technical issue that requires STEM-based solutions. This framing ignores the social, cultural and political dimensions of the crisis, at the expense of women, who are much better represented in the social sciences—they make up almost half of the workforce in the UK, for example.[18] So, women are marginalised within STEM, while social science is marginalised in climate debates. Is it any wonder that women haven't been accorded a significant voice in this conversation?

There's something else at play here, too—something more broadly to do with how we think about what constitutes knowledge. Back in the 1980s, feminist critics of science like Donna Haraway were challenging 'the God trick', through which 'Man' and 'White' were default positions from which supposedly objective, neutral knowledge flowed. The artist Grayson Perry has his own description of this privileged man (white, middle-class, middle-aged, heterosexual), who sounds a lot like Audre Lorde's "mythical norm". Perry calls him "Default Man". Default Man's worldview, he argues,

> now so overlaps with the dominant narrative that it is like a Death Star hiding behind the moon. We cannot unpick his thoughts and feelings from the 'proper,

right-thinking' attitudes of our society. It is like in the past, when people who spoke in cut-glass ... BBC tones would insist they did not have an accent, only north-erners and poor people had one of those. We live and breathe in a Default Male world: no wonder he suc-ceeds, for much of our society operates on his terms.[19]

One result of this situation is that knowledge produced by men has never been labelled 'men's knowledge'—it was just knowledge, plain and simple. By contrast, what women and people of colour have expressed has always been seen as partial; as shaped and limited by their social and biological position. The authors among them are not just 'writing', they are producing 'women's writing' and 'minority writing' respectively.

In truth, legions of sociologists have argued, what we know or discover can never come from nowhere: knowl-edge, whether it's produced by men or women, can only ever be partial; it's always a "view from somewhere".[20] Yet, decades after Haraway first made this argument, implicitly gendered views about knowledge are still play-ing a major role in shaping who gets to speak about the climate crisis, and on whose behalf.

## Climate agenda without gender

So, women's voices are being excluded from climate negotiations and policymaking. It's obvious why that should concern us as an equal opportunities issue in these powerful and well-paid jobs—but why is it bad news for women in general?

More women at the table doesn't guarantee that women's concerns or issues will automatically be considered. For instance, the key architects of the 2015 Paris Agreement were women—in addition to Figueres, Laurence Tubiana, CEO of the European Climate Foundation since 2017, helped guide it to the finishing-line—yet this landmark, legally binding international climate treaty contains just three passing references to gender.[21]

But the opposite is almost certainly true: exclude women and it's much harder to notice and address the effects of the climate crisis as they specifically play out in women's lives. Perhaps inevitably, when you have so few women involved in climate negotiations, the subject of gender rarely commands attention. There wasn't a single reference to women in the founding document of the UNFCCC, signed in Rio in 1992.

All praise, then, to the persistence of women activists, who struggled over many years to get gender on the international climate agenda, through advocacy groups like the Women's Environment & Development Organization, or GenderCC—Women for Climate Justice, formed at COP13 in Bali 2007, where the feminist rallying cry became "No climate justice without gender justice."[22] The COPs admit observers, loosely grouped together according to their shared interests in what are known as 'constituencies'. The women/gender constituency was only granted full status just before COP17 in Durban in 2011; it wasn't until COP18 (Doha, 2012) that the UNFCCC made an official commitment to include women in its activities, and to publicise women's participation in committees and negotiations—partly because of the pressure applied by GenderCC.

'Miraculous!' proclaimed Christiana Figueres.

Other landmarks have included the 2014 appointment of Mary Robinson as the UN special envoy for climate change. Robinson had previously been first the president of Ireland, and then the UN High Commissioner for Human Rights; she had been awarded the US Presidential Medal of Freedom, which recognises people who've made "an especially meritorious contribution to the security or national interests of the United States, world peace, cultural or other significant public or private endeavors". Telling, perhaps, that a woman apparently needs to have been both a former head of state and a UN bigwig before she can get a seat at the climate table...

Also in 2014, COP20 established the Lima Work Programme on Gender to increase women's representation in climate negotiations. This acknowledged that 'balanced' participation of men and women in COPs was linked to gender-responsive climate policies.[23] Another miracle, perhaps, but let's not get over-excited here. The following year, delegates from 196 countries spent nearly two weeks at COP21 huddled in marathon negotiations, debating every aspect of the climate crisis and trying to come up with a form of words that they could all sign up to. In that entire fortnight, they could only find time for one high-level plenary on the subject of gender, to mark 'Gender Day'.[24] Apparently everything else at the conference that delivered the Paris Agreement was ungendered and neutral...

## Engineering the climate crisis

It's clear, then, that the lack of women in climate policy-making has sidelined the consideration of gender. This is bad for women—but it's also bad for the planet. Remember Audre Lorde's maxim that you can't fix a crisis using the tools that caused it? Well, that's much more likely to be the approach if those participating in climate negotiations are those who benefit most from the status quo.

I saw this at the Massachusetts Institute of Technology in 2013, when I attended a three-day climate change boot camp for journalists. In a succession of intensive and brilliantly informative sessions, some of the most knowledgeable and influential figures in international climate change research and policy shared their knowledge and findings. But something perplexed me: a large chunk of time, a whole session, was given over entirely to the electric car, yet not a single one of the eight sessions mentioned public transport. When a climate policy expert from California described their modelling, which showed them how they could reduce carbon emissions by 80 per cent by 2050 but left them stumped about the last 20 per cent, I put up my hand and suggested that public transport might have a part to play in helping reach this target. They hadn't factored this in, replied the speaker, because anything involving a change in social behaviour would be "speculative".

This threw me somewhat, since the whole point about models, surely, is that they're speculative—that's why they're called models and not predictions. Anyway, how are we supposed to arrest the climate crisis without changing our behaviour, especially in the global North— behaviour which currently privileges car-drivers, most of whom, as we've seen, are men? Yet the sheer tangibility and relative novelty of the electric car hobbled any attempt to think through wide-ranging changes in transport policy.

Nowhere is this allure of the technological fix clearer than in the mega geo-engineering climate solutions often pushed by male scientists. Geo-engineering involves large-scale attempts to manipulate the natural environment, or 'hack' the climate, usually by sucking $CO_2$ out of the air or reducing heat. Geo-engineering solutions touted since the 2010s include: refreezing the poles with iceberg-making submarines;[25] fertilising the oceans using iron to encourage the growth of phytoplankton (plant-like organisms that sequester $CO_2$);[26] or a giant space umbrella to shield us from the sun. And if these phantasms are a mite too modest, how about 16 trillion flying space robots to deflect the sun's rays instead?[27]

All of these are genuine projects that have been taken seriously. What they have in common is their epic scale and the fact that they rest on untried technologies. They were also all conceived by male scientists, and none of them have come to fruition. Now, you could say that these men were prepared to think big and experiment boldly. On the other hand, without resorting to crude stereotypes like 'toys for the boys' (oh, I just did), such projects to control nature are hardware-happy and have a messianic hint of the 'masters of the universe' about them.

Hubris is definitely at work here. Female commentators have warned that attempting to engineer the earth or the atmosphere could do more harm than good.[28] So too have Indigenous groups, who are among the signatories to the 'Manifesto Against Geoengineering', which dismisses that approach as "an attempt to uphold a failed status quo", tackling the symptoms of the climate crisis and not its causes. Calling for geo-engineering to be banned, they argue that the effects of such projects are likely to be massive, irreversible and potentially catastrophic. And Indigenous lands, they say, are particularly vulnerable to being grabbed for experiments like this.[29]

Certainly, these 'climate hacks' fit in with that 'White Male Effect' we saw in the last chapter: men and women (and white people versus people of colour) regarding risk differently, for cultural reasons. For example, when a group of people living near a bay in Alabama were asked whether they were concerned about the highly polluted waters and the risk of eating seafood, white men were much happier to accept the risk than white women, or black men or women.[30] The same pattern surely helps to explain why the vastly male-dominated response to the climate crisis has become so enthralled by the idea of colossal, untested reworkings of nature as the solution to all our problems.

What makes these fanciful projects extra-interesting isn't their vast cost or their gigantism, but the fact that they've attracted the enthusiasm of climate change sceptics.[31] This suggests that at least some climate scepticism might come not only from a desire to protect one's status as an advantaged group, but also from a sense of powerlessness in the face of facts that one can't control. Domestic abuse following climate disasters, the aggressive nostalgia of workers in post-industrial communities, the fear that a bag-for-life is 'girly'—men's responses to climate breakdown often seem more about their own gender-normative insecurities than about climate science. You square up to the apocalypse with spectacular, macho technology, no matter the risks to the eco-system that might result. The climate is disrupted. The solution? Disrupt it some more.

## *On the altar of 2°C*

For another example of how climate policy is shaped by the marginalisation of women, take a look at the 'doctrine of 2°C': the commonly held idea that, if we can limit the rise in average global temperatures to 2 degrees Celsius above pre-industrial levels, then catastrophe will have been averted.

Geographer Joni Seager has traced the development of this near-religious creed, from its adoption in 2009 by the G8 group of wealthy countries, back to its creation in 1975 by Yale economist William Nordhaus, who based it on—well, definitely not science. Nordhaus arrived at this figure by exploring the "tradeoffs between economic growth and environmental policy". A 2-degree rise, Nordhaus concluded, would be modest enough not to be dangerous.

Not so, says Seager: there's no real safe geophysical threshold anymore, and to imagine that we can control the climate in this way, just switching it on and off, harks back to the Francis Bacon mechanistic view of nature that Carolyn Merchant identified so long ago. Writes Seager,

> For elites situated in Berlin or Paris or Washington DC, the dangers of global warming may appear to be comfortably manageable up to about 2° ... [if] the 2° warming cap looks like a safe bet, it is only so for temperate-latitude, rich countries. For the millions of peo-

ple in poor countries, low-latitude countries, low-lying states, and small island states, 2° is not acceptable.[32]

And within those poor countries, we know which section of the population is most likely to feel the devastating effects of 2 degrees of heating: women of colour and Indigenous people.

The reason why the 2-degree target has been touted unthinkingly as the thing to aim for, argues Seager, is because anything over that would mark the point when 'their' problems become 'ours'; when climate-related disasters start to threaten life in the wealthy countries, too. This isn't about the interests of the planet as a whole—the mythical climate 'we': it's about what's come to be called 'climate security', which is another way of saying our security in the global North.[33] Sociologist Joane Nagel has remarked upon an allied phenomenon she calls the 'militarisation' of climate change: high-income nations only really start to get concerned about the climate crisis when there's unrest in poor countries that might bring environmental migrants clamouring at their own borders.[34]

## Green colonialism and seeing REDD

It's not just women in general who've been excluded from the most influential climate discussions: it's Indigenous people in particular, and especially Indigenous women. In the conservation movement, sometimes called 'Fortress

Conservation', colonialism isn't only historical: there are harrowing tales of 'eco-guards' or park rangers, working today in areas of Africa and Asia managed by conservation groups, who subject Indigenous peoples to violent sexual and physical abuse and evict them from their ancestral lands, all in the name of conservation.

According to Survival International, an organisation that defends the rights of tribal peoples, the idea that Indigenous communities don't understand how to care for their environment "is nothing but old-fashioned racism". As Mordecai Ogada, co-author of *The Big Conservation Lie*, puts it: "The message is that African wildlife is in danger, and the source of the danger is black people..."[35] On the contrary, Survival International says, "Evidence from across the world shows that securing land rights for indigenous communities produces equal or better conservation outcomes" than the programmes designed and overseen by the major international conservation charities—and at a fraction of the cost.[36]

At the time of writing, there are international plans underway, backed by the big beasts of conservation like WWF, to turn 30 per cent of the earth into 'Protected Areas' by 2030, in the hope that this will mitigate climate change. Survival International calls this a "Big Green Lie", arguing that creating protected areas has "no effect on climate change" and suggesting that the evidence shows them to be poor at preventing loss of wildlife.

Who will suffer if 30% of Earth is 'protected'? It won't be those who have overwhelmingly caused the climate crisis, but rather indigenous and other local people in the Global South who play little or no part in the environment's destruction. Kicking them off their land to create Protected Areas won't help the climate: Indigenous people are the best guardians of the natural world and an essential part of [the] human diversity that is a key to protecting biodiversity.[37]

Survival International is joining calls instead to decolonise conservation. Indigenous women have a vital role to play in this, as we will see in the next chapter—but when you marginalise them in climate projects, the results can seriously backfire.

There's no clearer example of this than the UN initiative known as REDD: Reducing Emissions from Deforestation and Forest Degradation. In theory, REDD 'rewards' Indigenous people for 'good forest management', providing a financial incentive for them to change the ways that they use forests. It does this mostly through carbon trading: under REDD and REDD+, wealthy, high-emitting countries make cash payments known as 'carbon credits' to those in poor countries, to help them introduce practices that prevent loss or degradation of forests, a major cause (and result) of the climate crisis. Wealthy countries like this 'solution' to their own excessive emissions because it's cheap and doesn't threaten their own economic structure.

The view from the other side is rather different: those on the receiving end of REDD call it variously a "forest offset scam", "$CO_2$lonialism of forests" and "capitalism of the trees and air". Critics argue that, through this mechanism, "Indigenous Peoples, North and South, are forced into the world market with nothing to negotiate with except the natural resources relied on for survival." Under the banner of the No REDD Platform, these Indigenous voices claim that REDD is a false, greenwashing solution, one that commodifies nature and provides the global North with a licence to continue mining and burning fossil fuels. Propping up the extractive industries, it does nothing to stop dangerous emissions—indeed, it actually increases pollution. To stop deforestation, REDD's opponents call instead for a moratorium on oil extraction, alongside curbs on logging, agrofuels and commercial monoculture plantations.[38]

REDD has had a particular impact on Indigenous women dependent on forests. They're the ones so often responsible for gathering the firewood and collecting the water, and are keepers of the seeds: they rely on the forest for food and medicinal herbs, about which they've accumulated huge stores of knowledge. They also play a key role in conserving and managing the forest. Yet REDD+ was dreamt up without their participation, taking little account of their needs or what they're supposed to fall back on if they're denied access to the forest. They also haven't had equal access to information about REDD, or to training.[39]

This is what happens when you're gender-blind: you're also gender-unjust. Imagine what a climate change mitigation scheme would have looked like if those deforestation and climate change 'experts' had started by talking to Indigenous women—those with real expertise about forests—and asked them to help devise it.

In the last decade or so, there have been a number of attempts to make REDD+ more gender-sensitive and responsive,[40] although a 2018 study of villages participating in a REDD+ scheme found that the women living in them thought that their wellbeing had declined significantly because of it. What these women valued most in their lives, it turned out, was having an income of their own. Perhaps, the researchers speculated, the payments that resulted from REDD went to their spouse and weren't distributed to them, something that other REDD projects have found too?[41] Recent REDD+ initiatives, the researchers concluded, seemed to be repeating past mistakes by not paying enough attention to gender equality or to safeguarding women's rights.[42] Says the principal researcher, Anne Larson, "There is no gender neutrality when it comes to forests."[43]

But there's something else that the REDD saga makes clear: just adding in 'gender' isn't good enough either. Not all women are equally excluded from the processes of climate and policymaking; and women are not the only group struggling to get a seat at the table. Responses to the climate crisis have been informed, skewed and impoverished not only by the absence of women in general, but also by the absence of minorities.

## *The unbearable whiteness of green*[44]

In January 2020, 23-year-old Ugandan climate activist Vanessa Nakate appeared at a press conference at the World Economic Forum in Davos, Switzerland, alongside four other prominent young female climate activists. Yet, in the photo of the event that the news agency Associated Press dispatched all over the world, Nakate— the only black woman among the five—had been cropped out, leaving just the four white activists.

Nakate's tweet to the Associated Press, asking why both her image and her comments had been cut from their report, zipped through the press and social media, prompting the beginnings of an international debate about the whiteness of the climate movement. "It was like I wasn't even there," she remarked. "Climate activists of color are erased ... As much as this incident has hurt me personally, I'm glad because it has brought more attention to activists in Africa. Maybe media will start paying attention to us not just when we're the victims of climate tragedies."[45]

The incident dramatised something that environmental activists of colour have known for a long time: that environmental groups, unless they're campaigning intersectionally about environmental justice and racism, are unrepentantly white. This inequality was taken up in a June 2020 statement by twenty-five black environmental leaders from Africa, Europe and the US, condemning the "systemic and pervasive racism" in the environment movement and its "casual acceptance of white supremacy".

> There is exclusivity within the staffing of environmental organisations in Africa, the US and UK which is disproportionately white middle class, creating a 'green insiders club'. Historically an internal perception has developed within these organisations that they are the true custodians of the natural world and this is acted upon in their conduct towards Black people. Such organisations also have a tendency to frame people of African descent as being inferior and incompetent in nature, often whilst appropriating our traditional knowledge.[46]

These leading environmentalists' experience is backed up by a study that found the profession to be the second-least diverse occupation out of 202 in the UK, employing the princely percentage of 0.6% of non-whites.[47] In the US, less than 12% of leadership roles in environmental institutions are occupied by people from ethnic minorities, even though they make up nearly 40% of the population. The recruitment strategies employed—using informal networks and word-of-mouth—favour white workers, so that 'diversity' consists of promoting white women, as opposed to women and men of colour.[48] Green 2.0, which campaigns to increase racial and ethnic diversity in the mainstream environment movement, noted in its annual report on the composition of the largest US NGOs and foundations that 2020 had seen incremental progress in hiring people of colour—but that these organisations remain overwhelmingly white.[49]

The colonial aspect of the climate movement was re-enacted hilariously in Michaela Coel's acclaimed 2020 BBC TV drama series *I May Destroy You*. In Episode 7, Arabella, the black protagonist, is recruited as an influencer of colour to add a sheen of diversity to Happy Animals, a vegan start-up. Arabella's mates are sceptical about the whole thing, inveighing against those who "invade Hackney to talk about cows and carrots", a moralising attitude they liken to colonial missionary practices.[50] One in particular is riled by the eco-activists who come to his door to lecture him about electric cars after he's worked hard to save up and buy himself a Mercedes. Realising that she's been exploited by Happy Animals, Arabella sabotages a livestreamed ad by diving into a box of fried chicken.

In reality, since Coel herself eats little meat, the chicken was actually a piece of cauliflower.[51] Now I don't want to give the cauliflower-that-thinks-it's-a-chicken too much of a starring role but, if you were so inclined, you could read into its existence a paradox that goes way beyond the writer of this particular drama series. People of colour are regularly pictured as indifferent to climate and the environment, whereas the opposite is true. In the US, non-white minorities—especially Hispanics/ Latinos and African Americans—express consistently *higher* levels of concern about climate change than white people.[52] A 2018 national survey experiment found, unsurprisingly, that BIPOC—who are most threatened by the environmental perils of living near toxic waste or in areas of poor air quality—express high levels of concern about these harms.

Yet Americans stereotype environmentalists as white and highly educated, and significantly underestimate how concerned non-white, low-income Americans are about the environment. (Here again we see the White Male Effect: white men are more unconcerned about the environment than anyone else—but they also underestimate everyone else's concern!)[53] It's as if there's some kind of schism at play: white, middle-class-led climate movements are so cordoned off from everyday environmental hazards that they simply don't recognise the environmental justice movement, led by working-class people and people of colour, as occupying the same universe—and they certainly don't prioritise the concerns of those most exposed to environmental risk.

Extinction Rebellion, in particular, has been criticised for its race-blindness (although they've also been defended by some activists of colour who find the movement to be a welcoming environment, as we'll hear later on from Daze Aghaji). It took XR a while to recognise that its policy of mass civil disobedience was failing to reckon with the way it would imperil people of colour: it's all very well for white people to invite arrest, but quite a different matter for people of colour—regular victims of stop-and-search and police brutality.[54]

Some white XR activists have argued that inviting arrest is a good way for *them* to use their white privilege. But, in any case, there's an even broader race problem at the very heart of XR. Co-founder Roger Hallam rejects the ideas of "climate justice" and "identity politics"— hello again, you old euphemism for black politics—in favour of a "universalist language".[55] This seems to be what induced him, when comparing the Holocaust to the Belgian genocide in the Congo, to dismiss the Holocaust as "just another fuckery in human history". Hallam doesn't seem to realise that you don't need to play genocides off against each other—you can abhor atrocities committed by the Belgians as well as those committed by the Nazis against the Jews. Nor does he see that the two events were expressions of a similar racialised ideal. In other words, he fails to understand how different injustices might be linked, rather than ranked.

So too with Jonathan Logan, one of XR America's founders, who declared:

Let me put it this way ... if we don't solve climate change, Black lives don't matter. If we don't solve climate change now, LGBTQ [people] don't matter. If we don't solve climate change right now, all of us together in one big group, the #MeToo movement doesn't matter ... I can't say it hard enough. We don't have time to argue about social justice.[56]

In other words, put your parochial, individual concerns aside, in favour of the climate 'we'.

## *The queering of the climate debate*

On 29 October 2012, Hurricane Sandy wrecked its way across New York City, killing forty-four people and destroying 300 homes in the ill-prepared metropolis. Climate scientists believe that the rising sea levels and warmer oceans brought about by global heating made Sandy more destructive than it might otherwise have been. The religious right, though, had another explanation for its severity: it was God, punishing the city for its mayor's support for gay marriage.[57]

This wasn't the first time that right-wing pastors had invoked God's wrath for what some saw as a natural disaster and others as one intensified by climate change. After Hurricane Katrina had devastated New Orleans in 2005, submerging 80 per cent of the city, pastor Rick Joyner had thundered, "He's not gonna put up with this perversion anymore."[58] This God, as well as wrathful, seems to have been ineptly indiscriminate, seeing as He swept up so many heterosexuals and believers in His destruction. Unless, of course, there are far more gay people in New Orleans than we ever imagined. This God may also be a mischievous one: Joyner's own daughter is a climate activist.

Attitudes like Joyner's have been dubbed "climate change homophobia" by climate scholar Greta Gaard. Climate change, she argues, exacerbates pressures on marginalised people, because they're less likely to have access to the economic and cultural resources to mitigate its effects, but are also marginalised in policy-making bodies that could prevent it.[59] Others have remarked on the heterosexism of environmental movements, an exclusion that persists despite the fact that a far greater proportion of LGBTQ Americans than heterosexuals believe in global warming.[60]

Meanwhile, the 'queer ecology' movement has critiqued the ways in which the idea of the 'natural' has been used to invalidate queer and trans identities, as well as to define nature in a manner that excludes them.[61] We have so anthropomorphised, not to say Disneyfied, the 'natural' world that we often see animals and other species as just a reflection of human society—as 'naturally' heterosexual and procreative, although there's plenty of evidence of same-sex coupling in the animal world, and of sex for pleasure rather than to breed.[62] As a result, the actual sexual diversity that exists in the natural world goes unreported.[63]

Similarly, there's nothing 'natural' in what we think of as 'wilderness'. National parks like Yellowstone and

Yosemite, created in the US in the nineteenth and twentieth centuries, were designed as a response to anxiety about the emasculation of the white male body: the wilderness of the national park was seen as providing a curative environment—one where heterosexual masculinity could be restored.[64] And there is another erased history within the decidedly unnatural creation of the national parks: not coincidentally, they were places from which Native Americans were violently evicted. As Mark Spence has documented, this idealised wilderness was in reality a dispossessed landscape, now a spot for tourists to visit, but no longer for Native Americans to reside in.[65] It had been not only 'masculinised' but also whitewashed.[66]

So the exclusion and marginalisation of gay, trans and queer voices from the climate conversation isn't just a matter of inequity: it also changes the conversation itself.

## A disabling climate

It's 29 August 2005, in New Orleans. Benilda Caixetta, a quadriplegic woman, is trying to evacuate from her home as it's being buffeted by Hurricane Katrina. She keeps phoning the paratransit system—imperfect even in good weather—but nobody turns up. Speaking on the phone to Marci Roth of the Spinal Cord Injury Association, her voice is panicky as she tells her that "the water is rushing in". Then the phone goes dead.

There's no happy ending to this story. Five days later, Roth learned that Benilda had been found dead in her apartment, floating next to her wheelchair.[67]

Seventy-three per cent of Hurricane Katrina-related deaths were of people over 60, many of whom had a disability. Younger people with disabilities were also greatly affected.[68] 15 per cent of the global population live with a disability, according to estimates;[69] and yet, remarkably, disability has only really begun to enter the climate change conversation since the 2010s. Even then, people with disabilities are often lumped in with a catch-all group of 'vulnerable people', a mega-monolith that also includes women, children, older people and Indigenous people.[70]

In reality, of course, there are enormous differences between and within each of these groups—and you can be a member of more than one category at the same time. For instance, clearly age, gender and race will all affect a person's capacity to deal with the effects of the climate crisis, and people with disabilities are not magically excluded from this reality: a young deaf person will have different needs and resources from an older person with dementia. But all of them are more likely to be affected by things like disrupted health services, for example. According to a 2020 UN report, people with disabilities may experience greater difficulties in migrating because of mobility problems, and can find emergency shelters inaccessible.[71] Other research has found women with disabilities particularly at risk—especially if they live alone, aren't white and are poor.[72]

The various reports, reviews and discussions now emerging are unanimous: we need to enhance the resilience of people with disabilities in the face of climate emergencies. Yet, despite examples of good practice around the world,[73] we know little about what does work. Instead, we know rather a lot to suggest that they're falling through the gaps in existing programmes designed to address the problem.[74] A UN survey of 6,000 people with disabilities in 126 countries found that their needs were largely ignored in disasters: they're rarely consulted, and only about 20 per cent of them said that they could evacuate without difficulty.[75]

I've been writing about disability for over three decades now, and it's shocking to see the same old 'crippling images' recur.[76] It's only recently that guidance documents, toolkits and reports have come to recognise that people with disabilities have to be integrated fully into the climate debate, participating in climate policymaking, and shaping our adaptation and mitigation plans.

But even now, the subject of climate change and disability remains dogged by antiquated thinking. We still treat 'disabled' as a noun, rather than as the verb it really is. This reflects a failure to appreciate how we are disabled by the world in which we live, rather than by our own anatomy. If people with disabilities are especially vulnerable in climate-related disasters, this vulnerability isn't located in their bodies and doesn't come from any inherent, unavoidable 'impairment' per se: it's produced by their interaction with a physical environment and social and institutional structures or attitudes that don't take their needs into account.[77]

For example, when buildings and public transport are designed to accommodate people with all sorts of different needs, including people in wheelchairs, on crutches, carrying babies or shopping, pushing buggies, with a dodgy knee or just plain knackered, then in some sense none of them is disabled and all are mobile. If, on the other hand, you design purely for Audre Lorde's "mythical norm",[78] in this case a young person who can move fast and without impediment, then you disable all of the people above.

The environmental movement itself must bear some responsibility for the marginalisation of disability voices: it hasn't made itself accessible to disability rights activists, although disability rights organisations have themselves been working on climate resilience.[79] Elizabeth Wright, a disability activist and Paralympic medallist, has described feeling excluded from a movement that she'd love to participate in but feels alienated by: she is frustrated when environmental campaigners diss cars, on which she has to rely. She calls this "eco-ablism".[80]

But governments and international climate bodies, too, are to blame, for stressing the helplessness and vulnerability of people with disabilities in climate-related disasters and only ever seeing them, if at all, as victims. Above all, authorities are at fault for excluding people with disabilities from emergency planning and distribution of relief after disasters,[81] even though, through their often-daily experience of coping in a crisis, people with disabilities have valuable expertise, skills and resources.[82] They could and should be the leaders of the climate movement and of climate negotiations.

So many voices marginalised—when we say 'women', we mean women of colour, Indigenous women, LGBTQI+ women, women with disabilities. Imagine how enriched climate policy and debate would be if this whole panoply of voices were to be included, and if they brought all their energy, imagination and diverse experiences along with them.

In the second half of the book, we watch this begin.

# PART TWO

# WOMEN AND CLIMATE JUSTICE

## STELLA NYAMBURA MBAU, 32, KENYA

*I graduated with a PhD in technology in 2019. I was look-*
*ing at climate resilience—I designed an early warning*
*system for flash floods. I'm a member of Polluters Out, a*
*global youth coalition backed by scientists and grassroots*
*organisations, demanding that polluters be kept out of*
*COP negotiations. I also started a group with other activ-*
*ists: we call ourselves Afro Climate Warriors and have*
*members from both Fridays for Future and Extinction*
*Rebellion. I wanted to see if we could get a continent-wide*
*action going, because I haven't seen that yet: for the whole*
*of Africa. We advocate for better regional climate govern-*
*ance in Africa.*

*In Uganda climate change is a really big thing. I don't*
*know if it's because of the activists, Hilda [Nakabuye] and*
*Vanessa [Nakate], but there's more action there—in*
*Kenya, not so much, not many school strikes. In Kenya*
*they'd say, "Do you not have anything else to do?" And for*
*kids who are in school, you cannot leave school to go on*
*climate activism.*

*I'm also interested in food resilience: it could be a con-*
*tainer farm out the back to grow food in, because people*

might not have much space, but you might have space for a container. Communication gaps between the urban and rural areas are very prominent. People still think we just missed the rains 'this year'; it happens again the next year, but they're not making a connection yet. I think it's because weather is an everyday kind of thing, and climate is more co-ordinated. So they just see it as, "Oh, we have a flood today, a drought tomorrow and then the flood comes back again. A flood in a drought, a lot of water and no water: how can these two things be this same thing?" There's a lack of connection between them.

Awareness reduces vulnerability. I have an auntie who's visiting Nairobi now from the village. She told me that people are waiting for the rain: it's rain-fed agriculture. They did the planting maybe a couple of months ago when it rained. So now they need more rain to come for fruiting, but that's not happening. And if it takes too long before it comes, then all the crop dies. So that means all of that investment goes to waste. If they knew the rains were not coming, it would make a difference. It would mean you could be going to the river to fetch water, or whatever plan B is, instead of just sitting around waiting for the rain.

I focus on climate resilience. I wouldn't talk to anybody about reducing their carbon footprint here. It's important that we're careful about [our emissions], but my emphasis is definitely not on that. I'm a vegan, I talk about veganism and the need for people to just go back to traditional foods. Here the focus isn't just carbon, it's also health. I believe that less processed food is healthier.

*The Kenyan law banning plastics in 2017—introduced by Judi Wakhungu, the first female environment minister—was very commendable. It made the streets so clean, and people appreciate it. It made environmentalists in Kenya feel proud, even though people started smuggling in plastics from Uganda soon after. Our waste footprint mainly comes from plastic, a by-product of oil, which we don't produce. It's a result of capitalism in the sense that, without globalisation and the movement of goods that capitalism offers, plastic pollution here would probably have been a lot less.*

*Wangarī Maathai made environmentalists here feel proud to be Kenyan. She championed women's rights and environmental conservation; and, in the Green Belt Movement that she established to mobilise women to combat deforestation, she found a way to bring these two things together. She earned the Nobel Peace Prize in 2004, the first African woman to win the prize, and became an inspiration for environmentalists across the globe. Wangarī Maathai used young people, as well as women's groups, to distribute trees at the grassroots. My dad was part of the Kaharo University Students' Association that worked with Wangarī through the Green Belt Movement, and that way, through my dad and his childhood friends, trees got to our village.*

*Farmers need drought-resistant crops, and access to credit so that they have money at hand. In central Kenya, the level of alcoholism—mostly in men—is one of the worst globally, and many women are left with no option but to take on the role of breadwinner. There's a lot of anger towards men, spending the money on drink, leaving women to take care of the children, the house, the farming—everything. Some women kick out the men, so it would help for them to have access to credit.*

*Women don't inherit land from their parents. When they get married, they get to use the man's share but, in the case of separation, the woman is disinherited and has to fend for herself and the kids. At this point, for them to continue farming—which is the main economic activity in most of rural Kenya—these women have to rent out a piece of farm. It also means that, for the children to have access to customary land, women have to stick by their husbands—that or they lose everything.*

*The Kenyan government has very comprehensive climate plans but there's a big distance between those and action. I feel pessimistic about climate change. During Covid, the lockdown arrived within days and they had a very quick response. I wouldn't expect the same turnaround for climate change, but I'd like to see a bit more fire in how we do it. It's not only important to listen to the youth, women and Indigenous communities, it's also important to bank on them to execute climate goals. I see them as a resource—a human resource, a knowledge resource; and increasing their capacity could mean giving them money. I've started my own company, called Loabowa. We're hoping to help increase climate resilience in communities like ours by installing infrastructure like micro-grids, which means that during flooding, when the main grid often fails, people would still have access to electricity.*

# 6

# ECO-WARRIORS AND CLIMATE CHAMPIONS

## WOMEN AND GIRLS TAKING ACTION

There are not many women who know exactly their worth in gold, but Maria Leusa Munduruku does: 100 grams. This is the sum that illegal goldminers in Brazil's Tapajós River basin, where she lives, have offered as a reward to anyone who kills her.

Leusa, a member of the Munduruku Indigenous tribe, is undeterred. She leads perilous missions to protect her people's land in the Amazon from the mining, soya bean farming, cattle raising, road building and hydroelectrical plants on Indigenous lands sanctioned by Brazilian president Jair Bolsonaro. With her band of fellow Indigenous women, she destroys the miners' equipment and burns the boats built with timber stolen from the forest by loggers.[1] Leusa is one of many women and girls across the world who, despite their exclusion, are fighting for the planet—and in many cases winning. These activists are proving that there are solutions to climate breakdown, ones that can and do achieve real results, and they're prepared to use all sorts of fresh, original methods to get them.

When she speaks at public events, Leusa invariably has a baby at her breast or nestling in her arms; she takes children with her on her forays of nonviolent civil disobedience. Women haven't traditionally been Munduruku fighters,[2] but when some of the men in her tribe were co-opted by the gold prospectors, she formed a women's association to lead the fightback.

> Our women's group is very strong. We are now in the front because the men put too much trust in the authorities. We think differently. We think it is up to us to protect ourselves ... We are trying to show the men there is another way to make a living. It's true that mining makes more money, but we argue it destroys the future for our children ... mining brings death, not a future, to our children. Some of our people can be persuaded, but others won't listen. Some want to kill me. Even my own uncle has relatives that have threatened me ... Because of the government, our forest is shedding tears. Tears that fall like milk from our breast.[3]

In 2015, Leusa won a United Nations Ecuator Prize for successfully blocking the development of a Tapajós River dam complex that would have submerged her territory. She's one of a new generation of Indigenous South American women leaders fighting deforestation—women like Célia Xakriabá, who's been fighting for Indigenous rights in the Brazilian Cerrado savannah since she was 13, and who sees a deep connection between climate change and women's rights and knowledge:

> This 21st century, it's the century of the indigenous woman, because you can't cure with the same evil that first caused the sickness. You have to overcome this colonising power that is mainly male. I like to say about the matrix of destruction that it's not matrix, it's the *patrix* because it's based on patriarchy, not matriarchy. And the women, they are the ones who are in this century regaining power over the land, because they know how to cure the Earth. Women have this knowledge and that's why we are on the frontline right now.[4]

In 2019 Xakriabá took part in Brazil's first Indigenous Women's March. She was among thousands of women congregating on the capital, Brasilia, carrying banners with the slogan "Territory: our body, our spirit." They were there to denounce President Bolsonaro's policies that have violated Indigenous rights, brought violence to tribal peoples and helped deforest the Amazon—especially through illegal fires clearing the forest for agriculture, which proliferated in 2019 at an alarming rate.[5]

Also on the march was Nemonte Nenquimo, a Waorani leader in Ecuador and one of three generations of Waorani women who played a leading role that year in taking the Ecuadorian government to court, to block their planned auction of licences to drill for crude oil in the Ecuadorian Amazon. This drilling threatened half a million acres of Indigenous ancestral lands in some of the world's most biodiverse rainforest. Dozens of Waorani women participated in the court hearings; when they felt that they weren't being respected, they broke out spontaneously into song. They won, in the process saving the equivalent of greenhouse gases emitted by around 4 million cars in one year. Outside the courtroom, Nenquimo declared, "We are the caretakers of the forest and we will continue defending it as our ancestors have done for thousands of years."[6]

The link between Indigenous peoples and their lands is vital not just for historical reasons. There's clear evidence that, when Indigenous people are granted full property rights over their land, deforestation is reduced. They know how to protect the forest, by preserving biodiversity, by using collective management techniques and with a whole system of sanctions and conflict-resolution mechanisms.[7] Outside tribal reserves, deforestation can be up to twenty times greater.[8] Indigenous women, as carers of natural resources and managers of seeds and medicinal plants, now play an increasingly prominent role in defending these resources.

### Black and green

Non-Indigenous women of colour have also been among the campaigners shaping the climate movement—women like international lawyer Farhana Yamin, who played a key role in getting the Paris Agreement to include a target of net zero emissions by 2050, and who, as part of the XR campaign of civil disobedience, glued herself to the pavement outside the Shell building in London in March 2020. Or Rhiana Gunn-Wright, climate policy director at the Roosevelt Institute, and co-author of a Green New Deal paper on which US Congresswoman Alexandria Ocasio-Cortez and Senator Ed Markey based their congressional resolution of the same name. She sees part of her role as helping people to understand the link between racial justice and climate justice.[9]

A growing number of programmes and projects are setting out to develop a new generation of environmental leaders of colour, such as Bristol's Black and Green Ambassadors project;[10] but these often emerge from local environmental justice campaigns, frequently connected with air quality. After her 9-year-old daughter Ella died of asthma in 2013, Londoner Rosamund Kissi-Debrah campaigned long and hard to have air pollution listed on Ella's death certificate as the cause of death, galvanised by a medical report suggesting a direct link between her condition and the poor air quality near her home. In December 2020, Kissi-Debrah won the argument and, in the process, helped make legal history: for the first time in the UK, air pollution was recorded as a cause in an individual death.[11]

In Reserve, Louisiana, Mary Hampton wondered for years why, in almost every family in the area—known locally as 'Cancer Alley'—there was someone who'd died of cancer. In 2015, the Environmental Protection Agency confirmed that the risk of cancer from air toxicity was fifty times the national average. The reason? The 180 petrochemical plants nearby belching chloroprene and around fifty other toxic chemicals from its stacks. Hampton helped co-found the Concerned Citizens of St John the Baptist group, to put pressure on the plants.[12]

In the adjoining St James parish, eight other black women fighting environmental racism, who call themselves Women of Cancer Valley, have told their stories in a series of powerful films: of constant skin rashes and sinus infections; of families blighted by cancer (raging here at 800 times the national average); of stopping their kids from playing outdoors because of the contaminated air, soil and water, in an area where their families and other predominantly black communities have lived for generations, and where the emission rate of chloroprene is 100 times the suggested limit.[13] The petrochemical industry and its flagrant disregard—contempt is a better word—for the lives of African Americans has turned these women into steely environmental campaigners, fighting for the right to clean air, soil and water.

For the Women of Cancer Valley, the struggle continues; but they're part of a growing number of US communities rising up to protect their health and to hold to account the corporations and local governments that have endangered it. Communities led by both women of colour and white women, like the one in Flint, Michigan, whose tainted water supply has been identified by prosecutors as one of the worst human-made environmental disasters in American history.[14]

In 2014, after Rick Snyder, Michigan's governor, switched the city's water supply from Lake Huron to the Flint River to save money, residents noticed an immediate change to their tap water. Not only did it turn brown, but they also started to suffer skin rashes and lose clumps of hair and eyebrows. Nine people died of Legionnaire's disease. When unsafe levels of lead were found in children, including her own, LeeAnne Walters leapt into action, raising awareness among her neighbours and fellow citizens and helping collect water samples for testing. In 2018 she was awarded a Goldman Prize honouring grassroots environmental heroes.[15] In January 2021, nine city officials—including Snyder himself—were charged with various crimes relating to the scandal. Walters's persistence had paid off.

*The goal: no coal*

Another area in which women climate campaigners have notched up great success is in the fight against coal. The Berlin-based Europe Beyond Coal campaign is run by a coalition of NGOs, lobbying for Europe to be coal-free by 2030. Jobs in mining and extraction, campaign director Kathrin Gutmann argues, may be well-paid, but they're dangerous: EBC works with mining communities on energy transition to develop alternative jobs. It also raises awareness of coal's twin effects on the environment and human health: when coal is burned, it releases vast amounts of $CO_2$, but also toxic heavy metals like mercury, sulphur dioxide and nitrogen that pollute the air and damage health. Coal mining is also associated with water pollution.

> The vast number of negative impacts of coal have still not been priced in. If one did that, coal would be way more uneconomic compared to renewables; but we've got a political system that shields the industry, and that's why it requires campaigning by us to give all that visibility.[16]

Not only does EBC's argument make sense—it is working. Gutmann attributes Germany's recent decision to phase out coal by 2038 partly to the pressure exerted by the campaign:

> Every single government announcement on a coal exit had NGO and civil society campaigning behind it, so we made all that happen. We track how many coal plants there are still ... [and] the fact that there are increasingly tighter pollution standards that coal power plants have to be applying is also the result of advocacy work that members of our coalition have been doing.

In contrast to the pattern in most German environmental organisations—the higher up the hierarchy you go, the more male-dominated it becomes—EBC has made conscious efforts to ensure a gender-equal leadership. Their campaign secretariat contains a lot of women, and "in our different working groups—magically!—it's always a man and a woman who co-lead". Other campaigns, though, even if they're similarly determined to give an equal voice to everybody, have gone further to achieve the same goal. Gutmann recalls the German grassroots anti-coal action group Ende Gelände (Here And No Further!)—when it put up both male and female spokespersons at media briefings, it was invariably the man who'd be asked more questions, or end up being quoted more. As a result, Ende Gelände started promoting women speakers and putting forward *only* spokeswomen.

Ende Gelände is especially interesting because, although in some ways it's a single-issue campaign—conducting decentralised acts of civil disobedience against $CO_2$ emitters and mass actions to protect villages threatened by open-cast mining—the action group is hugely sensitive to broader issues in the way its members organise themselves. They define their struggle as feminist, antifascist, antiracist, anticapitalist, against antisemitism—in other words, against a lot of things besides the extraction of fossil fuels. And they live their politics, trying in different ways to avoid reproducing "toxic masculinity in dominant speech or appearance", and to make space for particular contingents, such a queer feminists:

We, Ende Gelände, do not just fight for the instant phase-out of coal—we fight for worldwide climate justice—and that has something to do with gender roles and power structures ... In the public debate about solutions to the climate crisis voices of women are under-represented, and people who do not identify themselves with the binary understanding of gender (e.g. trans or intersex people) are in an even worse position ... We must fight for equality within our own movements: Activists should not find themselves forced into gendered positions or experience gendered violence at actions like Ende Gelände.[17]

Sensitive to racism in the environment movement, the group also takes active steps to address this in its own campaign. And it makes provision for people who want to be involved, but aren't able to trudge for miles through fields or past police chains—those, for example, in wheelchairs or on crutches. Ende Gelände's blockades have temporarily closed pits and coal-power plants, and are credited with a role in Germany's decision to phase out coal. The group doesn't think this is fast enough—their direct action continues.

### Climate activists in the spotlight

What distinguishes many female climate activists today, especially those in positions of power, is this willingness to include ordinary people in the conversation, and in the action that needs to take place. These women leaders speak about the climate in a new way—one that resonates particularly with women. Alexandria Ocasio-Cortez, the young Democrat congresswoman who co-sponsored the Green New Deal bill, is a striking example. Defining herself clearly as a Latina American, she identifies more with her constituents in the Bronx and Queens, whose background she shares, than she does with the male politicians, often old and white, on Capitol Hill (Bernie Sanders excluded). She speaks eloquently, unequivocally and regularly through Twitter.

Like Ocasio-Cortez, Caroline Lucas uses her power to convince ordinary people that she shares their fight. The sole British Green Party member in Parliament, she joined her constituents in 2019 on a climate strike in Brighton, where she told them:

> Being the sole Green MP in Parliament has sometimes felt like a lonely job. But every time I see young people taking to the streets like you are today, I don't feel lonely. I feel among hundreds of thousands of friends here in the UK—and millions more across the world— who see the reality of the climate emergency. And who won't stop until our political leaders do too.[18]

Lucas works through raising the subject in Parliament: in 2019 she tabled a motion declaring a climate emergency that was picked up by the Labour Party and passed by the House of Commons. In 2020–21 she co-sponsored the Wellbeing of Future Generations Bill, which would require the UK government, in its planning, to prioritise the environment and the prevention of poverty. For over ten years, she's acted as the green conscience of the UK Parliament, its Greek chorus on the climate crisis. And for her, womanhood is not incidental to the cause. Lucas believes that women's unique experiences give them an important role to play in preventing a climate catastrophe. Among those who inspired her, she singles out the German Green MP Petra Kelly, and Rachel Carson, the American marine biologist whose 1962 book *Silent Spring* created enormous public concern about the harmful effects of indiscriminate pesticide use.

An important part of the Green MP's role in climate action is the fact that she is just as happy talking about the emotional side of the climate crisis as about the harmful effects of fracking. "Why is it that we're so squeamish about discussing how we *feel* about the climate crisis?" Lucas asks. "Only by talking through how we feel will we manage to dig deep enough to find the creativity and innovation that are needed to respond effectively to what many now recognise is the biggest threat facing humankind."[19]

A politician of another stripe, the former Irish president Mary Robinson, brought to bear her past experience as a UN commissioner on human rights in her two stints as the UN's special envoy on climate change during the 2010s. But Robinson takes the climate emergency far beyond the negotiating hall or the parliamentary committee room. Her special skill is talking climate justice in jargon-free language: she can make radical ideas sound like common sense, in her book, *Climate Justice*; on the podcast series about women and the climate crisis, *Mothers of Invention*, that she co-hosts with Irish comedian Maeve Higgins; and through the Mary Robinson Foundation—Climate Justice, which she established.

These women all use the power they have to tell human stories about the climate crisis. Margaret Atwood does it through fiction: the threat of extinction caused by environmental degradation has long hovered over her novels, notably *The Handmaid's Tale*, which hints that pollution and radioactive waste have caused mass infertility, the handmaids the only fertile exceptions. Atwood has articulated the same dystopian vision in interviews about the world today, predicting that the apocalyptic effects of environmental damage will hit women hardest,[20] and emphasising that the climate crisis and the rights of women are "very connected, so that people who want to suppress women also want to pretend that there is no climate crisis. So if you suppress women you suppress also some very strong voices about the climate crisis."[21]

Similarly, some actors use film to raise public awareness about the environment. Elliot Page, formerly Ellen Page, the award-winning Canadian star of *Juno*, directed and co-produced *There's Something in the Water*, a documentary about the effects of environmental degradation on First Nations communities in Nova Scotia. After Greta Thunberg thundered, "Our house is on fire," the actress Jane Fonda joined the weekly 'Fire Drill Fridays' rallies outside Capitol Hill in Washington DC, until Covid-19 forced them online.[22] Noting that two thirds of those at the rallies were older women, Fonda was arrested five times, but declared, "I'm almost 83 years old. What the heck can they do to me? ... So I'm willing to step into the fire—and there is a fire and I'm stepping into it."[23]

## Climate crimes

This willingness to take risks, and push a campaign to its very limits, has produced a whole raft of inventive new ways to try and force governments to make dramatic changes in their climate-related policies. In 2009, Scottish barrister Polly Higgins posed a problem of law that had never come up in the dusty tomes of legal precedent: "How do we create a legal duty to care for the earth?" The answer, she concluded, lay in recognising a new crime: ecocide.

Ecocide, she said,

is a crime against the living natural world—ecosystem loss, damage or destruction ... Dangerous industrial activity causes climate ecocide. Currently there is a missing responsibility to protect ... What is required is the expansion of our collective duty of care to protect the natural living world and all life. International eco-cide crime is a law to protect the Earth.[24]

Making ecocide an international crime would require an amendment to the 1998 Rome Statute of the International Criminal Court, which governs existing crimes against humanity. Ecocide was actually included in early drafts of the Rome Statute—until 1996, when it was dropped at the behest of the UK, France and the Netherlands.

For Higgins, its restoration was no abstract legal question: it became her life's work. Selling her house to finance her campaign, she drafted a model law to show what the crime of ecocide could look like.[25] Polly Higgins died in 2019, but a panel of international lawyers, convened by the Stop Ecocide Foundation, are carrying on her work. Seventy-five years after the concepts of genocide and crimes against humanity were established at the Nuremberg trials of high-ranking Nazi officers, they are drafting plans for a legally enforceable crime of ecocide—criminalising mass damage to and destruction of ecosystems.

Higgins wanted to create a new law, but other women climate activists have made imaginative use of existing laws to try and get greenhouse gas emissions lowered. Among the boldest is Maura Healey, the Massachusetts attorney general, who is suing Exxon Mobil—the world's largest publicly traded oil and gas company—for misleading and deceiving consumers and investors by omitting, denying and downplaying the risks of climate change. According to Healey's argument, Exxon knew decades ago that rising fossil fuel use was causing climate change that could be "catastrophic" for the world, and that maintaining a safe climate would require "sharply curtailing the use of fossil fuels". But rather than disclose these facts to consumers and investors, she alleges, Exxon engaged in a decades-long campaign to deceive them about the climate-related impacts of its products—a campaign that continues to this day.[26] The case is ongoing.

Another pioneer in legal climate activism is Urgenda, the Dutch citizens' action group founded by Marjan Minnesma in 2007. Backed by 886 concerned Dutch citizens, Urgenda started a legal case against the Dutch government in 2015. It took them four years to reach the Dutch Supreme Court but, in December 2019, it won in a milestone ruling: the Supreme Court ordered the government to reduce the country's emissions by the end of 2020 to 75 per cent of 1990 levels. David Boyd, the UN special rapporteur on human rights and the environment, judged it "the most important climate change court decision in the world so far, confirming that human rights are jeopardised by the climate emergency and that wealthy nations are legally obligated to achieve rapid and substantial emissions reduction".[27] I defy you not to shed a tear watching the 'aftermovie' of Urgenda's victory, as the activists, their supporters and even their male lawyer whoop with joy outside the courtroom, tearing up themselves.[28]

After Urgenda's success, Minnesma was invited to meet government ministers to discuss potential carbon reduction policies. She presented them with dozens. The victory has inspired campaigners in many other countries to try to litigate their governments into reducing emissions, among them Ireland, Belgium, Canada, France, Germany, India, Nepal, Pakistan and Switzerland (as we heard from Rosmarie Wydler-Wälti). Some cases were won, including in Ireland; others were lost, and still others are ongoing—as of November 2020, over 1,650 have been filed in total, from all six continents.[29]

One of the most famous has been *Juliana vs United States*. Originally filed in 2015, this case saw twenty-one young people, including Kelsey Juliana, take the US government to court, on the grounds that it had violated their fundamental rights by allowing greenhouse gases to rise despite the scientific evidence. Government lawyers responded, revealingly, that Americans do not have a right to "a climate capable of sustaining human life"—nothing if not frank.[30] In 2020, the lawsuit finally reached the US Supreme Court, which reluctantly concluded that, despite making an impressive case, it was beyond the Court's constitutional power to grant, and that the plaintiffs, now aged between 12 and 23, needed to take their case to the political branch of the government.

Much had changed in the five years since the case was first brought. Those five years were the hottest on record.[31] But it wasn't just the globe that had heated up: so had the climate movement. By the time the Supreme Court delivered its judgment, the idea of teenage climate activists had become much less astonishing.

## The Greta Effect—version 1

It began with a photo. A slight, 15-year-old girl with plaits, dressed in a yellow raincoat and blue trainers, sitting on a Stockholm street corner on a Friday, next to a hand-daubed sign reading *Skolstrejk för Klimatet*. She looked so young, so serious and so alone. Normally you only see homeless adults sitting on a street corner like this, begging for a few coins—not a teenage girl begging on behalf of the planet.

In 2018 when her protest began, it was almost comical, the idea of a school strike: strikes mean withdrawing your labour, but all that schoolkids can withdraw is going to school, and then they're called truants or slackers. Yet, as other young activists joined her under the banner Fridays for Future in 2019, Greta Thunberg's campaign rapidly acquired momentum. Almost instantly gaining an international platform, she became one of the most recognised young women on the planet, often referred to simply as Greta. Four months after the start of her school climate strike, she was already addressing COP24 in Poland; other major international gatherings were soon to follow.

Powered by anger, 'Greta' distilled the arguments about the climate crisis into a series of short, pithy but memorably explosive statements: "We are facing an existential threat," "Our house is on fire," and, to a UN Climate Summit, "How dare you!"

Thunberg became a meme that zipped through social media like a contagion—a positive one, in contrast to the deadly virus that would follow in 2020. Unable to vote, denied a voice through existing channels of political power or traditional media, young people turned to the forums that *they* dominated—Facebook, Twitter, Instagram and TikTok—to organise. Between 2019 and early 2020, until Covid-19 stopped them, they flooded the streets in more than 2,000 cities, in mass rallies that provided visual proof of their numbers, determination and verve. One lone climate striker even braved the streets in China—Ou Hongyi, a 17-year-old girl.[32]

Their sense of urgency had been crystallised by the 2018 IPCC report, which concluded that only twelve years remained to avoid environmental catastrophe. Unless, by 2030, global heating had been kept to no more than 1.5 degrees Celsius (2.7 degrees Fahrenheit) above pre-industrial levels, and unless carbon emissions had reduced by 45%, hundreds of millions of people would face dramatically higher risks of drought, floods, extreme heat and poverty.

That single fact—identifying a twelve-year window in which to save the planet—transformed the climate crisis from an abstract debate into something concrete and imminent, lapping at young climate activists' ankles. It brought environmental catastrophe into their imaginable individual lifespan: they added twelve to their current age and saw their future disappear. As Jamie Margolin, co-founder of the US youth climate movement Zero Hour, said, "In 12 years, I'll only be 28! My life will just be beginning when the world is ending!"[33] Do not waste time, the young campaigners urged adults: this time is not yours to waste. This is our time. To make this absolutely clear, the Zero Hour website features a countdown—in years, days, hours, minutes, seconds—to 2030.

Out on the streets, there was something infinitely touching about the school strikers' homemade banners and placards, fashioned out of whatever piece of cardboard was to hand. "There is no planet B" was a popular one, alongside "You will die of old age. I will die of climate change"; "The oceans are rising and so are we"; "Denial is not a policy"; and, my favourite, "Sorry, I can't clean my room—I have a planet to save." The protesters' festive air, face paint and exuberance accentuated their youthfulness, as they warned of destruction even while they noisily celebrated life. A new breed of campaigner had been born, the student climate activist—and most seemed to be teenage girls.

On the 15 March 2019 demo in London, I asked a group of four of them, with one lone boy, why they thought so many young women had got involved. Among their various theories was the idea that young women were more used to debating social issues. The boy had asked his male friends to come along, but they'd said that they couldn't be bothered. The girls, he said, alluding perhaps to the women's movement, were used to protesting.

At the 20 September 2019 climate strike in Quito, Ecuador, Maria Belen, the 22-year-old trainee physio-therapist who organised the event, told me, "I learned that when I have a strong belief I should speak out and now I don't feel scared anymore."[34] In fact, there were plenty of boys and young men on both the London and Quito strikes, it's just that they weren't in the majority nor, unusually, were they the leaders—and, interestingly, they seemed fine with that.

2018–19 was a thrilling, moving moment for the climate campaign, one when it broke through into the mainstream and captured the headlines. No longer could climate activism be dismissed as the preserve of backward-looking, hippy-dippy, sandal-wearing, lentil-munching jeremiahs, or whatever other patronising caricature fossil fuels' defenders chose to lob their way.

That said, the most prominent activists were still mocked and trolled, largely by older white men—although some older white women pitched in too. The antagonism of certain older women towards the young campaigners was memorably illustrated by the 2019 encounter between the US youth movement Sunrise, pushing for a Green New Deal, and Senator Dianne Feinstein, the Democrat from California. YouTube shows the impassioned child climate activists crowding into Feinstein's office, imploring her to vote for Ocasio-Cortez and Markey's Green New Deal bill, because only ten years remained to turn climate change around.[35] In a response later described by the movement as a "tour de force of tone-deaf condescension",[36] Feinstein insists,

> It's not going to get turned round in ten years ... You know what's interesting about this group? I've been doing this for thirty years. I know what I'm doing. You come in here and say it must be done my way or the highway. I don't respond to that. I've gotten elected.[37]

The senator was visibly riled by these small upstarts, clamouring to overturn business-as-usual and seeming to have come out of nowhere.

### The Greta Effect—version 2

Well, not quite. The youth climate movement came out of somewhere, and it wasn't created solely by Greta Thunberg. Jamie Margolin co-founded Zero Hour in 2017, at roughly the same time as Varshini Prakash was setting up the Sunrise movement—yet the spotlight never shone on them as individuals as much as it later did on Thunberg. Neither of them has acquired first-name-only fame.

Did this have anything to do with the fact that neither of them was white? Prakash's parents emigrated to the US from India. Margolin describes herself as a "queer mixed-race latina and daughter of a Colombian immigrant and an Ashkenazi Jew", and Zero Hour as a "color-led" movement.[38]

In *Winning the Green New Deal*, Prakash describes in fascinating detail the meticulous planning and forethought that went into developing Sunrise as a mass movement—no thin air about it.[39] On the contrary, the movement acknowledges some of its antecedents, like the Occupy movement of 2011. Almost certainly, the #MeToo movement fed into it somewhere too, along with the 2018 student-led March for Our Lives mass demo in favour of US gun control, itself boosted by the earlier, rousing "We call BS" speech of 18-year-old Emma Gonzalez, survivor of the Parkland high school shooting.[40] These green shoots of protest had fertilised each other.

And then there were the women out on the streets of Sudan, Algeria and Venezuela in 2019—women who wanted to be part of a mass public protest against the old white men running and ruining their countries. Movements rarely come out of nowhere: they seed and foment, seethe and bubble before they erupt. But such slowly unfolding growth comes onto the mass media radar only when it becomes an event, rather than when it's a process.

Thunberg herself has tried to share the limelight, encouraging reporters to interview not only her but also other young climate activists, particularly of colour. Yet many still bristle at the way in which she—a young white woman, born in a wealthy country to parents who could afford to accommodate their daughter's convictions—has been singled out, at the expense of young activists in the global South.

As the Nigerian writer Chika Unigwe put it,

> Frustratingly, these other activists are often referred to in the media as the 'Greta Thunberg' of their country, or are said to be following in her footsteps, even in cases where they began their public activism long before she started hers. ... This tendency of the media to present Thunberg as the one who calls, and the others existing only to heed her call, is problematic, especially for those black and brown activists whose media invisibility leads to invisibility [in the eyes of] organisations whose help they could greatly benefit from. This 'white saviour' narrative invalidates the impact of locals working in their communities and perpetuates the stereotype of 'the native with no agency' who cannot help themselves.[41]

This privileging of the Thunberg narrative, argues Unigwe, ends up impacting on the perceptions of young climate campaigners of colour themselves: it "creates a world where [15-year-old Ugandan activist Leah]

Namugerwa would mention a Swedish teenager she only heard about a year ago as inspiration, but not Wangarī Maathai, the environmentalist from neighbouring Kenya who won the Nobel peace prize in 2004."

While this is all true, and while there are plenty of valid criticisms that can be levelled at Thunberg's politics, the accusation of white privilege has also been appropriated by those who want Thunberg to stay quiet for very different reasons—those outraged that she, a mere slip of a thing, has been given a platform to challenge the white patriarchs overseeing the breakdown of the climate. She seems to have triggered an eruption of rage in a number of older white men. The attacks of these trolls and 'critics' are both opportunistic and deeply personal: they hope to shame her into silence by mocking her as 'freakish' or 'weird', without seeming to notice that she freely embraces such descriptions herself.

Thunberg was lionised for many reasons, among them her mediagenic appeal. The ferocity of her speech, set against her childlike appearance and the backstory of her Asperger's syndrome, made her distinctive, oddball—a 'character' rather than a regular protester.

But perhaps just as important in earning her the media spotlight was the simplicity of her declarations, and here perhaps she has a greater case to answer. Her call to "follow the science" seemed to blast a pure, clear path through all of the assertion and counter-assertion in the adult climate debate. But, while it's true that climate scientists are near-unanimous about the catastrophe that will unfold unless we decarbonise fast, "follow the science" is ultimately a reductive maxim; it's politics, not science, that will guide us out of this place of peril. 'Following the science' can't make for us the complex and challenging political and social decisions that will need to be made. Despite the consensus on the climate crisis, there's rarely just a single science, anyway—as became apparent in 2020 when Boris Johnson and his Conservative government in Britain seized upon Thunberg's "following the science" line to justify whatever current decision about the pandemic they were making that day, no matter how many scientists disagreed with it.

There were other disquieting strands to the Greta phenomenon. Her status as a child evoked all kinds of primitive fantasies about innocence, which she embodied particularly as a girl-child, implicitly a reproducer of the future.[42] It was interesting to see that alongside Thunberg and the school strikers sat another kind of protester: the mother or parent, as in Moms Clean Air Force or Parents for Future, groups whose very names seemed to suggest that their members' voices deserved to be heard on account of their maternity or paternity, as producers of the reproducers.

Thunberg hasn't represented herself as a young girl whose future fertility is at stake, but she's certainly been explicit in framing as unnatural and criminal the way that responding to climate breakdown has been "left" to kids who should be in school: a failure of responsibility on the part of "the grown-ups". This line of thinking has arguably contributed to a culture in which climate campaigning is understood as being driven by parental duty—simultaneously excluding those without children and perpetuating the often unhelpful 'Mother Earth' tropes explored in Chapter 4. Although some of the parents and grandparents campaigning for the end of fossil fuels have been at it for decades, others are simply responding to the call that they already should have cleared all this up, 'for the children'; that they have failed in their parental, often maternal, duties.

Another problem with Thunberg's discourse is the way it nourished the growing narrative among youth protesters around intergenerational unfairness: the one that blames old people for zero-hours jobs, soaring property prices and university tuition fees, and now the climate crisis. "Young people are being let down by older generations and those in power," Thunberg declared.[43] But the fact that the most powerful people in our societies are old doesn't mean that most old people are powerful—swathes of older people have neither money nor influence, and also support the climate strikes.[44] Other young climate activists have taken up the dismissive 'OK boomer' rhetoric; the singer Billie Eilish told *NME*, "Hopefully the adults and the old people start listening to us [about climate change] ...

Old people are gonna die and don't really care if we die, but we don't wanna die yet."[45]

Thunberg herself has admitted that "this is not a single-generation job. It's humanity's job ... We're asking adults to step up alongside us."[46] And the intergenerational turn-out at XR's sit-ins showed that plenty already had. We grow out of hope, it's sometimes said; but some people evidently grow into it as they age. Fighting for the right to clean air and water can't be a matter of indifference to those most likely next to die, any more than it can be the preserve of those most recently born. Yet sometimes the zest and resolve of young campaigners has ballooned into hubris, as when a 14-year-old American climate activist declared that "we are the generation that will fix this world".[47] Such inflated expectations, resting on such young shoulders. And they appear to be getting younger.

I spoke to Licypriya Kangujam, a 9-year-old Indian girl from an Indigenous family and one of the youngest child environmental activists in the world, who has already addressed the UN, at COP25 in 2019. Licy spends a lot of her time planting trees. She helped organise the 2019 Great October March of school students to the Indian Parliament, trying to get its members to pass a bill to control emissions and curb the country's severe air pollution. Temporarily dropping out of school to devote time to her climate activism, she helped design a "symbolic survival kit", SUKIFU, that acts as a filter for poor air.

Over the course of that year, Licy travelled with her father to more than thirty-two countries. She speaks fluently about the climate crisis, if sometimes a little over-fluently. Her parents make sacrifices, not just financial, to support her activism: they fear for her safety and the media attention trained on her—she's already been arrested once. A hostile Indian press has accused Licy's parents of all sorts of fraudulent activities, including using her as a tool to advance their own views.

Licy plans to attend COP26 in Glasgow—but it'll take her nineteen days to get there by a solar-powered vehicle. She's smart and sharp, telling the BBC, "If you call me the Greta of India, you are not covering my story ... I have my own identity." Although she and Greta respect each other, she said, "I already began a movement to fight climate change before Greta started."[48]

"People always tell me that you are too young to get involved in such activism," she said to me, "but I proved to them that age doesn't matter—you can make a difference, big or small. I am a girl child: I'm strong, smart, intelligent."[49] Beneath Licy's green girl 'empowerment' bravado, there's a wistfulness to both her and her father about the path that they've chosen. In 2019, she saw her mother for a total of thirty-five days—an average of twice a month—and missed her. She also missed her teachers and friends. Most parents of junior school children try to limit the time they spend messing around on social media; Licy's try to limit the hours she devotes to her activism. When I reached her on a video call, she'd been playing with a friend, and admitted that she was tired: "I don't get the free time to play with my friends." The costs of child climate activism can be high.

## Youth climate activism at large

With her Fridays for Future strikes, Greta Thunberg undoubtedly hit upon a quiet but novel way of raising the alarm about the climate crisis. Yet there is arguably as much cause for concern as for celebration in the explosion of the youth movement. While the 'Greta effect' of mass global rallies showed that concern and anger about the environment wasn't confined to the global North, commentators rarely recognised that striking from school has a different meaning in countries where receiving an education is regarded as a privilege, and where parents might have struggled hard to find the funds for school uniforms and textbooks.

There's another aspect to the globalisation of this youth movement that I find disquieting. I spoke to young female activists in Senegal and Nepal. In 2019, Nepal was responsible, per capita, for 0.04% of the world's $CO_2$ emissions, and Senegal for 0.03%; yet these climate campaigners are urging their fellow citizens to ditch their plastic bags and turn vegetarian—similar agendas to many of their counterparts in the US and Europe, whose contributions to world $CO_2$ emissions are 13.43% and 8.69% respectively.[50]

Where's the sense in that? Have we exported our slogans along with our trash? I worry that these fine young campaigners of the global South have been subjected to a kind of climate campaign colonialism, distilled in the climate 'we'. Although their concern for the environment is informed and not misplaced, they live in countries already suffering from the rampaging effects of the climate crisis to which their contribution has been pitiful—they're not the climate guilty. Aware of the imbalance, the young people I speak with still maintain that everyone can and should do their bit, even though, as I suggest to them, our bit in the global North needs to utterly dwarf theirs. But then I check myself: a 'reverse' white saviour is a white saviour, nonetheless—especially when they're engaged in 'Northsplaining'.

The chief vector for climate activism has been social media: this is what enabled it to ripple so far, so fast. This is brilliant, but also disturbing, because it made climate campaigning cool, creating climate celebrity along the way. Instagram, which had already birthed a whole troupe of young influencers, now found many suddenly choosing to style themselves as sustainability ones. Some influencers had a go at others for posting about the devastating fires in Australia and then, barely pausing for breath, promoting a sponsored deal with a fast fashion brand. Is sustainable fashion even possible, wondered the *Fashionista* website.[51] The whole point of being an influencer, surely, is to get free clothes and be paid to push products. As *Elle* magazine put it, "Instagram wants you to buy things, and it doesn't really care whether they're eco-friendly or not."[52] Some sustainability influencers, it concluded, really were on a journey to help young people ditch over-consumption; but others were engaged in little more than greenwashing.

It can indeed sometimes seem as if some 'climate influencers' are just pouting for the planet. The signs they hold up may display a green message, but equally important in their highly filtered, likes-chasing photos are the artfully arranged hair and the head tilted just so. (Do male climate influencers feel a pressure to display themselves like this? The photos of young 'climate men' on Insta seem to focus more on the landscape behind the body; but then, fewer of them post about sustainable fashion—so perhaps they have a freedom that the women don't.)

It's too easy, though, to just dismiss this as hashtag activism or clicktivism. Yes, these young activists may have posed for the camera; but this doesn't mean that their concern for the earth is merely a pose. Greta Thunberg herself may eschew such frivolities, but then in some ways she's an old soul—most young people aren't as single-minded as she is, and on Insta they display their many simultaneous interests and concerns to others who share them.

Still, more interesting to me is what's happening around climate activism on TikTok, the app where young people—800 million of them a month, mostly aged 16 to 24—upload 60-second videos.[53] Their very brevity, echoing Thunberg's direct mode of address, forces them to get speedily to the point.

Chinese-owned, TikTok launched in 2019 but really took off in 2020's lockdowns. There are sustainability and repair videos here too, but also huge numbers of other climate videos, under hashtags like #GlobalWarning. Bespoke groups of environmental influencers such as EcoTok pool their talents and experience. This group has come up with really interesting ways of popularising some quite heavy content—"monoculture", "carbon sequestering", the climate problems of Mauritius. EcoTok's chatty but punchy style is undoubtedly helping the youth climate movement to reach new audiences with serious messages.

This is a visual generation, for whom optics and aesthetics matter as much as politics, and indeed are a branch of it. It's thrilling to see each generation develop its own inventive ways, platforms and channels to agitate about the climate crisis, and to see young women playing a key role—though TikTok as a whole is slightly male-dominated, EcoTok is led by women. But what's less thrilling is the burden repeatedly placed on young women to be the agents of change. We sometimes seem to invest them with magic powers: here come the Super-Girl Climate Crusaders, lacking only a cape and the ability to fly.

They may not be able to fly but, along with the other women who have featured in this chapter, they've been remarkably effective in changing the attitudes of ordinary people to the climate crisis, and in driving home to them the urgency of the situation. At the same time, and just as important, these girl and women activists' efforts are an antidote to the feeling of helplessness that can often come with greater understanding; and their victories, however small or local they might be, engender a sense of hope.

# ANNETTE WALLGREN,
## 35, SWEDEN/THAILAND

*I'm a Programme Manager for gender and climate change at the UN Environment Programme (UNEP). I've seen myself how environmental degradation has a different impact on men and women, and how the inequalities in many countries have been deepened because of climate change and will get worse if we don't act now.*

*In Asia-Pacific, where I have most of my experience, women often manage natural resources like water, wood and fodder, and are dependent on them for income, food or medicine. But because of climate change and biodiversity loss, they're losing access to these resources. They then face particular challenges because they don't have the same ability to resort to other roles as men, the same access to markets, land, education, training, credit.*

*In India and Bangladesh, women work as waste-pickers in the informal sector, so their exposure to these hazards and chemicals is way bigger. But when we try to make waste management more environmentally friendly, and these jobs become formalised and better paid, we see that women lose access to them and they become more run by men. So, in countries like Mongolia, Bhutan and Nepal, UNEP looked at who, from the waste-pickers up to the managers, would be affected by the transition to a greener sector. And once you do that, you understand the impact that your actions will have, and you make sure that a certain percentage of the employment is given to women. This is why, in our environment programmes, we need to consult with both men and women and learn from their experiences, skills and needs: with a stronger gender perspective we can design more realistic solutions.*

*Renewable energy, for example, is traditionally a male-dominated area: we really need to involve women in the solution or we'll fail in our attempts to implement it properly. Often countries have a national policy on renewable energy but rarely talk about what people use the energy for. In those countries that I work in—Cambodia, Bangladesh and Vietnam—women are often the energy managers, they're the ones actually using energy in the households; yet it's not designed for them. Bangladesh has made great advances in renewable energy but, in some regions, women don't have the same access as men. Women don't use the mini-grids in certain urban areas outside the household, because of the gender norms and roles. But what if we could run these programmes more at the household level? How could that benefit women?*

*Through the project EmPower: Women for Climate-Resilient Societies, which is a joint initiative between*

*UNEP and UN Women, we're trying to put gender equality and human rights at the heart of climate action, by supporting women entrepreneurs in the renewable energy sector and helping make sure that governments' climate change policies include a gender perspective and support women's civil society organisations. We've identified a few enterprise models, where women can use renewable energy in different kinds of businesses to increase their income. So in each of these three countries, Bangladesh, Cambodia and Vietnam, we've selected a few women, community leaders, as managers.*

*For example, a woman in North Vietnam from an Indigenous community is running this company where they're drying fruit, vegetables, mushrooms. She began to engage more and more women in the community, selling these products to nearby provinces and tourists, and now they're looking into a solar drying system that can generate further income for this community. So the role she's playing is really as a key leader of this group of women that started very small and is now expanding. We've also learned that renewable energy can support these communities in getting back on their feet after the pandemic.*

*You need to be really careful that the interventions where you challenge the gender norms don't backlash onto the women. So, if we're supporting women in accessing renewable energy, we always make sure that the men are involved as well. In Cambodia, when we started in 2018, we wanted to have all these consultations with women to understand how they'd use renewable energy if it was more available to them. We wanted women-only groups but then slowly realised that, in Cambodia, if you do that, you risk some resistance because people live so connected, men and women, though they have very separate roles. So then we understood that every step along the way, to provide this economic opportunity for the women, we also need to have the men and the boys involved, making sure that this change is supported by the whole community.*

*I started my journey as a feminist when I was quite young as it was obvious to me that boys and girls didn't have the same opportunities. Understanding and wanting to make a change has shaped me both personally and professionally. Looking back to my grandmother's generation I see the huge progress since then for women's rights. That's why I'm hopeful that we're capable of change. I feel a responsibility to the next generation, and to my son who was born in the middle of a climate and pandemic crisis, that we have to fix this!*

*Sometimes I become a bit like Greta Thunberg and wish everyone would understand the urgency. People are already impacted by climate change, it's already happening. And of course the situation is worsened by the Covid-19 pandemic. People have to move to a new home because of climate change; they lose their income. Women in particular have to take on new burdens to adapt to the new realities. What I've seen—from communities in Myanmar, the Philippines, the Lao PDR, Cambodia, Bangladesh and Vietnam—is that those already suffering from lack of access to resources, decision-making and livelihoods will be most affected.*

*Climate change comes back to inequality. That's why, when you talk about transitioning to a green economy and climate action, we need to make sure that a gender-equality and a human-rights perspective is included. If it isn't, you can actually increase inequalities. This is why I feel my job working on gender and environment is so important, and can hopefully make a difference.*

# 7

# ENGENDERING CLIMATE SOLUTIONS

Meet Hilaria. A farmer, she also weaves beautiful baskets and makes jewellery; but, until recently, she could only do this during the day, because Mwada—her village in northern Tanzania—lacked electricity. In 2013, though, she learned about Solar Sister, an initiative supporting African women to start clean-energy businesses in off-grid communities. After getting trained in everything from budgeting to customer care, and with a loan from her husband, Hilaria bought twenty-five lights. She sold the first one back to her husband, who became her ambassador, and she later added phone chargers and clean ovens to her stock.

Today Hilaria has over 2,000 customers. She has organised her fellow weavers into a group called Mshikamano (solidarity in Swahili) so that they could become solar energy entrepreneurs too. The bulk of Hilaria's income has gone into her daughters' education: Gladness, 15, is in secondary school, while Theresia, 18, is studying accounting. Hilaria herself couldn't afford to stay beyond primary school. In 2017, she won €1,000 as Woman Entrepreneur of the Year from the International Network on Gender and Sustainable Energy: travelling to New York to collect the prize, she spoke at the Sustainable Energy for All Forum.[1]

Hilaria's story is one of tens of thousands around the world that show the huge potential impact of climate-friendly schemes, training and resources targeted at women—the effects are multiplied many times over. These examples also show, paradoxically, that the support and encouragement of a husband can be a critical factor in helping women become more independent.

In this chapter, we dive into stories of women-led sustainable initiatives and policies that bring hope into these women's lives, and offer some welcome relief from the gloomier climate narratives. Alongside the fleet of gender-responsive climate initiatives like Hilaria's, launched in rural areas by international agencies and charities, there are also gender-sensitive approaches to the climate crisis in cities, driven by local women politicians in both the global North and South.

Alas, there are no panaceas that can be plucked out of this trove: reasons for climate optimism yes, but also caveats and reservations aplenty. Before we celebrate these women-led climate solutions, we need to look critically at how easily they can be transformed into a troubling narrative: the narrative of women-as-climate-saviours.

*Yes, but...*

One word is (deliberately) missing from this chapter: empowerment. Once a feminist rallying cry, its meaning has become so debased that it can now be stretched to include 'leaning in' to become a high-paid corporate exec, and even Gwyneth Paltrow's jade egg for vaginas, supposed to balance your hormones. (Cost: $66; fine for making unsubstantiated scientific claims about it: $145,000.)[2] This is how far 'empowerment' has been rebranded, from a political struggle into the kind of self-care that requires purchasing a load of pricey goods and services.

'Empowerment' has now become something of a development cliché, too, with almost every climate-connected project promising to promote it in women of the global South. On the surface, 'empowering women', and its sister slogan 'investing in women', seem attractive and liberal; radical, even. The reality, though, is often conservative: Andrea Cornwall, a professor of global development and anthropology, has called it "empowerment lite".[3]

'Empowerment lite' may seem like a feminist project, but it's one that has been emptied of anything that destabilises the gendered status quo. It encourages women to become entrepreneurs and participate in markets, while doing nothing to reduce their caring responsibilities.[4]

Even worse, if you focus all your energies on boosting women's climate resilience, so that they can cope with oppressive situations, 'empowerment' can actually divert them from becoming part of collective challenges to those oppressions. The whole idea of empowerment, critics have argued, has become a useful plank of neo-liberalism: suggesting that you tackle inequality by 'empowering' individual women, instead of homing in on the structures that produce and maintain gender inequality and trying to dismantle them.[5]

The star of the 'empowerment lite' narrative is the small-scale woman entrepreneur, endowed with the power, and perhaps also the duty, to 'lift' her family and community out of poverty.[6] Yet for every Hilaria whose life has clearly been improved by participating in such schemes, there are scores of others for whom 'entrepreneurship' is another word for 'more work': women-as-agents-of-change mutates all too easily into women-charged-with-the burden-of-delivering-change, another example of our old friend the 'feminisation of responsibility'. When the story is told this way, power—the actual, real power of elite countries, global companies and rich individuals identified in Chapter 3—magically evaporates. Pouff! It's gone. In its place is the woman smallholder or solar power entrepreneur who can counter climate change and reverse inequality, one field and one solar lamp at a time.

You can see why this narrative would appeal, not just to development agencies financed by wealthy countries, but also to transnational corporations, investment banks and management consultancies. These big businesses—not famed for their commitment to social justice or equity—have readily co-opted the idea of women's empowerment, purring about its economic benefits. They have come to regard women as a good investment, one that can accelerate economic growth—because these women become not only producers but also consumers. Jackpot! "Gender equality is smart economics," the World Bank declared in 2007. "Invest in Girls & Women: Everyone Wins," trilled a development toolkit launched in 2014.

Alongside the small-scale woman entrepreneur, empowerment lite has another figure in its sights: the teenage girl. "Girls as economic actors can bring about change for themselves, their families, and their countries," predicted Bloomberg. "Conversely, ignoring the girl effect can cost societies billions in lost potential."[7] "Girl Effect" was actually the name of a campaign launched by Nike through its philanthropic wing, the Nike Foundation, in 2008. "Girls are the most powerful force for change on the planet," proclaimed *Nike News*, adding that "the girl effect is about the unique potential of adolescent girls to end poverty for themselves and the world."[8]

Of course it's good to encourage confidence in girls and young women, but the eradication of world poverty? Seems like a bit of a load to lay on teenage girls when they might just feel like scrolling through cat videos. And which ones are we asking to do this work—the English girls aged 17–19, almost one quarter of whom experience mental health problems?[9] The nearly one third of young women aged 16–24 in the UK who are depressed or anxious?[10] Or would it be the almost two thirds of students in higher education who thought that their wellbeing had worsened in the course of a single term during the pandemic (autumn 2020)?[11] Oh, ladies, do put away your phones and get on with saving the planet...

The 'girl effect' also echoes, uncannily, the burden placed on the young climate activists described in the last chapter—right down to the remarks of Jennifer Buffett, president of a foundation partnering with Nike on the Girl Effect, that "Girls and women are the mothers of every child born."[12] (This in an article entitled "Save a Girl, Save the World," where Buffett is pictured in unabashed white saviour mode, the sole white person surrounded by a crowd of brown girls.) Buffett was engaging in that same 'girls as reproducers of the future' story, referring to the need to educate and nourish them and improve their health, so that they can do the same for the next generation. Is it too cynical to add, so that they can also buy Nike trainers? Is it that Nike will save girls, or that girls will save Nike?

Nike's 'girl effect' has undeniably done some good things in its campaigns on HIV and girls' education, but its own workers' rights and living wages are strikingly missing from its roster of causes—perhaps, as Al Jazeera America witheringly pointed out, because Nike moved much of its business to China and Indonesia after the Korean women working for the company successfully lobbied for higher wages. The girl effect, Al Jazeera concluded, is "a corporate fable that keeps the system intact, turns girls into consumers, expands market power and diffuses blame".[13]

These are the faux-feminist climate solutions; the ones that seem progressive, but actually aren't. But there are genuinely uplifting stories to be told here too—of women-led climate initiatives that are successful, emancipatory and deserving of our cheers.

## Women-shaped solutions

Women, as Chapter 1 showed, are routinely excluded from preparations for disasters. Often the last to hear about an imminent calamity, women are also often the last to leave home after everyone else has evacuated.

This is what Women's Weather Watch set out to tackle. Co-run in Fiji by ActionAid and the feminist NGO femLINKPacific, the programme uses community radio and a mobile phone network to connect 350 women, many in remote areas, and warn them of an impending cyclone or flood. These women can then escape their homes and shout to their friends and neighbours about the storm on its way—just as they did when

Cyclone Winston barrelled down on rural Fiji in 2016. In that crisis, the women took on the role of first responders, protecting food in containers and burying crops to save them from the destruction. The network works both ways: women connected through it were also able to provide femLINK with information that has strengthened attempts to prevent gender-based violence following a climate disaster.[14]

Women's lives can also be dramatically improved by basic upgrading of infrastructure. Let's go back to Fatuma, the water pilgrim we left in Chapter 1, inching her way home to her Ethiopian village of Afdera, weighed down by the equivalent of a long-haul luggage allowance: Ethiopian droughts haven't disappeared, but Fatuma's long daily trek to collect water has, thanks to the arrival of a nearby desalination plant, funded by anti-poverty charity Care International. This pipes water from the salt lake to a collection point near Fatuma's home, after the salt has been removed. With the time that she's saved, Fatuma now has a paid job as a cleaner in a government department, and has become her community's representative in the district office for women's affairs, organising meetings and urging the local women to vote and form co-operatives. As in Hilaria's family, and to Fatuma's delight, her two young daughters attend school.[15]

Meanwhile in Kenya, over 95 per cent of the population cooks with polluting solid fuel, and more than 21 million people suffer ill health due to household air pollution—the second most frequent cause of premature death. Peninah Nabwire, 48, has been involved in a pilot scheme helping to refine the design of the EcoZoom clean cooking stove, produced by a social enterprise. Not only was she given a prototype herself, which she got to keep—saving her time and money and protecting her health—Peninah has also become a local EcoZoom advocate.[16]

Effective projects like these don't just come up with solutions to a climate-linked problem: they use those solutions to bring lasting changes to the position of women in their communities. So WELFARE Togo, a scheme launched in the West African country in 2015 to conserve endangered mangrove trees in Lake Togo, trains fisherwomen in a new technique, using ropes and baits tied to mangrove trees instead of fishing nets or motorised boats. Making the mangroves essential to the process ensures preservation of their fragile ecosystem, and women using the technique have been able to put nutritious food on the table for their children. Organising themselves into community mangrove watch groups, the women also monitor planted areas and reforest them. By 2025, they'll have planted 200,000 mangrove trees, which are also brilliant 'storm buffers', helping to prevent flooding.

At the same time as strengthening mangrove and human health, WELFARE Togo strengthens the position of fisherwomen within their communities: it provides them with some economic independence, and they benefit from the flexibility of this particular technique—fishing from the shore allows them to stay closer to home and fish during the day. The scheme also offers knowledge and activity to those who participate, including single mothers, widows and "street girls"; they are given information about unwanted pregnancies and forced marriage, and encouraged to engage in social and political activities.[17]

One of the most remarkable examples of a project that simultaneously improves the land and women's lives is Bhungroo. In Gujarat, India, monsoon floods alternate with drought, creating food insecurity and debt. Bhungroo, a locally developed rainwater management technology, deals with both problems, stopping farmers' crops from getting waterlogged during the monsoon while keeping them properly irrigated during the dry season. Each Bhungroo system is jointly owned by five of the poorest or most marginalised women in the community. After being trained as climate leaders, they promote, construct, install and maintain the Bhungroo themselves. The ownership groups they form enable them to provide a service to other farmers. As a result, income is expected to treble and, in what had become wastelands, harvests have been restored. By ensuring that the groups owning the Bhungroo system consist only of women, and that the water is provided directly to them, the men's control over irrigation water has been "curtailed down".[18]

The knock-on effects have been extraordinary. Like most Indian women, the Bhungroo owners started off without any land rights—Indian women make up over 40 per cent of the country's agricultural labour force, yet own less than 2 per cent of its farmland.[19] But once they gained water irrigation rights, the government revenue department transferred formal land ownership to them. Emboldened, they started "to take on local political positions, helping with other issues around gender relations … and negotiating with the government for irrigation cooperatives". What started off simply as a way of managing water has ended up transforming the status of women within their communities. 20,000 farmers have been involved, and over 6,000 who'd left for the cities because of drought have come back—a reverse migration.[20]

Bhungroo is a technological solution, but not a technological fix: it doesn't simply insert a new piece of kit into the old gendered social and economic relationships. Instead, it uses the new technology as a vehicle to boost and transform local women's power and rights.

Although most of these initiatives originated outside the local communities where they now operate, there's also a long tradition of powerful, women-led, local climate initiatives, like the Chipko movement that developed in the foothills of the Himalayas in the 1970s. To protest against the commercial exploitation of the forest by private contractors and prevent logging, village women threatened to put their bodies on the line and 'hugged' a row of threatened ash trees. Through their nonviolent protests, the Chipko campaigners became celebrated icons of eco-feminism and women's environmental activism.[21]

And then there's Vandana Shiva, an Indian environmentalist who was appalled by international corporations' attempts to patent seeds and genetically modify them—a move she regards as "biopiracy". Regarding seeds instead as part of "the commons" that needs reclaiming, in 1991 she created Navdanya, a flourishing network of seed-keepers and organic producers across sixteen Indian states that preserves and promotes biodiversity through sixty-five community seed banks.[22] Navdanya's seeds are open-source: free for ordinary farmers to use, unlike patented seeds. This matters in particular to women farmers, in India and elsewhere, who often can't easily access financial services, including loans or credit.

Shiva sees women as the main savers of seeds: Navdanya runs a Grandmother's University to transmit farming knowledge, from older women with tremendous expertise who are unable to read and write, to literate younger women and children, who can then enshrine it in community biodiversity registers. The women also swap climate-resilient crops between communities: because they plant crops like millet that can withstand drought and don't need irrigation, Indian women, Shiva argues, can make a good income and also feed their families—in contrast to the many male farmers chasing cash crops like genetically modified cotton, 300,000 of whom have committed suicide.

The blame for these suicides, Shiva claims, lies with transnational companies: their patented seeds (often based on traditional knowledge, frequently women's) extract royalties from the poor farmers who use them.[23] She contends that this is all part of the "masculinization of agriculture", observing that companies like Monsanto give their herbicides names like 'Machete', 'Pentagon', 'Prowl', 'Squadron' and 'Avenge'. "This is the language of war, not sustainability."[24] To Shiva, it's clear: you can't save the planet without equality.[25]

The gender dimension was baked into these projects from the very start. Those climate schemes that see themselves as 'gender-neutral', on the other hand—whether they're mitigation ones that aim to reduce or eliminate greenhouse gases, or adaptation ones dealing with emissions' effects—often end up exacerbating existing inequalities. They can even inadvertently discriminate against women, as in the case of energy schemes that ignore the informal sectors that women work in, for instance as micro-entrepreneurs.[26]

At COP25 in Madrid (2019), the UNFCCC agreed a new and ambitious five-year Gender Action Plan, which commits to "gender-responsive climate action", as well as "full, meaningful and equal participation and leadership of women" in future COPs and the broader UNFCCC process. Acknowledging the importance of human rights and Indigenous rights, this recognises the need to understand the different effects of climate change on men and women, and to scale up gender-just solutions.[27] Fine and significant words, and women climate activists and scholars have applauded the Gender Action Plan as a potentially valuable tool—but they reserve judgement about whether and how it will be fully implemented by each of the more than fifty countries signed up to it.[28]

## Madam Mayor

The stories above feature poor rural women in the global South, in keeping with the iconography of climate change victims highlighted in Chapter 1. In reality, though, it's cities where most the world's population now lives, and where two thirds of us are predicted to be living by 2050; cities that are the main producers of $CO_2$ emissions (over 70 per cent) and the major consumers of energy; and cities where many of the sharpest effects of global heating will be felt.[29] And so cities, long seen as the chief cause of the climate crisis, are increasingly viewed as places where many of the solutions will need to lie.

There's an intriguing but little-known story about women fighting climate change: the prominent new role being played by women mayors. Their number is increasing rapidly around the globe—perhaps because the route to getting elected mayor is swifter than the slow progress up the ladder into parliaments and national governments. Women start from behind, politically, and therefore need to make up ground fast. Mayors are also in control of their own budgets and so can introduce innovative programmes more nimbly and decisively than national politicians.

Climate crisis policies introduced by women mayors have sneaked in somewhat beneath the international and national political radar. Leading them is Anne Hidalgo, who became the first woman elected mayor of Paris in 2014. She is particularly sensitive to women's greater vulnerability to the climate crisis. In 2017 Hidalgo launched a Women4Climate initiative, gathering together the women among the C40 Cities Climate Leadership group. Originally the C40 represented forty cities, but today they number ninety-seven, and the number of women among the mayors increased five-fold in just four years, from four in 2014 to twenty as of 2018.[30] These Women4Climate meet annually to discuss how to use their power to tackle climate change, to mentor young female climate champions and to run an annual competition, spotlighting innovative climate crisis solutions designed by women in tech.

Most of the women in the C40 have got to work pretty speedily to find ways of reducing their city's carbon dioxide emissions. Muriel Bowser (Washington, DC) is funding a Green Bank to support building improvements that lower emissions.[31] Valérie Plante (Montreal) has a climate plan pledging to make the city zero-waste by 2030.[32] Clover Moore (Sydney) is steering her city to 100 per cent renewable energy, with a target of cutting emissions 70 per cent by 2030—Sydney is on track to meet that target six years early, by 2024.[33]

Sustainability rhetoric may be cheap these days—today, we all speak green fluently—but concrete plans cost. Ada Colau, mayor of Barcelona since 2015, worked with 200 local organisations to make it the first major Spanish city to put its fine words into concrete action. In 2020 she announced €563 million to be spent on 103 different plans, including the creation of low-emission zones and the building of "100 'climate shelters' in municipal facilities where people can go during heatwaves", as well as the introduction of organic food in schools. Over the decade to 2030, almost all of the centre of Barcelona will turn car-free.[34] Colau also plans to create twenty-one public squares, "so that no citizen is more than 200 metres from a small square or park";[35] she has called for "a 'paradigm shift' to a new green economic model rooted in justice and sustainability".[36] The Carbon Disclosure Project, which scrutinises such climate plans, rates Colau's very highly, ranking Barcelona in the top 7 per cent among a total of almost 600 cities.[37]

Perhaps it was no accident that initiatives like this took off in the middle of the pandemic, as lockdowns in 2020 enabled people to experience, for a while, cities that weren't choking with dirty air from motorised transport. This stimulated creative thinking among city leaders about how their metropolis could be greened. Colau has inspired Poitiers's 30-year-old mayor: Léonore Moncond'huy, a member of the green Europe Ecologie-Les-Verts party voted into office on the green surge of 2020, who campaigned under the slogan "Poitiers is the new Barcelona!" Moncond'huy's ambitious climate plans involve using her public procurement powers to avoid the city buying non-reusable and non-recyclable products. As *Politico* has reported, she plans to launch programmes to "improve waste management, reduce water consumption, cut air pollution, restore biodiversity and create a method to measure the carbon impact of the municipality's actions", and how much they contribute to reducing $CO_2$ emissions.[38]

Hidalgo hasn't let up on her own efforts, either. Her Plan Vélo, introduced in 2017 during her first term as Paris mayor, made the city vastly more pedestrian and bike-friendly, increasing the number of bike lanes by 50 per cent to a total of 620 miles, and raising Paris from seventeenth to eighth on the list of bike-friendly cities—to the rage of its motorists. "Part of it has to do with being a woman," she has suggested. "And being a woman that wants to reduce the number of cars meant that I upset lots of men. Two-thirds of public transport users are women."[39] She's right: across the world, women make up the largest share of public transport users.[40] In England, one third more women than men travel by bus.[41]

Re-elected in 2020, Hidalgo's plans now include the creation of eco-urban forests; the pedestrianisation of part of the Champs Élysées, so that the road becomes 'an extraordinary garden'; but also, most innovatively, the idea of the '15-minute city', who residents can meet all their needs—"for work, shopping, health and culture"— within 15 minutes' walking or cycling distance from their own doorstep. This Paris en Commun initiative goes against all the 'zoning' tendencies of the modern city, built upon the separation of work and home.[42] But, again, the Covid pandemic has seriously challenged that principle: with so many people working from home, employers are rethinking the need for city-centre offices, and employees have reoriented themselves in relation to their neighbourhoods. Hidalgo's aim is to reduce Parisians' need for motorised transport. Inflaming motorists even more, her second term (2020–26) will remove half of the city's remaining parking spaces.

Equally importantly, she's also stumbled into a key argument about the gendered geographies of cities. Marxists and feminists have long claimed that the separation of housing from workplaces created the home as a private sphere where women's labour was free, and the office or factory as a public sphere where labour was paid—making it particularly hard for women (and the men who choose to do so) to combine paid work with childcare.[43] Under Hidalgo's plan, local Parisian areas, instead of being seen as corridors to go through or past, a route to somewhere else, become places in their own right. Re-envisaging the city in this way has massive implications, not just for the use of energy, but also for the ways in which human energy is expended. It could revitalise swathes of the French capital, and is being trialled in other large cities like Melbourne.

Hidalgo is not without her critics—and they're not confined to drivers. She's been accused of being too soft on developers and of simply pushing Paris's pollution problems out to the suburbs.[44] In any case, the link between being a woman mayor and being a climate-sensitive one might be tenuous: there are plenty of men introducing green urban policies too, and not all of the women can reel off a slate of ambitious or successful green initiatives. Take Virginia Raggi, the first woman to serve as mayor of Rome: she signed up to all the usual sustainability pledges, but since 2016 her term has been distinguished more by the capital's water crises, hundreds of toppling trees, overflowing street bins (attracting wild boars, pigeons and rats—who needs a city zoo?), the collapse of an escalator in the Metro—oh, and the odd bus bursting into flames.[45] Not so much the Eternal City, then; more of a seemingly eternally chaotic and unsustainable one.

Even so, it's clear that a number of women mayors do see confronting the climate crisis and its impact on women as among their most urgent challenges, and not all of them are in the global North. Yvonne Aki-Sawyerr has been mayor of Freetown, capital of Sierra Leone, since 2018. Freetown doesn't contribute to greenhouse gas emissions in a big way, but it certainly suffers from them, with past municipal decisions making it especially vulnerable. In 2017, three days of torrential rain triggered huge mudslides from Sugar Loaf mountain overlooking the city: "In just under five minutes," according to Aki-Sawyerr, "over a thousand people died." More than 3,000 were left homeless.[46]

There were a number of reasons for the disaster: natural drainage systems have been destroyed by construction and "unrestricted deforestation", man-made drains had been left blocked, and the deforestation "weakened the stability of nearby slopes", causing soil erosion. And, as Aki-Sawyerr has said, "Climate change for us here in Freetown looks like extreme weather conditions. It looks like terrible rainfall, which ... led to the deadly mudslide." Her three-year Transform Freetown plan involves flood mitigation, creating carbon sinks and natural flooding protection by increasing vegetation 50 per cent, partly by planting 1 million trees in 2020 alone. She has also strengthened the city's drainage systems—unblocking drains and repairing underground channels—so that, when 176 millimetres of rain fell on the city over 3 hours in August 2019, this time it could run off, with far fewer deaths than in 2017: only four.

Aki-Sawyerr is not only thinking about the city's environment, but about how its problems relate to the city's women. Between 60 and 70 per cent of Sierra Leoneans affected by natural disasters are women, and so the council has brought in the Sierra Leone Institute of Women Engineers to advise those among them who want to help devise solutions: "The women are bearing the brunt ... And we see a situation where those who feel it most are also in a position ... to build those ideas into something practical in terms of solutions."

## Greening the government

In 2019, 34-year-old Sanna Marin was elected prime minister of Finland, becoming the youngest prime minister in the world. She formed a coalition government made up of five parties, all led by women—four of the five were under 36. The Finnish government immediately vowed to make the country carbon-neutral by 2035. Their aim, said the leader of the Greens, was to make Finland "the world's first fossil-free welfare society".[47]

A few months before Marin's election, Mette Frederiksen became Denmark's youngest ever prime minister at 41, committing her own country to a 70 per cent reduction in greenhouse gas emissions by 2030.[48]

Was it their youth, or just coincidence, that led these premiers to prioritise decarbonising their countries in this way? Or was it also because they were women? Half a dozen major pieces of research since the mid-2000s have suggested that gender plays a significant part: countries with a higher proportion of women in parliament are more likely to ratify environmental treaties.[49] Again and again, researchers have ended up with parallel findings: governments with more women in decision-making roles are more likely to create protected areas like nature reserves; so, if you increase the proportion of women in cabinet, you're more likely to have protected lands.[50] More broadly, $CO_2$ emissions per head of population are lower in countries where women have higher political status—in other words, having women in positions of power is associated with greater environmental protection.[51] Companies that have a higher proportion of women directors on their board are more likely to frankly and fully disclose their greenhouse gas emissions.[52]

A word of caution: most of these studies find a strong 'association' between more women and better environmental policies, not necessarily a causal link—although one 2019 piece of research was less hesitant in claiming that having more women in parliament leads a country to adopt more stringent climate policies, and that such countries have lower carbon footprints. "Female political representation," it concluded, "may be an underutilized tool for addressing climate change."[53]

Now, let's not elevate women as the magic ingredient that turns countries green—there are some contradictions here. Norway, for example, is ranked third in the global table of gender equality, and second for state environmentalism;[54] nonetheless it's the world's fifth-largest exporter of oil and third-largest exporter of natural gas.[55] The Norwegian state may have good domestic environmental policies, but it also exports vast amounts of fossil fuels all around the world. Yet, since so much research has come up with similar (significant) results, from robust statistical studies—studies, incidentally, that go out of their way to consider alternative explanations for their findings—it's reasonable to ask the question. Why do women tend to produce greener governments?

Let's rule out straightaway any answer that rests on the idea of women as innate 'Earth Mothers' or Mothers of the Earth, programmed by evolution to protect the planet. That narrative was laid to rest in Chapter 4. A more plausible explanation lies in women's attitude to risk. A number of studies show that they tend to worry more than men about the health-related aspects of climate change and, along with people of colour and working-class people, to see global environmental problems as posing more of a risk to themselves than men do—especially white and better-off men.[56] Women take risk more seriously, and are less willing to impose risks on other people.[57]

There are a bunch of perfectly sensible explanations for this, and they are about social realities and cultural norms, not biology. Women—like people of colour and working-class people—really are at greater risk from climate breakdown, and experience its effects in distinctive ways, as we've seen. Since they're more likely to be harmed by environmental degradation, they're understandably more sensitive to the problem; and, having participated in and benefited from the extractive industries much less than men, they are also less invested in them, and more able to admit the harm they cause: women are both more aware of the problem and more inclined to a profoundly new solution. So it's logical that, when women attain positions of power, they mostly make different environmental decisions from those made by men.[58]

Another reason is women's attitude to the natural world. Women, it seems, are less likely than men to hold narrow views about nature as something that exists mainly for humans to exploit. Again, this is hardly surprising. Cast from an early age in the role of carers, women grow up with an implicit understanding that their expected role is to nurture people and places. They are also often the ones who have to pick up the pieces after climate-induced disasters. Men, on the other hand, are encouraged to treat nature with a certain bravado, as explored in Chapter 3; and failure to do so—by taking the radical step of bringing their own bag to the shop, for example—seemingly threatens their masculinity.

Whatever the precise explanation (and most likely it's a combination), the conclusion is clear: promoting women into positions of political and executive authority, and improving gender equality more broadly, are not only valuable in their own right. They can also be important routes to tackling the climate crisis.

For some reason, this whole subject reminds me of the Joel Pett *USA Today* cartoon of a climate summit. While a male expert stands on the podium in front of a screen, listing decarbonising policies like "Preserve Rainforests", "Green Jobs" and "Clean Water, Air", an angry man in the audience pipes up: "What if it's a big hoax and we create a better world for nothing?"[59]

# DAZE AGHAJI, 20, UK

*When I was around 7 or 8, there was a tree in front of our house that my mum really wanted to cut down. I literally stood out there and said, "You're not going to cut down that tree." This was the first time I remember feeling that I needed to protect nature.*

*I moved back to London when I was 16 and I started experiencing a lot of issues around my skin and breathing. I grew up having asthma, but when I was in Lincolnshire, I didn't have it. Then I found out about air pollution and climate change, and spent more years than I would like to admit just being really angry at how little organisations and governments were doing on climate change. Do you know, the first thing that most people do when they first come to activism is focus on individual change? This is because many industries have spent millions in creating the narrative that the individual is to blame for climate change. Plus it's something that we feel like we have so much more control over: it feels easier to fix. Don't eat meat, use recycled bog paper—recycle, recycle, recycle! This is what we are told; this is what I believed too.*

*On a cold Wednesday in the winter of 2019, I went to an Extinction Rebellion meeting by chance. I was super-depressed and my friend invited me to join her. Before this meeting, people always told me I was an alarmist, but I met people there with the same urgency as me. In the meetings, we do things called check-ins. This was the first time I was meeting people outside of my family who asked how I was doing and cared about the answer. Without that kindness, I don't know whether I would have stayed. It was mostly white but there were people of colour there as well— I wasn't the only one.*

**One of the main criticisms of XR has been that its tactic of civil disobedience and inviting arrest is appropriate for white people but not black people.**

*I don't entirely agree with this. Extinction Rebellion has used tactics that were created by and used by people of colour, from Gandhi to Martin Luther King. We need to recognise that the most popular civil disobedience movements have been led by people of colour, who have been using it as a form of resistance for a very long time. I do think we haven't done so well in explicitly acknowledging that there is a difference in the treatment of marginalised groups when using the arrest tactic. It is something we need to get better at.*

*I recently MCed in Parliament Square at the start of ten days of protests to demand government action on the climate crisis. I was doing the introductions for the speak-*

ers, *in front of thousands of people, getting them excited for the activities to come. I never had the confidence to do this kind of thing before I had the community in XR believing in me. They raised my confidence, helped me find my voice and told me, "Whatever society tells you, you're worth being heard," and from then this idea of caving into society's expectation of perfection, or trying to fit in, just melted away.*

*XR takes care of its rebels in different ways, from providing holding and care to providing living expenses (when there's money) for people who are having a difficult time and need help to stay in activism. This really helps many people from marginalised backgrounds to be activists.*

*I ran as an independent candidate in the 2019 European elections under the banner of climate and ecological emergency. I got over 1,000 votes—I was pretty chuffed because independents normally get like 200 votes. My mum gets how important this is to me, especially the way that the climate crisis is now affecting my family in Nigeria. My auntie's house got flooded in Lagos: she's no longer able to live there and she's had to relocate to my cousin's.*

*I do a lot of work around advocating for a regenerative culture: the idea that we need to transition into a just society, and we can actually start cultivating these ways of living. In XR we see our regen culture as having five pillars: self-care (how can you take care of yourself?), interpersonal care (how can you bring your healthy self into relation with other people?), community care (how can you bring your healthy self and new skills to talk to one another in your community?), action care (how can you take care of your community in really high-stakes moments?) and people and planet care. It's basically: how can we bring love, duty and compassion onto the earth and stop destroying it, because the climate crisis has come from destructive behaviours—from us learning how to use and abuse people through things like colonisation, racism.*

*The system has told us, "Oh you can't do this, you can't do that," but Covid-19 has really shown us that if they do want to put things in place to help people, they can—and I think we need to aim for what's seen as impossible. My heart is in raising public consciousness and bringing us together to create community. Obviously carbon reduction is something that we really need to do ASAP, but the way that we actually get the sustained health of the planet and of the people is by addressing these behaviours that we've learnt. Covid-19 highlighted the injustices in our system— there was no hiding it. We could see who was hit first and hit the hardest. In this crisis, we saw what we can do—we saw people coming together to create mutual aid organisations and caring for one another.*

*I think Black Lives Matter was almost a byproduct of seeing black and ethnic people die at higher rates, and a young black man yelling "I can't breathe" and losing his life. People were saying, "Now I have to put this energy into my community." The environment, LGBTQ+, women's rights, Black Lives Matter—I see them as all in the same fight, just coming from different angles.*

# 8

# A GREEN NEW DEAL FOR WOMEN

She wasted no time. In February 2019, five weeks after she was sworn in as a congresswoman, Alexandria Ocasio-Cortez co-sponsored (with Senator Ed Markey) a Green New Deal. A non-binding resolution rather than a bill, it called for the US to take a lead in the reduction of global carbon emissions to net zero by 2050, through a ten-year mobilisation investing in jobs, affordable housing, renewable energy and high-quality health care.[1]

The Republican reaction was a touch theatrical: one of them warned that the Democrats want to "take away your hamburgers";[2] another that the Green Deal was "tantamount to genocide".[3] President Trump had a pop too. Calling Ocasio-Cortez (with his customary wit) a "wonderful young bartender", he maintained that the Green New Deal would cost $1 trillion annually and amount to "the biggest government power grab in US history".[4]

This was hardly surprising, perhaps, since the original New Deal—the 1930s relief and stimulus programme introduced by Roosevelt to create jobs during the Depression—was also opposed by Republicans. But the hostility to Ocasio-Cortez's Green New Deal wasn't confined to the GOP. Nancy Pelosi, then the Democrats' minority leader of the House of Representatives, also mocked the resolution as "The green dream or whatever they call it, nobody knows what it is, but they're for it right?"[5] Pelosi, the arch-pragmatist, had been riled perhaps by the whoops of joy and applause greeting Ocasio-Cortez when, the previous November, she'd dropped in on a sit-in of Pelosi's office by the Sunrise group, which was urging the veteran congresswoman to take stronger climate action.[6]

The key ideas in Ocasio-Cortez's Green New Deal were dismissed by many on both sides of the aisle as unfeasible. But in reality, according to a business survey, almost all of them were supported by more than 80 per cent of Americans.[7] Less of a blueprint than a progressive manifesto, whose (deliberately) vague ideas were designed to be fleshed out later, the resolution inspired a number of local variants: a European Green Deal (no surprise that the 'New' was dropped, when you look at the compromise they ended up with);[8] a British version produced by a Green New Deal Group, convened by Colin Hines, which had been meeting to exchange ideas on the subject since 2007;[9] and a separate British Green New Deal campaign.[10] There were even versions particular to individual cities such as Coventry, or to a university (Goldsmiths, University of London).[11]

As this book has said over and over, gender inequality and the climate crisis are intimately connected, and in equal need of transformation. By focusing on this very connection, you can produce a double solution: policies that address both the role of gender in creating the climate crisis and women's needs can save human life on Earth from extinction *and* hugely improve women's lives at the same time. Yet Ocasio-Cortez's Green New Deal had a curious blind-spot around gender. Apart from one mention of the gender earnings gap, the entire document contained just two other references to women, subsumed into a long list of groups referred to under the umbrella term "frontline and vulnerable communities".[12] It's an omission repeated in the joint Green New Deal proposal of economist Robert Pollin and Noam Chomsky, the political activist and professor of linguistics;[13] the European Green Deal brokered by European Commission president Ursula von der Leyen in 2019, which was also entirely lacking a gender analysis;[14] all the other versions mentioned above, and more;[15] and even the Green New Deal of the UK Student Climate Network.[16]

In the run-up to the UK's December 2019 general election, more Green New Deals appeared, as British political parties came up with prototypes of their own. Although the Green Party's was part of a broader election manifesto with plenty of good policies concerning women, there was no reference to gender in the party's Green New Deal itself.[17] The Green New Deal passed overwhelmingly by the Labour Party at its autumn conference contained a single mention of gender.[18]

Out of frustration and in response, feminist environmental activists have set about composing their own alternatives. One Feminist Green New Deal, launched in 2019 by a coalition of American groups including the Women's Environment and Development Organization, includes pretty much everything that the Ocasio-Cortez resolution doesn't. It prioritises women's leadership, and calls for paid family leave and free childcare. It recognises the specific and disproportionate challenges facing Indigenous women and women of colour. It mentions corporate greed, toxic chemicals affecting the reproductive rights of women, and the problem of "patriarchal and male-dominated power structures". Its ambitions include an end to US extractivism overseas, as well as reparations for those most affected by America's world-leading damage to the planet.[19] If you're going to set out a manifesto for a radically better future, you might as well make it comprehensive, visionary and a white male climate denier's nightmare.

Over in the UK, however, those feminist environmentalists scrutinising the various Green New Deals homed in on something else: green jobs.

## Green jobs—for the boys?

Has there ever been a happier pairing than the words 'green' and 'jobs'? Long assumed to be mutually incompatible—isn't the greening of the environment all about closing down things like coal plants and oil refineries?— the now increasingly popular prospect of green jobs seems like a magic formula to tackle the climate crisis at the same time as solving the economic one.

From the 2008 crash until the outbreak of Covid-19, it was common to hear people say that an economic recovery had to take place before we could turn our thoughts properly to the climate. Yet, in the age of the pandemic, that view has been increasingly replaced by the idea of a 'green recovery', to be brought about by environmental stimulus packages, often centred on the energy industry. So, for example, launching its "green recovery roadmap" in September 2020, the Confederation of British Industry identified as areas for growth the construction of low-carbon electricity generation, developing sustainable aviation fuel and retrofitting buildings to be more energy-efficient.[20] This last area was also one of the policies promoted by a University of Oxford study, authored by a quintet of (male) climate economists who believed that investing in "clean physical infrastructure" was the route to financial recovery.[21]

The language used to express this vision often has a macho whiff to it—these projects, the study suggested, were "shovel-ready", a term also used by the UK government in its post-Covid recovery New Deal plans to "build, build, build".[22] Not that there's anything intrinsically male about a shovel: women are perfectly capable of wielding one and of doing the jobs that require them to—mostly in energy, construction and transport. It's just that, at the moment, not many women do. As critics have pointed out, the kind of green jobs integral to most climate programmes are occupied mainly by men; so if you use a green stimulus package to turn only *these* jobs into sustainable ones, yet again you'll be leaving out half the workforce. Green jobs propaganda almost never addresses issues of gender.[23]

This is certainly true of both the Oxford and Confederation of British Industry proposals—no mention of gender—and it's true even of the Green New Deal drawn up by the Vermont senator, Bernie Sanders, which references women twice, but focuses its promises on the creation of millions of jobs "in steel and auto manufacturing, construction, energy efficiency retrofitting, coding and server farms, and renewable power plants".[24]

It's not as if they haven't been warned. A paper presented to the European Parliament by the International Labour Organization back in 2012 estimated that 80 per cent of green jobs would be related to green technologies in industry and manufacturing; and that, under such programmes (unless they got targeted support), women would miss out on training opportunities and learning new skills—facing much the same obstacles, in fact, as they did in the 'brown' economy.[25] Indeed, as economist Maeve Cohen and environmental researcher Sherilyn MacGregor have pointed out, when green jobs don't address gender inequalities, they can entrench them even further.[26] In order that these new, climate-friendly jobs aren't de facto male jobs, women need to be actively encouraged to take them up, by properly designed, well-aimed outreach campaigns and training. 'Gender-neutral' won't hack it.

Intriguingly, there's another kind of job with even greater potential to deliver a green economy—although it's one that's routinely overlooked when sustainable employment is discussed. So, before we get too carried away by the whole idea of decarbonising jobs building physical infrastructure, we need to look in an altogether different direction: the social infrastructure.

### *The care economy*

If 'green' plus 'jobs' seems magical, 'care' plus 'economy' sounds strange: we associate care with everything that *isn't* included in the economy. And what does care work have to do with the climate crisis?

Consider these striking facts. Gross Domestic Product measures the value of a country's goods and services (more on this below). The Women's Budget Group has found that investing as little as 1 per cent of UK GDP in the care sector would create 2.7 times as many jobs as the same sum invested in construction.[27] Even if wages paid for care work were raised to the level of those in construction (which would need them to more than double), 60 per cent more jobs would be created by investment in care. So far, so good.

Now here's the green pay-off: investing in care is *30 per cent less polluting* than investing the same amount in the construction industry. Care jobs, it turns out, are green jobs. And then there's the gender angle: while investment in construction increases the gender employment gap by creating far more jobs for men than women, investment in care narrows it.

Of course there's something chilling in talking about care work in such cold, monetary terms, when it's about human vulnerability and need: a decent society should regard it as precious, whatever its economic benefits, and not just value it when you can put a positive figure on it. But even when subjected to the unfeeling calculus of numbers, jobs in the care sector trump those in construction, for sustainability, gender equality and economic value.

In many different ways, as the psychoanalyst and environmentalist Sally Weintrobe has argued, the culture that we live in is actually one of "uncare", a situation fomented by neoliberalism.[28] This means that putting care jobs at the heart of a Green New Deal has the potential to make it really transformative. Nowhere is this enshrined more than in *Creating a Caring Economy*, the Women's Budget Group's 2020 call to action. What, it asks, would a society look like if it prioritised care— paid and unpaid—rather than economic growth? A society that both recognised the value of unpaid care, and gave men and women equal legal entitlement to paid caring leave, alongside free universal childcare? One in which people have "time to care, as well as time free from care"?[29]

The Women's Budget Group set out a roadmap of eight steps to get there. The first, and perhaps most important, is to "Re-envision what we mean by 'the economy'", so that it includes, rather than excludes, care. Part of this involves seeing care as work in the first place. My neighbour told me that her husband used to say that any tasks ending in 'ing'—cooking, cleaning, hoovering, ironing, sweeping—were hers, while his didn't end in 'ing': it was work. He's now her ex-husband.

Once you organise the economy around the wellbeing of all its members, instead of around one gender, or around those financial transactions that create most profit for the tiny elite identified in Chapter 3, then profit and loss take on fresh meanings. You then start to appreciate how the social arrangements that support the neediest and most vulnerable benefit everyone else too—partly because we're all vulnerable, needy and dependent at some stage or other in our life's arc.[30] But partly too because, even if you're only interested in the balance sheet, investing in care saves huge sums of money.

If you make care jobs more appealing by paying and training carers properly, and by raising the status of their work, you attract many more people into the sector—

men as well as women—and therefore increase your revenue from taxes. If care in the community becomes a real thing, and not just a slogan, you free up the NHS to concentrate on those physical cases and conditions that really do need to be dealt with in hospitals and clinics. As for mental health problems, these have been estimated to cost employers anything between £35 billion and £45 billion.[31] In all areas of healthcare and social care, proper preventative care and support saves money by reducing the need for costly crisis interventions. It also enables people to lead happier lives and to indulge in less destructive behaviour, which can often involve environmentally damaging, careless over-consumption.

Viewed like this, care is the marrow of the economy, which is why the Women's Budget Group urges us also to re-imagine what we mean by costs, efficiency and productivity: these look rather different when not only market value, but "social value, environmental value, wellbeing and unpaid time" are factored in. The idea behind the roadmap is that every policy should be assessed for its impact on our ability to receive and provide care, paid or unpaid, and the Group goes on to spell out the kinds of initiatives that could bring about such a transformation. These include free, universal childcare, and "a free-at-the-point-of-use, high-quality Universal Care Service, financed centrally by the public purse, closely connected to the National Health Service, locally run in consultation with users, [and] with a well-trained and well-paid care workforce".[32]

"Who'll pay for it?" the sceptics cry, seemingly unaware of the costs of our present arrangements, or of the fact that the Office for National Statistics has estimated unpaid work as equivalent to 56 per cent of the UK's GDP, and unpaid childcare alone as equal to 18 per cent.[33] So, someone is already paying for it—and if you have to ask who, it's probably not you. Care, Sherilyn MacGregor has observed, is the free subsidy given to people in power.[34] They are only able to do what they do because someone else is looking after their child or aged parent, someone who's most likely a woman or a person of colour, under-valued as well as under-paid.

As with so much of women's work, care like this is mostly taken for granted and invisible. At least, in non-pandemic times. Covid-19 suddenly beamed a light on care work in 2020, so that it flared into public consciousness: its sometimes gruelling and relentless nature, the way it sets off powerful feelings of gratitude and a recognition of the fragility of the human condition—a feeling we often run away from, because it's so frightening. Weekly clapping was a brief collective acknowledgement of this feeling, before gratitude fatigue set in.

Nevertheless Covid-19 allowed us to see care as an expression of compassion and love, speaking to our deepest identification with the Other, tapping into instincts way beyond the transactional—what social scientist Richard Titmuss, in a different context, called "the gift relationship".[35] But the pandemic also showed everyone the ways in which care can be thankless work—messy, repetitive and physically demanding, calling on stoicism as well as empathy. Sentimentalising it is a sure sign that we're not going to acknowledge these other dimensions, by paying care jobs with a decent wage or allowing time for them to be done properly. These are the ways we can truly recognise care work's vital place at the heart of daily life and human experience. Coronavirus also brought this fact home to some of the public: they responded not just by clapping their appreciation of health and care workers, but also through signs put up in windows, demanding better pay for NHS staff and, in the crisis of the first wave, adequate personal protective equipment too.

There's nothing utopian in these ideas. Nearly every one of the Women's Budget Group's proposals is being tried out somewhere, in some form. Iceland, Scotland, New Zealand and Wales, for instance, have all begun taking steps to integrate wellbeing into their economic policy. Danish care workers are now paid a salary more akin to that of teachers. In the UK, Norwich's Goldsmith Street—an award-winning, high-density, high-spec, sustainable social housing project—was delivered economically and is beloved by residents, all of whom pay a 'social rent' that's determined by their income.[36] Models exist for all of these innovative practices; they just haven't yet been wrapped together into a larger parcel bound by prioritisation of the principles of care.

And, just like the Green New Deal, these policies are popular: more than 50 per cent of those surveyed in 2020 (on some questions, a much higher percentage) thought that wellbeing should be used to measure the success of economic policy; agreed that a better balance is needed between paid work, caring responsibilities and free time; felt investment in social care, health and education to be more important for the future of the economy than investment in transport and technology; agreed that social care should be available to everyone based on their care needs, not their wealth; and that the government should encourage and financially support men to provide a more equal share of care work. Three in four agreed that "economic equality between women and men is the mark of a good society".[37] These ideas form the basis of the Feminist Green New Deal Manifesto that WEN (Women's Environmental Network) and the Women's Budget Group planned to launch at COP26 in Glasgow.

So if these are the green jobs and policies with the real potential to kickstart the economy and make it more gender-equal, why does our world look so different? What stands in the way of such a sensible Green New Deal for Women?

## G(ross) D(amaging) P(olicies)

One major obstacle is the measure through which a nation's wealth is calculated: GDP. Baked into GDP are a load of absurdities and gender biases. Marilyn Waring, a former New Zealand MP, was one of the first people to zero in on them in her 1988 book *If Women Counted: A New Feminist Economics*. Not only was women's labour invisible to GDP, she observed, but so too was the environment. GDP didn't distinguish between clean air and polluted; it was indifferent to whether drinking water was safe or tainted.[38] Think back to the toxic water in Flint that campaigners had to battle against for so long: all of that pollution would entirely escape GDP's gaze and interest, despite the costs to the local and state economy due to workers and citizens getting sick.

Of course, trying to monetise women's labour or to find ways to include it in GDP plays into the whole idea that nothing has any value beyond the market. Arguing later that she'd been playing economics at its own game, Waring has been critical of her own work and conceded that ascribing a monetary value to the tasks that women do might prove problematic.[39] Nonetheless, her book was important and influential in pointing out what GDP is blind to, and how this disadvantages both women and the planet.

Waring's misgivings about the biases inherent in GDP had been voiced by others too. As a fugitive from economics (abandoning it at university), I remember coming across a slim pamphlet in the 1970s called *Health, the Mass Media and the NHS*. Written by Peter Draper, a public health campaigner who'd set up the Unit for the

Study of Health Policy at Guy's Hospital, this showed how manufacturing more cigarettes would show up in GDP as an example of economic growth, and so would be treated as a good thing. Reading it helped me understand for the first time how the economic status quo benefited the producers of ill health, whether ours or the earth's. What's more, as others have remarked, if the increased production of cigarettes meant that the NHS had to carry out more operations for cancer, this too would add to GDP.[40] By contrast, if swathes of the population gave up smoking and took up running instead, GDP would be reduced: we'd all supposedly be poorer.

No one has demonstrated more eloquently that a nation's wealth, as measured by GDP, isn't the same as its health than Bobby Kennedy, scion of the Kennedy clan, when he was a candidate for the Democratic presidential nomination. On the campaign trail in 1968, he pointed out that the production of napalm and nuclear warheads counted towards GDP, but the health and joy of America's children didn't, declaring in soaring rhetoric that GDP:

> does not include the beauty of our poetry or the strength of our marriages, the intelligence of our public debate or the integrity of our public officials. It measures neither our wit nor our courage, neither our wisdom nor our learning, neither our compassion nor our devotion to our country. It measures everything, in short, except that which makes life worthwhile.[41]

## Green growth or degrowth?

Inherent in GDP is the idea that economic growth is a very good thing; yet, as the 1960s turned into the 1970s, environmental concern and unease over the effects of untrammelled growth began to mushroom, driven partly by a highly influential 1972 report, 'The Limits to Growth'. Based on a two-year study at the Massachusetts Institute of Technology, this sold 30 million copies, was translated into thirty languages, and predicted the collapse of civilisation by 2100 if economic and population growth continued at the same rate.[42]

Like Paul Ehrlich's 1968 book *The Population Bomb*, 'The Limits to Growth' succeeded in awakening alarm about the planet's limits in a great many people, without helping them to develop a rounded understanding of the causes of environmental degradation. It saw the scale of the problems facing the planet; but, conceiving them in global terms (a "world model"), it never identified who was chiefly responsible for the extraction of fossil fuels or who was consuming them. Instead, in an early outing for the climate 'we', it promoted the idea of a universal "self-imposed limitation to growth" to achieve a global "equilibrium society".[43]

Thirty years later, one of the report's authors, Donella Meadows, was still pushing sustainable growth as the solution to the climate crisis, envisaging a supposedly hopeful scenario in which "the world decides on an average family size of two children"—without ever specifying which particular body in the world would make this decision, or how; or, indeed, the key question: how it would be enforced.[44]

In the meantime, sustainable growth and 'green growth' have remained attractive to many people, especially through successive economic crises—first the 2008 crash and then, as we've seen, the economic crisis brought about by Covid-19. Yet critics maintain that the optimism of the green growth brigade is unfounded, because you can't decarbonise at the speed needed to meet the limit set by the Paris Agreement while continuing to grow in an ecologically sound way. 'Green growth' is a dummy; a comforter for those who accept the reality of climate breakdown, but can't stomach the idea of questioning economic growth.[45]

Young climate strikers have no such inhibitions: when she spoke to the UN Climate Action Summit in 2019, Greta Thunberg denounced the continued belief in "fairytales of eternal economic growth" at the beginning of a period of mass extinction.[46] But if economic growth is the chief planetary villain, and green or sustainable growth isn't the solution, then what is?

Another concept has come increasingly to dominate the climate conversation: 'degrowth'. Coining the phrase in 1972, the Austro-French philosopher André Gorz argued that capitalism and the economic growth on which it depended were incompatible with maintaining the earth's ecological balance.[47] What was needed wasn't 'just' zero growth, but degrowth—an idea revived in the 2010s through a flurry of enthusiastic books, seminars and websites. 'Degrowthers' don't believe that technology will ride to the planet's rescue. They don't fall back on financial mechanisms like carbon trading or carbon offsetting that allow high-income countries to continue polluting. They don't think that, if you simply replace fossil fuel energy with renewable, you're sorted. They argue instead for living within the planet's boundaries by radically reducing production and consumption in the global North.

Degrowth isn't a magic wand. Just think of the change in mindset needed to disrupt the global North's 'upgrade culture', which pressures people to trade in a perfectly functioning electronic product for a more recent version. Each autumn, the major manufacturers release newer models that purport to render older models if not redundant, then somehow lacking. Soon this turns out to be true, as the older models are 'no longer supported', their obsolescence built in.

For this is the lie fundamental to the upgrade: selling itself as the definitive product, the ultimate satisfier of needs, it conceals its own transience—the fact that it, too, will soon be superseded. It makes us buy the same object, tweaked, many times over. Resistance can be hard, because material objects are freighted with personal and cultural meanings: by upgrading our gadgets and gizmos, it can feel as if we're upgrading ourselves.[48]

The degrowth movement forces us to think about what we need, rather than what we want, and about what makes a fulfilling life. Campaigners are trying to steer climate futurism away from pious, austere visions of a post-growth society stressing what will have to be given up, in favour of more joyous and celebratory predictions of what will be gained. The philosopher Kate Soper, in particular, rejects the idea of sacrifice: consuming less, she insists, doesn't mean having less pleasure. On the contrary, she argues, consuming less and distributing work more fairly will produce an "alternative hedonism", one based less on polluting products and experiences, and rooted instead in more joyful relationships with the earth and each other. This, she suggests, is the real meaning of "a good life".[49]

What are the implications of degrowth for women? There's no evidence that women are immune to the blandishments of the upgrade. On the contrary, degrowth often involves swapping goods for labour: so, if we don't watch out, we could end up with a situation where it isn't the economy that grows exponentially, but women's unpaid labour. Who makes the slower meals when fast food is eschewed? Whose day will be lengthened by avoiding motorised transport to take the kids to school? One woman told me, after a webinar on women and the climate crisis, that her friends spent hours vexing over whether to use disposable nappies, but when they turned—with the best of intentions—to nappy laundering services instead, they inadvertently played a part in exploiting the cheap labour of the refugee and immigrant women providing them. These aren't problems that lend themselves to individual solutions, although women are increasingly thrashing out the question of how degrowth can become gender-equal.[50]

The answer, of course, as it has been throughout this book, is to take women and gender into account when formulating our climate solutions. Degrowth can't simply be about individual consumers refraining from buying new things; it has to be about a systemic change in the way our society and economy are organised. In her bestselling 2017 book *Doughnut Economics*, economist Kate Raworth offers a roadmap to this destination. Like Waring three decades earlier, she challenges the fixation on GDP as a primary measure of progress, and starts instead with humanity's long-term goals, plotting a viable economic system that would help us achieve them.

Raworth insists that it's possible to achieve equitable human rights and social rights while meeting basic human needs, in a way that respects the planet's limits and also meets the UN's Sustainable Development Goals, agreed by every UN member-state in 2015 and to be achieved by 2030.[51] She calls her model "doughnut economics" because it consists of two concentric rings: at the outer ring are the planet's limits, while the inner ring marks the place where every human's basic needs are met. Between them, she concludes, is the safe and just space for all.

*"System change, not climate change"*

All these are compelling alternative visions—a Green New Deal for Women. A feminist degrowth plan. So, to return to my earlier question: what's preventing them from coming to fruition?

The ultimate answer lies in the global money markets, which were designed expressly to thwart such scenarios. Telling this shocking story in her book *The Case for the Green New Deal*, economist Ann Pettifor singles out the 1944 Bretton Woods Conference as a critical historical moment when, against opposition, the US Federal Reserve (the American equivalent of the Bank of England) was installed as the 'lender of last resort'—the world's central banker, if you like.

The result is that the US dollar—in concert with a globalised monetary system run by private, deregulated financial markets—works to accumulate and safeguard the wealth of a tiny international minority protected from national, democratic oversight. As we know from Chapter 3, this is a mostly male minority, and one which gorges on fossil fuel extraction.

The 1930s New Deal was a job-creating bonanza, despite the often-overlooked fact that it excluded African Americans from some programmes. Roosevelt was able to create it because he had the courage and skills to challenge Wall Street. But the globalised monetary system has become even more powerful in the decades since then. Today's leaders couldn't do a Roosevelt after the 2008 crash, because of the limited powers over capital that remain with national governments. That crash, far from threatening financialised capitalism, only strengthened it, leaving workers to take the hit.[52]

It's a staggering story, and a terrifying one. The only way of introducing a Green New Deal, Pettifor concludes, is by dismantling and transforming the current globalised financial system, which is designed to exploit at least half the world. Africa, she points out, is rich in natural resources:

> Africa is not poor, it is impoverished ... it has been made poor, mainly by free trade, liberalisation and privatisation, all of which exacerbate the massive losses, extraction and slavery associated with colonial exploitation ... far from being backward and dependent on our help, Africa pays more money to rich countries than it receives in aid. We need to face up to the uncomfortable truth: Africa is aiding rich Western nations.[53]

Pettifor walks us over the bumpy path through which countries can reclaim those regulatory powers and financial privileges long ago surrendered to 'the market'. This is the only way that a Green New Deal of any stripe, especially one grounded in a care economy, can ever hope to come into being.

It will involve heavy state spending in the form of government borrowing (through government bonds), but it also requires us to unlearn the neoliberal falsehoods that have brainwashed whole swathes of the population, some of whom should know better. Among them has been BBC Political Editor Laura Kuenssberg: in response to figures on government spending during the pandemic, she reported, "This is the credit card, the national mortgage, everything absolutely maxed out"—as though government spending were similar to a splurge in Topshop that tips you over into personal debt, rather than an essential plank of social and economic policy. Twenty-four leading economists wrote to the BBC to complain, one of them adding later: "All this new debt is owed to ourselves, so the choice is who pays whom rather than how the country collectively finds the money."[54]

The reform needed for a Green New Deal will also require an internationalist perspective, because, as we've seen, it's all too easy for rich countries to extract new forms of energy from the global South, which gets nothing back in return except toxic e-waste. But it's the green economy, they cry! *The Independent* has reported that Anglo-American, the mining giant, plans "to extract 400,000 tonnes of copper per year for the next 40 years from Chile's Andean glaciers"; it justifies this by saying that "our products are essential to the transition to a low carbon economy".[55]

Asad Rehman, executive director of the charity War on Want, has warned that "The new wave of green extraction promises to be as deadly and dirty as fossil fuel extraction."[56] In 2020, as an alternative to this new form of green colonialism, War on Want, joined forces with The Leap (a progressive climate organisation co-founded by the campaigner Naomi Klein), launching a movement for a Global Green New Deal. Although its details have yet to be spelt out, its heart clearly lies in the area of international climate justice.

## Knit your own Green New Deal for Women

With so many different versions swilling around, what additional features would a Global Green New Deal for Women need to have?

The care agenda is vital, and so is the inclusion of women's voices and gender considerations in all Green New Deal proposals. Disaster planning, as we've seen, changes if women's needs and voices are included. The mayor of Poitiers wants to use her procurement powers to reduce the city's carbon emissions. Could she ensure that they advance gender equality at the same time?

Sometimes it's hard to see how existing polices and spaces are already gendered. Take cars, for example. They spend 95 per cent of the time parked and only 5 per cent in use.[57] There are a billion parking spaces in the US (four for each car), and at least half of the downtown area of American cities is made over to the car.[58] The sociologist Richard Sennett has argued that "paid-for parking on streets is a daily privatis[ation] of public space".[59] But, if we think back to Chapter 3, it's also a masculinisation of public space, since women are far less likely to own cars than men.

There's another side to this. When researchers at Stanford University used data from the smartphones of nearly three quarters of a million people in 111 countries, they discovered something that they called "activity inequality", with a sharp gender dimension. In cities with high "walkability", there was less gendered inequality governing who gets to move around; in less walkable ones, women's activity was reduced much more than men's.[60] The researchers didn't peer into the reasons for this, but safety is clearly a major concern for women, plus the need to bundle many different activities into one trip due to women's greater burden of unpaid domestic labour.

In other words, Anne Hidalgo's proposed 15-minute city turns out to be particularly relevant to women. So too would the banning of private cars (people with disabilities exempted), and their replacement by plentiful, free public transport in a wide variety of forms—a plan currently being trialled in Luxembourg, a number of American cities and the German city of Monheim.[61] We know that women use public transport a lot more than men.[62] This is how you combine gender equality and environmental sustainability in a single policy.

As urban designer Christele Harrouk has remarked, "Although cities are supposed to be built for everyone, they are ... most of the time thought, planned and designed by men."[63] Women make up just one third of British architects.[64] Urban planning hasn't yet caught up with demographic changes that could seriously drive up consumption of domestic goods, unless ways are found for people to share them: the increase in single-person households is one example.[65] Another is the fact that, although the gap is narrowing, there are significantly more older women than older men living on their own, partly because women live longer than men.[66] Over the years, a great many visionary projects have shown how cities can be re-imagined to enable the sharing of resources, in ways that both save energy and encourage collective life—projects like the Older Women's Co-Housing Project in London. Urban historian Dolores Hayden has unearthed scores of other examples of pioneering feminist projects—from co-ops to community kitchens—developed to 'design out' the isolation of American housewives.[67]

My own fantasy is of a paid helper on every block, ready to chip in when an extra pair of hands is needed— whether after the birth of a baby, following a discharge from hospital, or for an ageing resident who wants to remain in their own home. These would be green jobs, unreliant on technology: a local human to pitch in with eldercare, rather than a robot. They'd enshrine, in architectural design and everyday life, a recognition that we all need help at some stage; that 'assisted living' shouldn't be the preserve of old people, since most of us need assistance with living occasionally (and some of us often).

At the heart of a Green New Deal for both women and men is the idea of the commons: those shared resources that are collectively owned by the public, who become its custodians and stewards, rather than its owners. As the writer George Monbiot has observed, "there is neither the physical nor ecological space for everyone to pursue private luxury. Instead we should strive for private sufficiency, public luxury."[68]

Stewardship is a reminder that we're here only temporarily and hold public goods in trust, to be handed on to the next generation in at least as good and sustainable condition as we inherited them, if not better. Alternatively, you could call us guests in public space. Guests seem to exist only in private settings: why not also in the public domain? But we are also hosts—on behalf of the future.

More and more, campaigners and critics have begun to think about what a feminist commons would look like.[69] And doesn't it work the other way round too? Won't more gender-equal societies be more receptive to the idea of shared ownership of public goods? It's not such a fanciful idea, when you look at some of the surprising effects of gender equality that have already been discovered.

## The gender equality bonus

'Gender' has come to be equated with 'women'; but, as this book doesn't stop chanting, it refers not only to women's roles but also to men's. And here there's an intriguing side story to demands for gender equality. All too often, it's assumed that extending the rights of women involves reducing those of men, in a zero-sum game, yet there's now a stack of evidence showing the opposite: that men too benefit from living in more gender-equal societies, and that policies promoting gender equality improve the quality of life of everyone, not just women.[70]

A recent World Health Organization report comparing forty-one European countries found that men's health was poorer in more unequal societies—gender stereotypes and the sexual division of labour harm men, as well as women.[71] When the sexes are more equal, men say that they're more satisfied with life.[72] In more gender-equal societies such as Nordic countries, both men and women, apparently, even sleep better.[73] To me this last finding, from a recent European study, suggests that men in more equal societies are encouraged to look after themselves. (And here, surely, is another bonus for women: those men are presumably no longer relying on women to look after them so much; perhaps—who knows—they might even be doing more of those '-ing jobs' for themselves.)

In more gender-equal societies, men are half as likely to be depressed and less likely to commit suicide, and have around a 40% less risk of dying a violent death.[74] Adolescent boys in those countries complain of fewer psychosomatic complaints,[75] and are more likely to use contraceptives.[76] Speaking of sex, contrary to the stereotypes, one study found that men with feminist partners reported greater sexual satisfaction—as did women with partners who supported feminism.[77] Icelandic men have the second-highest life expectancy in Europe.[78] That's not just down to the bracingly cold air and herring with everything: Iceland also has a smaller gender gap than any other country.[79]

How realistic is the prospect of such transformative programmes being adopted worldwide, at least in this millennium? Picking holes in other people's visions is certainly a popular pasttime, but the environmentalist Mayer Hillman had a ready reply to those happy detractors who bat down any proposals for serious, climate-linked policy changes: "If you don't think these solutions will work, there's an obligation on you to think up a better one. So often, ideas are rejected on the grounds that they are not perfect in all respects, in favour of the status quo, which is far more imperfect."[80]

So, to those who persist in dismissing the idea of a gender-equal, ecologically balanced society as an unworkable fantasy, let me ask this one thing: did you say the same thing to those male geo-engineers who proposed combating global heating by spraying aerosols of sulphate into the stratosphere, or "refreezing rapidly warming parts of the polar regions by deploying tall ships to pump salt particles from the ocean into polar clouds"?[81] Thought not.

# CONCLUSION

We have arrived at a hinge in history—a moment like no other. The conclusions of the 2018 IPCC report were clear and commanding: rapid, far-reaching and unprecedented changes are needed, in all aspects of society.[1] The rich world has awoken: the report, plus raging fires in Australia and California, and flooding in European cities and towns, made the imminence of climate catastrophe real, in a new and urgent way. (The poor countries of the world already knew what climate disaster looked like: each year Bangladesh experiences catastrophic floods, even if these scarcely register in the wealthy countries.)

Now, with the syndemic of the Covid-19 and racism crises as well as the climate one, how do we balance optimism with realism, temper pessimism with hope? Perhaps we need what the British activist Shaun Chamberlin calls "dark optimism", which allows you to be "unashamedly positive about what kind of a world humanity could create, and unashamedly realistic about how far we are from creating it today".[2]

At the start of the pandemic, a curious climate euphoria seemed to set in. People talked as if it were a dress rehearsal for a future decarbonised life. We're all in it together, they chanted—a Covid 'we' to add to the climate one. Many enthused about a slower pace of life, about their fresh appreciation of nature, the emergence of mutual aid groups and a sudden outbreak of neighbourliness. Working from home promised to cut transport emissions at a stroke. When $CO_2$ levels dropped dramatically as the result of planes being grounded, some believed that the rich countries had started down the path to net zero emissions.

But it soon became apparent that Covid-19 wasn't the great leveller: people of colour died in much greater numbers, especially those living in small and high-density accommodation, working in frontline jobs, and with underlying conditions caused by poverty. Globally more women than men lost their jobs, while also doing most of the childcare and home schooling during lockdown—care tasks distributed unequally once again.[3] The ability to learn, when socially distanced and locked down, was unequal too: the gap between disadvantaged students and their peers widened by 46 per cent in the UK. By September 2020, only 1% of teachers at the most affluent schools were reporting that pupils were six months behind in their learning, against 11% of teachers at the most deprived schools. Black and minority-ethnic pupils were especially affected.[4] Those without cars had to bike, stay within walking distance of their home, or risk their lives on public transport—and for those whose job couldn't be done from home, there was no choice.

Meanwhile, those who lived in houses with space and gardens survived lockdown more easily. Africa's death rate from the pandemic was lower than elsewhere in the world during the first wave, but in most poor countries of the global South that lacked halfway decent infrastructure, bodies piled up in the streets for days or sometimes weeks before being removed for burial; and millions living on the breadline tipped over into severe poverty.

Covid, then, did have something to tell us about the climate crisis. In early 2021, Oxfam published a report called 'The Inequality Virus'. You can substitute 'climate' for 'virus' throughout without noticing any difference. "The virus has exposed, fed off and increased existing inequalities of wealth, gender and race," it declared. Inequality, the report said, had risen during the pandemic in virtually every country at the same time. Surveying 295 economists from seventy-nine countries, Oxfam reported over half of them predicting that coronavirus would increase gender inequality, and two thirds believing that it would increase racial inequality.[5]

In fact, much of the optimism of the early days soon turned out to have been little more than a puff of magic thinking. Within mere weeks of the UK's first lockdown ending, the carbon savings of the locked-down period had halved;[6] and, according to one poll, large numbers of people who accepted that humans were responsible for the climate crisis nevertheless planned to fly more after the pandemic.[7] This was true of motorists too: although there was a dramatic drop in traffic levels during the first lockdown itself, UK drivers admitted that they were relying on their cars more than ever, because they felt safer in their own vehicles than on public transport.[8]

And those hopes for a post-Covid 'green recovery'? Countries around the world have poured money into the fossil fuel economy instead, with pandemic rescue packages streaming into high-carbon sectors.[9] For all the fine talk of "building back better", the British government directed most of its funds into building back the same or worse, committing £30.9 billion of its Covid-19 recovery plans to fossil fuel industries, and £27 billion to road building.[10] It has approved a huge new gas station in Yorkshire (Europe's largest, which could eventually account for three quarters of the UK's power-sector emissions); sanctioned the opening of a new coal mine in Cumbria; and given a £1 billion loan guarantee for a Mozambique gas pipeline.[11] Oh, and some of the world's biggest fossil fuel companies got added to the London Stock Exchange's 'ethical' investment list—all this in the year before Britain was to host, with its all-male delegation, the COP26 international climate conference in Glasgow.

There's another thing that happened during the pandemic. Think back to the gendered causes of the climate emergency and that handful of rich white male high-emitters. You might have imagined that their prosperity would have taken a hit during the pandemic, but the Institute for Policy Studies, a progressive American think tank, discovered something disturbing: between 21 March and 26 December 2020, over 73 million Americans lost their jobs, while US billionaire wealth increased by $1.1 trillion, a gain of almost 40%. Over the first ten months of the pandemic, billionaires' combined fortunes grew nearly 40%.[12]

Black and Latino families in the US, the researchers observed, were twice as likely to have zero or negative wealth, even before the pandemic; but in the first three months of 2020, eight of the US's richest billionaires saw their net worth surge by over $1 billion—pandemic profiteers, the Institute called them. Seven are white men, and the eighth, Mackenzie Bezos, is the ex-wife of the richest among them.[13] Their wealth had ballooned partly through Covid-induced demand for tech companies' goods and services, but also because they had bet on the recovery of global stock markets by buying shares in the early months of lockdown, when they were at their lowest.[14]

Oxfam has come to similar conclusions, adding that the world's ten richest billionaires had seen their wealth increase since the start of the pandemic by an amount "more than enough to prevent *anyone on Earth* from falling into poverty because of the virus, and to pay for a COVID-19 vaccine for *everyone*" on the planet.[15] In reality, by late January 2021, more than 71 million vaccine doses had been administered around the world, but only fifty-five of those doses—yes, you read that right—had been given to people living in the twenty-nine poorest countries.[16]

Curiously, although the Oxfam report identified the world's thousand richest people as "mainly White men", almost all the coverage referred to these billionaires' gender only in passing, if at all; nothing that I could find mentioned their ethnicity. We've so severed wealth from its roots in gender and racial inequality, so degendered and deracialised it, that we treat these billionaires almost as if they're incidentally men and white, rather than recognising the key role of those characteristics in enabling them to amass their money.

In among these dispiriting effects of the pandemic, though, you could spot saplings of fresh ideas and buds of promise: real reasons to be hopeful. Local low-traffic schemes sprung up and, in cities from Milan and Brighton to Vancouver and Bogotá—whose female mayor, Claudia López, is the first openly gay mayor of a Latin American capital—whole roads were closed off to cars during lockdown, to facilitate social distancing and accommodate the increased numbers of cyclists.[17] Some of these cities are hoping that the normalisation of pedestrianisation and of limitations on driving will encourage a permanent, post-lockdown move to greater cycling or walking.[18] Clean air became not just a health issue but also a human rights one, thanks to the persistence of Ella Adoo-Kissi-Debrah's mother and the human rights lawyer she hired to persuade a London coroner's court to admit air pollution as a cause of fatality on her daughter's death certificate.

Oxfam has identified another reason for hope. "Transformative policies that seemed unthinkable before the crisis," remarks 'The Inequality Virus', "have suddenly been shown to be a possibility."[19] The urgency of the pandemic, and the dramatic impact of lockdown on every aspect of public and private life, mandated a massive intervention of governments into the economy. The whole neoliberal ideology of a lean state melted before our eyes, like the Wicked Witch of the West. Overnight, governments began to pour billions into furlough schemes that provided a safety net for employers and employees. Controversially, in the UK, the state even subsidised citizens eating out.

True, in the UK some of the huge sums allocated for personal protective equipment, Covid-19 tests and the (unsuccessful) attempt to set up an efficient track and trace system were funnelled straight into the coffers of inexperienced private companies, often run by colleagues or friends of government ministers; this came to be called the 'chumocracy'. But the point is this: never again will it be possible to maintain that the only good state is a small one. Crises on this scale, it's plain, require government intervention. And never again will it be possible for governments to claim that they've run out of money: after all that insistence upon 'austerity' (for some), just like that, they have managed to pull billions out of the hat or from under the mattress when they thought the need was urgent—as they always manage to, curiously, whenever they decide to go to war.

This book has charted the devastating effects of carbon emissions on women, particularly women of colour, who've contributed the least to them. The climate crisis, I've suggested, is a crisis of masculinity, or of one particular form of masculinity, with a small number of rich white men holding the world to ransom, and women— again women of colour and Indigenous women in particular—excluded or marginalised from negotiations or plans to arrest and reverse the emergency.

We know what has to be done. There are hundreds— no, thousands—of international reports, from governments, relief agencies, NGOs and charities, not to mention a wealth of academic research over nearly two decades, all pointing in the same direction: the need for a colossal transformation in our social, political and economic systems, with women's voices and concerns at its heart. Gender inequality is a driver of the climate crisis, as well as its result; gender equality—which can only be achieved alongside racial equality—offers powerful channels to stop it. The 'vulnerabilities' of women and people of colour have been structured in—and can be structured out.

We've seen some of the forces lined up to prevent change, and they're gathering even more resolutely now that Joe Biden has replaced their cheerleader Donald Trump in the White House. This obstructionism has a long history: check out the University of Maine's 'Climate Chronology' report, which sets a history of knowledge about greenhouse gases' impact on global heating against a history of American resistance to curbing emissions.[20] Seeing these two timelines side by side—how long the basic facts have been known, and how little has been done about them—makes you boil over with rage and frustration. But it isn't only the decisions made in boardrooms, negotiating halls and government chambers that stand in the way of the radical, viable and affordable changes sketched out in the last chapter: it's also what's been done to our minds.

You have to be able to imagine change before you can fight for it; but, increasingly since the 1980s or so, neoliberalism has colonised our imagination in the global North, cloaking itself in inevitability, claiming for 'the market' an almost elemental power, as if it came about by some organic process and not the special interests of elites. As for the global South, North-controlled neoliberal institutions like the World Bank and the International Monetary Fund have made sure that no country in need of financial assistance can escape the strings of doctrine and policy that come attached with loans and aid; so long as this is true, nations impoverished by the neoliberal order cannot introduce the massive transformation that's needed to overthrow it.

We are told that this system, which so assaults and degrades nature, is natural! Margaret Thatcher famously proclaimed that "There is no alternative," and neoliberal economies nod their heads in agreement: it can't be other than this. Anything else would be worse, or against human nature. Instead of recognising that our damaged planet is dystopian, they dismiss radical visions of change as utopian.

What a remarkable sleight of hand: to have persuaded so many people that their achingly sombre engagement with the brutal facts of the climate emergency, their sense of grief at what's been done to the earth and its poorest inhabitants, is exaggerated and delusional; that any powerful programme of practical steps to escape the crisis is a juvenile fantasy. Get real, they chorus—by which they mean nothing more than tinkering with the plundering industries, a slight adjustment to their extractive spoils. This is a Wonderland that Alice would have recognised, and that Lewis Carroll would have been proud to have invented.

Someone once said that it's easier to imagine the end of the world than the end of capitalism. Covid-19 has certainly shown us a kind of end to our world; might it also enable us to imagine the end of capitalism? And help us to understand that one era's utopianism is another's pragmatism?

Those of us old enough to have lived through the Cold War, apartheid and the Irish Troubles know that seemingly indestructible systems *can* get dismantled, sometimes pretty quickly. The eruption of rage around the world triggered by the killing of George Floyd in May 2020 showed how dramatically and suddenly a consciousness—in this case white—could belatedly but powerfully be raised in allyship with people of colour, rising up against structural racism. Climate campaigners also like to cast back to the Second World War for an example of a mass mobilisation in the collective interest, and the pandemic, in its early days, exemplified this: it was extraordinary how speedily wealthcare took a back seat to healthcare, for a while at least.

The Indian novelist and campaigner Arundhati Roy has put it eloquently. The pandemic:

> has mocked immigration controls, biometrics, digital surveillance and every other kind of data analytics, and struck hardest—thus far—in the richest, most powerful nations of the world, bringing the engine of capitalism to a juddering halt. Temporarily perhaps, but at least long enough for us to examine its parts, make an assessment and decide whether we want to help fix it, or look for a better engine ... It is a portal, a gateway between one world and the next.

> We can choose to walk through it, dragging the car-
> casses of our prejudice and hatred, our avarice, our data
> banks and dead ideas, our dead rivers and smoky skies
> behind us. Or we can walk through lightly, with little
> luggage, ready to imagine another world. And ready to
> fight for it.[21]

It won't be an easy fight. We know who the climate guilty are, and how ruthlessly and shamelessly they'll defend their interests—through slippery language, for instance. In December 2020, ExxonMobil, the eleventh biggest climate polluting company in the US, proudly unveiled its 2025 greenhouse gas reduction plans, parading its support of the Paris Agreement. Yet its 15–20 per cent reduction in emissions is far from the decarbonising push that it claims to be.[22] If you peer more closely, as Emily Atkin, editor of the HEATED newsletter has done, you'll see that the plan commits to reducing not the corporation's overall greenhouse gas emissions or oil production, only their intensity—making it less carbon-intensive to produce a barrel of oil.

In fact, Atkin maintains, "this could still result in the company increasing its overall carbon footprint over the next five years, if it significantly ramps up oil produc-tion—which, it turns out, is exactly what Exxon intends to do".[23] Documents leaked to Bloomberg earlier in 2020 showed that Exxon planned to increase its annual $CO_2$ emissions by as much as the entire pre-pandemic output of Greece.[24] So far there's no indication that these plans have been cancelled, only delayed.

We know that false solutions will masquerade as authentic ones. Under Peru and Switzerland's trumpeted "world-first" carbon offset deal under the Paris Agreement, Switzerland invests in Peruvian sustainable development projects and gets to claim the resulting emission cuts against its own national targets, even though the money for the projects comes from Swiss motor fuel imports.[25] So, no change there. This is what they used to call creative accounting.

Ill-thought-out solutions don't help either. France's plan to move to clean energy by raising fuel and petrol prices brought tens of thousands of '*gilets jaunes*' protesters onto the streets in 2018: without working out a transitional strategy or alternative support for drivers, the state had simply offloaded the costs of climate policy straight on to the low-income consumer. "The elites talk about the end of the world," one *gilet jaune* told *Le Monde* newspaper, "while we are talking about the end of the month."[26]

We know that change is hard: it demands a reckoning. As the climate debt owed by the rich world to the poor becomes ever clearer, calls for climate reparations grow louder: for a repayment of the debt not just between nations, but also to those within them who've been victims of the fossil fuel industry. Yet for this to happen, as the African American environmentalist Tamara Toles

O'Laughlin has observed, the US would have to admit "the harm that it did to other people ... that it's been a bad actor ... The US has been reluctant to do that because it means admitting liability."[27]

So, a time for optimism, or for pessimism? Trump has gone. President Biden immediately rejoined the Paris Agreement; cancelled the Keystone XL oil pipeline; has paused new oil and gas drilling on public lands and off-shore waters; intends to commit $2 trillion to clean energy and infrastructure (yes, those green jobs again); and has ordered the Justice Department to consider establishing an environmental justice office.[28] No word on women and the climate crisis—Biden has appointed a good one, Gina McCarthy, as his White House National Climate Advisor, although in her early state-ments she hasn't mentioned gender either—and, as an American climate campaigner told me, "The Biden administration hasn't made gender equality as visible a priority as other issues, such as climate—but we will make sure they get better soon." Conservative news out-lets, of course, have immediately begun to forewarn about the jobs that will be lost.[29] You might interpret their panic as a sign that Biden's policies risk accelerating the end of fossil fuels...

Another cause for optimism: we've watched school-strikers, mostly girls and young women, refuse to be overwhelmed by a sense of helplessness, instead mobilis-ing their helplessness as a campaigning tool. They started not from what's politically feasible, but from what's most environmentally urgent, galvanising each other and crashing through adult defences. Some of them came to this action from a gentle place, a love of nature and animals and fears for their extinction. Others saw how rural racism interfered with their access to countryside and resolved to clear a space for themselves in it, like Mya-Rose Craig, AKA Birdgirl, or groups such as Black Girls Hike. It's been thrilling to watch their diverse efforts light up a whole generation.

You can't organise a climate movement through zeal alone, though. The founders and co-founders of youth climate justice organisations Zero Hour and Sunrise have put together how-to guides for building a protest movement, showing, in the case of Zero Hour, their painstaking steps to raise $80,000.[30] Varshini Prakash of Sunrise gives a fascinating account of that movement's strategy to build an active base through canny use of social media.[31] Nothing serendipitous there: just graft, belief and brilliant organising skills.

Women should not be tasked with doing this alone, nor should BIPOC. I've watched on Zoom as my interviewees, most of them women of colour, have described their campaigning life and the high personal costs it exacts in time and energy. I've worried about them and their friends, about the impact of meeting the unending demands of activism through traditional and social media, as well as on the streets and in groups, on podcasts and via public speaking. This is a time for allies.

We need a coalition of hopers, enablers and imaginers. Of climate champions matching the ferocity of those Indigenous climate warriors in the Amazon and the Cerrado. Visiting hours for despair will be strictly limited. Here all are welcome, whatever their gender, sexual identity and preference, abilities or disability, age or social class, and however they've been racialised—a glittering social diversity to equal the earth's biodiversity. A dance of human ingenuity, a hubbub of hope, and a synchrony of voices, united to create a healthy planet; one that is gender-equal, racially equal and climate-just. It is time.

# WHAT NOW?

## FURTHER RESOURCES

*Groups and websites*

**Black Girls Hike** is a UK-wide hiking network for black women, helping them to reconnect with nature while building a community.

**Climate Wise Women** supports grassroots women and women's groups to participate in international climate events.

**Flock Together** is a support group for young Londoners of colour who want to bird-watch and reconnect with nature.

**Fridays4Future** is a part of the global climate strike movement launched after Greta Thunberg began her School Strike for Climate in 2018.

**GenderCC—Women for Climate Justice** is a global network of activists and groups working for gender equality, women's rights and climate justice.

**HEATED** is a trenchant newsletter reporting on the climate emergency.

**The Mary Robinson Foundation—Climate Justice** is a centre for education and advocacy on the struggle for global climate justice.

**The NAACP Environmental and Justice Program** supports US communities of colour in addressing climate change and environmental injustice.

**OUT for Sustainability** is a North American nonprofit mobilising the LGBTQ+ community on sustainability and environmental issues.

**Queers X Climate** is a queer-led initiative promoting climate activism in the global LGBTQ+ community.

**Sunrise Movement** is a US youth movement against climate change and in support of a Green New Deal.

**Survival International** is a human rights organisation campaigning for the rights of Indigenous, tribal and uncontacted peoples.

**UK Student Climate Network** is a UK activist group of mainly under-18s.

**WECAN** is an international, intersectional feminist network of global climate justice advocates.

**The Women and Gender Constituency** is a coalition of women's groups that represents women's interests at the UNFCCC's COP summits.

**Women4Climate** is an initiative by the C40 mayors to mentor women climate leaders in cities.

**The Women's Environment and Development Organisation** is a global women's advocacy organisation and creator of the Gender Climate Tracker App. It monitors gender-responsive climate policy and participation of women in climate negotiations. WEDO was part of the coalition that launched the Feminist Green New Deal.

**The Women's Environment Network** is a UK-based charity promoting environmental justice and women's climate action.

**Wretched of the Earth** is a UK-based grassroots collective of Indigenous, black and brown individuals and groups for climate justice, in the UK and the global South.

**Zero Hour** is an intersectional US youth movement organising mass actions for climate justice and in support of a Green New Deal.

### *Podcasts, talks and short films*

*10 Solutions for Feminist Climate Resilient Recovery* (podcast from Women Organizing for Change in Agriculture and Natural Resource Management).

'A Message From the Future With Alexandria Ocasio-Cortez', video from *The Intercept* and Naomi Klein's The Leap.

'A Message From the Future II: The Years of Repair', video from *The Intercept* and Naomi Klein's The Leap.

'Does climate activism have a privilege problem?', episode of *Beyond Today* (BBC podcast).

'Ecofeminism and Queer Ecology', episode of *The Ecopolitics Podcast* (environmental politics podcast).

*Hot Take* (intersectional feminist climate podcast).

*How to Save a Planet* (podcast on climate solutions).

'Is climate breakdown sexist?', episode of *How to Save the Planet* (podcast from Friends of the Earth).

*Mothers of Invention* (podcast on feminist climate solutions).

'Queer and Trans Liberation', episode of *In Conversation: A Listening Series on Climate Justice and Collective Liberation* (podcast from Our Climate Voices).

'To stop the climate crisis, let's dismantle the system that caused it' (TEDxYouth talk by Jamie Margolin of Zero Hour).

*What Planet Are We On? ... with Liz Bonnin* (BBC climate solutions podcast).

'Why climate change is sexist', episode of *Tea with Mama Cash* (feminist politics podcast).

*YIKES* (podcast on climate justice and human rights).

### Books

Christiana Figueres & Tom Rivett-Carnac, 2020. *The Future We Choose: Surviving the Climate Crisis*. London: Manilla.

Friends of the Earth & C40 Cities, eds, 2018. *Why Women Will Save the Planet*. London: Zed.

Ayana Elizabeth Johnson & Katharine K. Wilkinson, eds, 2020. *All We Can Save*: *Truth, Courage, and Solutions for the Climate Crisis*. New York: One World.

Naomi Klein, 2015. *This Changes Everything: Capitalism vs. the Climate*. London: Penguin.

Jamie Margolin, 2020. *Youth to Power: Your Voice and How to Use It*. New York: Hachette.

Ann Pettifor, 2019. *The Case for the Green New Deal*. London: Verso.

Varshini Prakash & Guido Girgenti, eds, 2020. *Winning the*

*Green New Deal: Why We Must, How We Can.* New York: Simon & Schuster.

Mary Robinson, 2018. *Climate Justice: Hope, Resilience, and the Fight for a Sustainable Future.* London: Bloomsbury.

# NOTES

## INTRODUCTION

1. Lorde, A., 2019. *Sister Outsider*. London: Penguin.
2. MacGregor, S., 2019. 'Zooming in, calling out: (m)anthropogenic climate change through the lens of gender.' In: Bhavnani, K-K. et al., eds. *Climate Futures*. London: Zed Books.
3. Bem, S., 2008. *The Lenses of Gender: Transforming the Debate on Sexual Inequality*. New Haven, CT: Yale University Press.
4. Wallace-Wells, D., 2019. *The Uninhabitable Earth*. London: Penguin Books.
5. Milam, L., 1975, p. 351. *Sex and Broadcasting*. Berkeley, CA: Dildo Press.
6. Author interview, Jacqui Patterson, by Zoom, 5.8.20.
7. Yurcaba, J., 11.11.19. 'Activists Explain Most Gen Z Girls Have Climate Anxiety.' https://www.bustle.com/p/most-gen-z-girls-have-climate-anxiety-activists-explain-why-19199853. Accessed 2.2.21.
8. Pearson. A., et al., 2017. 'Race, Class, Gender and Climate Change Communication.' *Oxford Research Encyclopedia of Climate Science*. Oxford: OUP.
9. Patterson, op. cit.
10. Acha, M., 2019. 'Climate justice must be anti-patriarchal, or it will not be systemic.' In: Bhavnani, op. cit.
11. 'Inequitable Exposure to Air Pollution from Vehicles in the Northeast and Mid-Atlantic', 21.6.19. Union of Concerned Scientists. https://www.ucsusa.org/sites/default/files/attach/2019/06/Inequitable-Exposure-to-Vehicle-Pollution-Northeast-Mid-Atlantic-Region.pdf. Accessed 2.2.21; Washington, H., 19.5.20. 'How environmental racism is fuelling the coro-

navirus pandemic.' *Nature*. https://www.nature.com/articles/d41586-020-01453-y. Accessed 2.2.21.

12. 'Does exposure to air pollution increase the risk of dying from the coronavirus (COVID-19)?', 13.8.20. Office for National Statistics. https://www.ons.gov.uk/economy/environmentalaccounts/articles/doesexposuretoairpollutionincreasetheriskofdyingfromthecoronaviruscovid19/2020-08-13. Accessed 2.2.21.

13. Modarressy-Tehrani, C., 1.8.20. 'Women of color hardest hit by pandemic joblessness.' NBC News. https://www.nbcnews.com/news/us-news/women-color-hardest-hit-pandemic-joblessness-n1235585. Accessed 2.2.21.

14. Elwell-Sutton, T., 20.5.20. 'Emerging Findings on the impact of COVID-19 on black and minority ethnic people.' *The Health Foundation*. https://www.health.org.uk/news-and-comment/charts-and-infographics/emerging-findings-on-the-impact-of-covid-19-on-black-and-min. Accessed 2.2.21.

15. 'Gina McCarthy Talks About the Intersectionality of Climate Change', 30.1.21. The White House. https://www.youtube.com/watch?v=z9RfN375QDI. Accessed 3.2.21.

16. Raworth, K., 20.10.14. 'Must the Anthropocene be a Manthropocene?' *The Guardian*. https://www.theguardian.com/commentisfree/2014/oct/20/anthropocene-working-group-science-gender-bias. Accessed 4.1.21.

1. ON THE FRONTLINE: HOW THE CLIMATE CRISIS IS HARMING WOMEN

1. 'Breaking the cycle of Turkana's drought crisis', 8.5.17. Oxfam. https://reliefweb.int/report/kenya/breaking-cycle-turkanas-drought-crisis. Accessed 21.8.20.

2. 'Water and women's rights in Ethiopia—Fatuma's story', 6.6.16. CARE International. https://www.careinternational.org.uk/stories/water-and-womens-rights-ethiopia-fatumas-story. Accessed 21.8.20.

3. 'How Long Does It Take to Get Water? For Aysha, Eight Hours a Day', 1.3.08. Unicef USA. https://www.unicefusa.org/stories/how-long-does-it-take-get-water-aysha-eight-hours-day/30776. Accessed 21.8.20.

4. Ibid.

5. La Frenierre, J., 1.6.09. *The Burden of Fetching Water: Using Caloric Expenditure as an Indicator of Access to Safe Drinking Water—a Case Study*

*from Xieng Khouang Province, LAO PDR*. Graduate thesis, University of Denver. https://digitalcommons.du.edu/cgi/viewcontent.cgi?article=1351&context=etd. Accessed 9.2.21.

6. 'Women and drought in Southern Mozambique: more responsibilities, less power and increased vulnerabilities', 2016. UNFPA ESARO. https://www.open.ac.uk/technology/mozambique/sites/www.open.ac.uk.technology.mozambique/files/files/Women_and_drought_in_southern_Mozambique-2016.pdf. Accessed 25.8.20.

7. Geere, J. et al., 2018. 'Carrying water may be a major contributor to disability from musculoskeletal disorders in low income countries: a cross-sectional survey in South Africa, Ghana and Vietnam.' *Journal of Global Health* 8(1).

8. 'Gender and sustainable energy', 2016. Policy Brief 4, UNDP. https://www.who.int/news-room/fact-sheets/detail/household-air-pollution-and-health. Accessed 2.9.20.

9. 'Burden of Disease from Household Air Pollution for 2012', 2014. WHO. https://www.who.int/airpollution/data/HAP_BoD_results_March2014.pdf?ua=1. Accessed 1.9.20.

10. Fullerton, Duncan G. et al., 2008. 'Indoor air pollution from biomass fuel smoke is a major health concern in the developing world.' *Transactions of the Royal Society of Tropical Medicine and Hygiene*, 102(9). https://www.ncbi.nlm.nih.gov/pmc/articles/PMC2568866/. Accessed 25.8.20.

11. Health Effects Institute, 2020. 'State of Global Air: Impacts on Newborns'. https://www.stateofglobalair.org/health/newborns. Accessed 5.2.21.

12. 'State of Global Air', 2020. Health Effects Institute. https://www.stateofglobalair.org/. Accessed 21.10.20.

13. 'Gender and Livelihoods Impacts of Clean Cookstoves South Asia Study', 2014. Global Alliance for Clean Cookstoves. https://www.cleancookingalliance.org/binary-data/RESOURCE/file/000/000/363-1.pdf. Accessed 2.9.20.

14. 'Women and Climate Change', 2015. Georgetown Institute for Women, Peace and Security. https://giwps.georgetown.edu/wp-content/uploads/2017/09/Women-and-Climate-Change.pdf. Accessed 4.12.20.

15. 'Gender and disaster risk reduction', 2013. UNDP, Policy Brief 3. https://www.undp.org/content/dam/undp/library/gender/Gender%20and%20Environment/PB3-AP-Gender-and-disaster-risk-reduction.pdf. Accessed 2.9.20.

16. 'The tsunami's impact on women', March 2005. Oxfam International

Briefing Note. https://oxfamilibrary.openrepository.com/bitstream/handle/10546/115038/bn-tsunami-impact-on-women-250305-en.pdf?sequence=1&isAllowed=y. Accessed 27.8.20.

17. 'Climate Displacement in Bangladesh', n.d. Environmental Justice Foundation. https://ejfoundation.org/reports/climate-displacement-in-bangladesh. Accessed 27.8.20.

18. Nagel, J., 2016. *Gender and Climate Change*. New York: Routledge.

19. 'The Impact of Livelihood Recovery Initiatives in Reducing Vulnerability to Human Trafficking and Illegal Recruitment: Lessons from Typhoon Haiyan', 2015. International Labour Organization and International Organization for Migration. https://publications.iom.int/system/files/impacts_of_livelihood.pdf. Accessed 3.11.20.

20. Gerrard, M., 2018. 'Climate Change and Human Trafficking After the Paris Agreement.' *University of Miami Law Review*, 72(2).

21. 'Brides of the Sun: An Investigation into How Climate Change is Creating a Generation of Child Brides'. https://bridesofthesun.com/brides-of-the-sun1. Accessed 27.8.20; 'The Global Girlhood Report, 2020', 2020. Save the Children. https://resourcecentre.savethechildren.net/node/18201/pdf/global_girlhood_report_2020_africa_version_2.pdf. Accessed 21.10.20.

22. Haynes, A., 2017. 'Everyday life in rural Bangladesh', pp. 141–56. In: S. Buckingham and V. Le Masson (eds), *Understanding Climate Change Through Gender Relations*. Abingdon, Oxon: Routledge.

23. 'Marry Before Your House is Swept Away: Child Marriage in Bangladesh', 2015. Human Rights Watch. https://www.hrw.org/report/2015/06/09/marry-your-house-swept-away/child-marriage-bangladesh. Accessed 03.10.20.

24. 'Climate Change and Land', 2019. IPCC. https://www.ipcc.ch/srccl/chapter/summary-for-policymakers/. Accessed 28.8.20.

25. Negi, B. et al., 2010. 'Climate Change and Women's Voices From India', pp. 72–78. In: I. Dankelman (ed.), *Gender and Climate Change: An Introduction*. London: Earthscan.

26. Brody, A. et al., March 2008. 'Gender and climate change: mapping the linkages'. BRIDGE, Institute of Development Studies, Sussex for DFID. http://www.bridge.ids.ac.uk/sites/bridge.ids.ac.uk/files/reports/Climate_Change_DFID.pdf. Accessed 27.8.20.

27. Wainaina, B., 2.5.19. 'How to Write About Africa.' *Granta*. https://granta.com/how-to-write-about-africa/; Accessed 26.8.20.

28. Dogra, N., 2014. *Representations of Global Poverty*. London: I.B. Tauris.
29. Ibid., p. 40.
30. Röhr, 4.7.11. 'Beyond Women and Girls' Vulnerability: a debate on gender, climate change and disaster risk reduction'. Institute of Disaster Studies, Brighton.
31. Andrea Cornwall, quoted in 'Current challenges for women's rights and development', 30.11.11. Womankind.org. https://www.womankind.org.uk/blog/detail/our-blog/2011/11/30/current-challenges-for-women-s-rights-and-development. Accessed 27.8.20.
32. Dogra, op. cit., p. 3.
33. 'The Role of Women in Agriculture', March 2011. ESA Working Paper No. 11–02. FAO, UN. https://www.empowerwomen.org/en/resources/documents/2013/9/the-role-of-women-in-agriculture-esa-working-paper-no-1102?lang=en. Accessed 9.2.21.
34. Maslog, C., 8.1.15. 'Asia-Pacific Analysis: Asia's Invisible Women Farmers'. *SciDevNet*. https://www.scidev.net/asia-pacific/gender/columns/asia-pacific-analysis-asia-s-invisible-women-farmers.html. Accessed 28.8.20.
35. Okanle, O. et al., 2017. 'Gender Paradoxes and Agricultural Monopoly in Nigeria: Implications for Policy and Food (In)Security in Africa'. *Gender and Behaviour*, 15(3).
36. Béné, C. and Merten, S., 2008. 'Women and Fish-for-Sex: Transactional Sex, HIV/AIDS and Gender in African Fisheries'. *World Development*, 36(5).
37. Jones, G.W., 2005. 'The "Flight from Marriage" in South-East and East Asia'. *Journal of Comparative Family Studies*, 36(1).
38. Dwyer, E. and Woolf, L., 2018. *Down by the River*. Oxfam Research Reports. https://www.gdnonline.org/resources/Down-By-The-River_Web.pdf. Accessed 03.10.20.
39. van Oldenborgh, G. et al., 2020. 'Attribution of Australian bushfire risk to anthropogenic climate change'. *Natural Hazards and Earth Sciences*, 69.
40. Abdo, M. et al., 2019. 'Impact of Wildfire Smoke on Adverse Pregnancy Outcomes in Colorado, 2007–2015'. *International Journal of Environmental Research and Public Health*, 16(19).
41. Robertson, S., and Hull, L., 2020. 'Commentary: Pregnant women at risk in Australian bushfires'. https://www.channelnewsasia.com/news/commentary/pregnant-women-australia-fire-smoke-haze-air-pollution-health-12250794. Accessed 12.10.20.
42. 'The tsunami's impact on women', op. cit.

43. Seager, J. 2014. 'Disasters are gendered: what's new', pp. 265–282. In: Z. Zommers and A. Singh (eds), *Reducing Disaster: Early Warning Systems for Climate Change*. New York: Springer.

44. 'Bangladesh Media and Telecoms Landscape Guide', May 2012. *infoasaid*. http://www.cdacnetwork.org/contentAsset/raw-data/38d6a8d4-c96c-4583-bf8b-a402e7413ca7/attachedFile. Accessed 14.1.21.

45. 'Fact Sheet: Climate Change and Women', Winter 2008/9. Oxfam America. https://s3.amazonaws.com/oxfam-us/www/static/oa3/files/climatechangewomen-factsheet.pdf. Accessed 28.8.20.

46. Whittaker et al., 2015. 'Gendered responses to the 2009 Black Saturday bushfires in Victoria, Australia'. *Geographical Research*, 54(2), pp. 203–215.

## 2. CRISIS MULTIPLIER: HOW GLOBAL HEATING HURTS WOMEN INDIRECTLY

1. Black, G., 30.7.13. 'Your Clothes Were Made by a Bangladeshi Climate Refugee'. *Mother Jones*. https://www.motherjones.com/environment/2013/07/bangladesh-garment-workers-climate-change/. Accessed 3.9.20.

2. 'Global Report on Internal Displacement', 2020. Norwegian Refugee Council. https://www.internal-displacement.org/sites/default/files/publications/documents/2020-IDMC-GRID-executive-summary.pdf. Accessed 28.8.20.

3. 'Evicted by Climate Change: Confronting the Gendered Impacts of Climate-Induced Displacement', 6.7.20. CARE. https://careclimatechange.org/evicted-by-climate-change/. Accessed 21.10.20.

4. Brown, O., 2008. 'Migration and Climate Change'. International Organization for Migration.

5. 'Promoting Gender-Responsive Approaches to Natural Resource Management for Peace in North Kordofan, Sudan', 2019. UNDP. https://postconflict.unep.ch/publications/Sudan_Gender_NRM2019.pdf. Accessed 3.9.20.

6. 'Women and Girls in Internal Displacement', March 2020. IDMC. https://www.internal-displacement.org/publications/women-and-girls-in-internal-displacement. Accessed 28.8.20.

7. Ibid.

8. Thuringer, C., 22.8.16. 'Left Out and Behind: Fully Incorporating Gender into the Climate Discourse'. *New Security Beat*. https://www.newsecuritybeat.org/2016/08/left-behind-fully-incorporating-gender-climate-

discourse/. Accessed 13.10.20; 'In Conversation: Climate Justice and Queer and Trans Liberation', n.d. Podcast. https://www.ourclimatevoices. org/listening-series/queer-trans-liberation. Accessed 13.10.20.

9. Castañeda Camey, I. et al., 2020. 'Gender-based violence and environment linkages: the violence of inequality'. IUCN. https://portals.iucn.org/ library/sites/library/files/documents/2020-002-En.pdf. Accessed 03.10.20.

10. Ibid.

11. Ibid.

12. Ibid.

13. 'Climate Change, Disasters and Gender-Based Violence in the Pacific'. 2013. UN Women. https://www.preventionweb.net/files/52741_52741 sidsbrief2climatechangedisaste.pdf. Accessed 4.9.20.

14. 'How climate change impacts have challenged men's masculinity.' Tracy Kajumba blog, https://kajumbatracy.blogspot.com/2018/11/how-climate-change-impacts-have.html. Accessed 23.1.21.

15. Luft, R., 2008. 'Looking for Common Ground: Relief Work in Post-Katrina New Orleans as an American Parable of Race and Gender Violence'. *Feminist Formations*, 20(3); Austin, D., 2016. 'Hyper-masculinity and disaster'. In: E. Enarson and B. Pease (eds), *Men, Masculinities and Disaster*. Abingdon, Oxon: Routledge.

16. Thomas, E., 2017. 'Domestic Violence and Sexual Assault in the Pacific Islander Community'. Asian/Pacific Islander Domestic Violence Research Project. https://dvrp.org/wp-content/uploads/2017/05/GBV-in-the-PI-Community.pdf. Accessed 4.9.20; Sotero, M., 2006. 'A Conceptual Model of Historical Trauma: Implications for Public Health Practice and Research'. *Journal of Health Disparities Research and Practice*, 1(1); Kalei Kanuha, V., 2002. 'Colonization and Violence against Women'. *Asia Pacific Institute on Gender-Based Violence*. https://www.api-gbv.org/ resources/colonization-violence-against-women/. Accessed 13.10.20; Sotero, M. 'A Conceptual Model of Historical Trauma: Implications for Public Health Practice and Research'. *Journal of Health Disparities Research and Practice*, 1(1).

17. Le Masson, V. et al., 2016. 'Disasters and violence against women and girls'. *Overseas Development Institute*. https://www.odi.org/sites/odi.org.uk/ files/resource-documents/11113.pdf. Accessed 4.9.20.

18. Lakhani, N., 17.9.18. 'Berta Cáceres murder trial delayed after judges accused of abusing authority.' *The Guardian*. www.theguardian.com/

world/2018/sep/17/berta-caceres-trial-postponed-judges-accused. Accessed 13.10.20.

19. Ervin, J., 27.11.18. 'In defence of nature: women at the forefront'. United Nations Development Programme blog. https://www.undp.org/content/ undp/en/home/blog/2018/in-defense-of-nature-women-at-the-forefront. html. Accessed 13.10.20.

20. Houghton, R., 2009. '"Everything Became a Struggle, Absolute Struggle": Post-flood Increases in Domestic Violence in New Zealand', pp. 99–111. In: E. Enarson and P. Dhar Chakrabarti, eds. *Women, Gender and Disaster*. Sage: New Delhi.

21. Schumacher, J. et al., 2010. 'Intimate partner violence and Hurricane Katrina: predictors and associated mental health outcomes.' *Violence and Victims*, 25(5).

22. Parkinson, D., and Zara, C., 2013. 'The hidden disaster: domestic violence in the aftermath of natural disaster'. *Australian Journal of Emergency Management*, 8(2).

23. 'Canada: Out of Sight, Out of Mind: Gender, Indigenous Rights and Energy Development in Northeast British Columbia', 2016. Amnesty International. https://www.amnesty.org/en/documents/amr20/4872/ 2016/en/. Accessed 6.10.20.

24. Brown, O. and Vivekananda, J., 22.10.19. 'Lake Chad shrinking? It's a story that masks serious failures of governance'. *The Guardian*. https:// www.theguardian.com/global-development/2019/oct/22/lake-chad-shrinking-story-masks-serious-failures-of-governance. Accessed 10.10.20.

25. 'Lake Chad's Unseen Crisis'. 2016. Oxfam. https://www-cdn.oxfam.org/ s3fs-public/file_attachments/bn-lake-chad-refugees-idps-190816-en.pdf. Accessed 10.10.20.

26. Gouby, M., 25.9.20. 'Chad tries to keep lake off heritage list to search for oil'. *The Guardian*. https://www.theguardian.com/world/2020/sep/24/ chad-halts-lake-world-heritage-status-request-over-oil-exploration-unesco. Accessed 9.2.21.

27. Frank, C. and Guesnet, L., 2009. '"We were promised development and all we got is misery"—The Influence of Petroleum on Conflict Dynamics in Chad'. Brief 41, Bonn International Center for Conversion. https:// www.bicc.de/uploads/tx_bicctools/brief41.pdf. Accessed 20.10.20.

28. Author interview, Adenike Oladosu, via Zoom, 13.08.20.

29. Ribot, J. 2017. 'Vulnerability does not Fall from the Sky: Addressing a Risk Conundrum'. In: R. Kasperson et al. (eds), *Risk Conundrums: Solving Unsolvable Problems*. London: Earthscan.

30. Rothe, D., 2017. 'Gendering Resilience: Myths and Stereotypes in the Discourse of Climate-Induced Migration.' *Global Policy*, 8(1).

31. Cornwall, A. and Rivas, A-M., 2015. 'From "Gender Equality and Women's Empowerment" to Global Justice: Reclaiming a Transformative Agenda for Gender and Development.' *Third World Quarterly*, 36(2).

32. See MacGregor, S., 2010. 'Gender and climate change: from Impacts to discourses'. *Journal of the Indian Ocean Region*, 6(2); Arora-Jonsson, S., 2011. 'Virtue and vulnerability: Discourses on women, gender and climate change'. *Global Environmental Change*, 21(2); Resurrección, B., 2013. 'Persistent women and environment linkages in climate change and sustainable development agendas'. *Women's Studies International Forum*, 40; MacGregor, S., 2017b. 'Moving beyond impacts'. In: Buckingham, S. and Le Masson, V., eds. *Understanding Climate Change through Gender Relations*. Abingdon, Oxon: Routledge.

33. Emphasis in original.

34. Mollett, S., 2017. 'Gender's critical edge', p. 148. In: S. MacGregor, ed., 2017a, *Routledge Handbook of Gender and Environment*. Abingdon, Oxon: Routledge.

35. Nagel, J., 2016. *Gender and Climate Change*. New York: Routledge.

36. Keller, R., 2015. *Fatal Isolation: The Devastating Paris Heatwave of 2003*. Chicago, IL: University of Chicago Press.

37. Röhr 2011, op. cit. Emphasis in original.

38. Weller, I., 2017. 'Gender dimensions of sustainable consumption.' In: S. MacGregor 2017a, op. cit.

39. Ngozi Adichie, C., 2009. 'The danger of a single story'. *TEDGlobal*. https://www.ted.com/talks/chimamanda_ngozi_adichie_the_danger_of_a_single_story. Accessed 13.10.20.

40. Mies, M. and Shiva, V., 2014 (18th ed.). *Ecofeminism*. London: Zed Books.

41. Draper, R., Feb. 2019. 'This metal is powering today's technology—at what price?' *National Geographic*. https://www.nationalgeographic.com/magazine/2019/02/lithium-is-fueling-technology-today-at-what-cost/?awc=19533_1602247266_f29117d3ed372524e995d91e60a170be. Accessed 11.10.20.

42. Aronoff, K. et al., 2019. *A Planet to Win*. London: Verso.

43. Balch, O., 8.12.20. 'The curse of "white oil": electric vehicles' dirty secret.' *The Guardian*. https://www.theguardian.com/news/2020/dec/08/the-curse-of-white-oil-electric-vehicles-dirty-secret-lithium. Accessed 16.1.21.

44. Friends of the Earth Europe, Feb. 2013. 'Lithium.' http://www.foeeurope.

org/sites/default/files/publications/13_factsheet-lithium-gb.pdf. Accessed 5.2.21.

45. Forti, V. et al., 2020. 'The Global E-waste Monitor'. United Nationals University. http://ewastemonitor.info/wp-content/uploads/2020/07/GEM_2020_def_july1_low.pdf#. Accessed 20.10.20.

46. 'Holes in the Circular Economy', 2019. Basel Action Network. http://wiki.ban.org/images/f/f4/Holes_in_the_Circular_Economy-_WEEE_Leakage_from_Europe.pdf. Accessed 20.10.20.

47. McAllister, L. et al., 2014. 'Women, E-Waste, and Technological Solutions to Climate Change'. *Health and Human Rights Journal*, 16(1); Heacock, H. et al., May 2016. 'E-waste and Harm to Vulnerable Populations: A Growing Global Problem'. *Environmental Health Perspectives*, 124(5).

48. McAllister, L., 8.10.20. 'Women, E-Waste and Technological Solutions'. Paper presented at 'Confronting the Climate Crisis: Feminist Pathways to Just and Sustainable Futures', The Consortium on Gender, Security and Human Rights.

49. Jian, M., 2014. *The Dark Road*. London: Vintage.

50. Oladosu, op. cit.

51. Author interview, Jacqui Patterson, by Zoom, 5.8.20.

52. Carmichael, S. and Hamilton, C., 1992. *Black Power: The Politics of Liberation in America*, p. 5. New York: Vintage.

53. Moore-Nall, A., 2015. 'The Legacy of Uranium Development on or near Indian Reservations and Health Implications Rekindling Public Awareness'. *Geosciences*, 5(1).

54. Lewis, J. et al., 2017. 'Mining and Environmental Health Disparities in Native American Communities'. *Current Environmental Health Reports*, 4(2).

55. 'Coal-Blooded: Putting Profits Before People'. 2016. National Association for the Advancement of Coloured People. https://www.naacp.org/wp-content/uploads/2016/04/CoalBlooded.pdf. Accessed 10.10.20.

56. Milman, O., 20.12.18. 'Robert Bullard: Environmental justice isn't just slang, it's real.' *The Guardian*. https://www.theguardian.com/comment-isfree/2018/dec/20/robert-bullard-interview-environmental-justice-civil-rights-movement. Accessed 16.1.21.

57. Patterson, J., 27.2.16. 'Geopolitics of Climate Change—a Civil Rights Perspective'. Speech given at the University of California, Santa Cruz. https://www.naacp.org/latest/geopolitics-of-climate-changea-civil-rights-perspective/. Accessed 10/10/20.

58. 'Exposure to Toxic Environmental Agents, 2013', 2013. The American College of Obstetricians and Gynaecologists. Committee Opinion no. 575. https://www.acog.org/-/media/project/acog/acogorg/clinical/files/committee-opinion/articles/2013/10/exposure-to-toxic-environmental-agents.pdf?_ga=2.4016944.1046525431.1602337418-959776673.1602337418. Accessed 10.10.20.

59. Ibid.

## 3. MAN-MADE: THE ORIGINS OF THE CLIMATE CRISIS

1. 'David Attenborough: A Life on Our Planet', 2020. *Netflix*.
2. Ritchie, H., 2018. 'Global Inequalities in CO2 emissions'. *Our World in Data*. https://ourworldindata.org/co2-by-income-region. Accessed 10.11.20.
3. Ibid.
4. 'Average Brit will emit more by January 12 than residents of seven African countries do in a year', 2020. Oxfam. https://oxfamapps.org/media/press_release/average-brit-will-emit-more-by-12-january-than-residents-of-seven-african-countries-do-in-a-year/. Accessed 10.11.20.
5. Kommenda, N., 19.7.2019. 'How your flight emits as much CO2 as many people do in a year.' *The Guardian*. https://www.theguardian.com/environment/ng-interactive/2019/jul/19/carbon-calculator-how-taking-one-flight-emits-as-much-as-many-people-do-in-a-year. Accessed 3.11.20.
6. 'An Open Letter to Extinction Rebellion'. 3.5.19. *Red Pepper*. https://www.redpepper.org.uk/an-open-letter-to-extinction-rebellion/. Accessed 10.11.20.
7. 'Each Country's Share of CO2 Emissions', 12.8.20. Union of Concerned Scientists. https://www.ucsusa.org/resources/each-countrys-share-co2-emissions. Accessed 10.11.20.
8. 'Is the World Outsourcing Its Greenhouse Emissions to China?', 5.11.09. *Scientific American*. https://www.scientificamerican.com/article/earth-talks-outsourcing-greenhouse-china/. Accessed 10.11.20.
9. 'Latest data shows two million Londoners living with illegal toxic air', 1.4.19. Mayor of London. https://www.london.gov.uk/press-releases/mayoral/two-million-londoners-live-with-illegal-toxic-air. Accessed 16.1.21.
10. Vaughan, A. and Addley, E., 17.5.16. 'Boris Johnson "held back" negative findings of air pollution report.' *The Guardian*. https://www.theguardian.com/environment/2016/may/17/boris-johnson-held-back-negative-findings-of-air-pollution-report. Accessed 16.1.21.

11. 'UK Government loses third air pollution case as judge rules air pollution plans "unlawful"', 21.2.18. https://www.clientearth.org/latest/latest-updates/news/uk-government-loses-third-air-pollution-case-as-judge-rules-air-pollution-plans-unlawful/. Accessed 16.1.21.

12. 'The Carbon Majors Database', 2017. CDP. https://b8f65cb373b1b 7b15feb-c70d8ead6ced550b4d987d7c03fcdd1d.ssl.cf3.rackcdn.com/cms/reports/documents/000/002/327/original/Carbon-Majors-Report-2017.pdf. Accessed 11.11.20.

13. Heede, R., 2019. 'Carbon Majors'. Climate Accountability Institute. https://climateaccountability.org/carbonmajors.html. Accessed 11.11.20.

14. Robinson, E. and Robbins, R.C., 1968. 'Sources, abundance, and fate of gaseous atmospheric pollutants. Final report and supplement.' Menlo Park, CA: Stanford Research Institute. https://www.smokeandfumes.org/documents/document16. Accessed 16.1.21.

15. 'The Climate Deception Dossiers', 29.6.15. Union of Concerned Scientists. https://www.ucsusa.org/resources/climate-deception-dossiers#:~:text=The%20documents%20clearly%20show%20that,campaign%20of%20deception%20continues%20today. Accessed 16.1.21.

16. 'Women in Energy—Gas, Mining and Oil: Quick Take', 29.3.19. *Catalyst* website. https://www.catalyst.org/research/women-in-energy-gas-mining-oil/. Accessed 11.11.20.

17. 'Women CEOs of the S&P 500', 2.12.20. *Catalyst* website. https://www.catalyst.org/research/women-ceos-of-the-sp-500/. Accessed 9.2.21.

18. Pettifor, A., 2019. *The Case for the Green New Deal*. London: Verso.

19. 'Asset Management and Climate Change', 2019. *InfluenceMap*. https://influencemap.org/report/FinanceMap-Launch-Report-f80b653f6a631c ec947a07e44ae4a4a7. Accessed 16.11.20.

20. 'Is Your Money Destroying Rainforests or Violating Rights?', 2020. forestsandfinances.org. https://www.ran.org/wp-content/uploads/2020/09/FF_Briefing_2020-EN.pdf. Accessed 16.11.20. Banks aren't the only financial culprits: the British government also, oh-so-quietly, helps finance, to the tune of billions of pounds, fossil fuel projects overseas that emit greenhouse gases equivalent to seventeen coal plants, according to a BBC/Greenpeace joint investigation. Barratt, L., 23.1.20. 'Revealed: UK government financing millions of tonnes of emissions overseas.' *Unearthed*. https://unearthed.greenpeace.org/2020/01/23/uk-boris-johnson-financing-coal-fossil-fuels-carbon-emissions/. Accessed 24.11.20.

21. Cheek, S., 4.3.20. 'Number of female managers stagnates as funds universe

balloons'. *Portfolio Adviser*. https://portfolio-adviser.com/number-of-female-managers-stagnates-as-funds-universe-balloons/. Accessed 16.11.20.

22. 'Women in Financial Services: Quick Take', 29.6.20. *Catalyst* website. https://www.catalyst.org/research/women-in-financial-services/. Accessed 16.11.20.

23. 'Carbon emissions of richest 1 percent more than double the emissions of the poorest half of humanity', 21.9.20. Oxfam International. https://www.oxfam.org/en/press-releases/carbon-emissions-richest-1-percent-more-double-emissions-poorest-half-humanity. Accessed 9.2.21.

24. Byanyima, W., 18.12.15. 'What to do about climate change? Ask women—they have the most to lose.' *The New Humanitarian*. https://www.thenewhumanitarian.org/opinion/2018/12/18/what-do-about-climate-change-ask-women-they-have-most-lose. Accessed 16.1.21.

25. 'Carbon emissions of richest 1 percent', op. cit.; 'The Carbon Inequality Era', 2020. Oxfam. https://oxfam.app.box.com/s/q36ywh37ppur8gl276z-we8goqr6utkej/file/720283965204. Accessed 4.11.20.

26. Gössling, S., and Humpe, A., 2020. 'The global scale, distribution and growth of aviation: Implications for climate change.' *Global Environmental Change*, 65.

27. Neate, R., 9.1.21. 'Gates bids for jet firm puts climate book under a cloud.' *The Guardian*.

28. Kenner, D., 2019. *Carbon Inequality: The Role of the Richest in Climate Change*. Abingdon, Oxon: Routledge.

29. 'Koch Industries: Secretly Funding the Climate Denial Machine', n.d. Greenpeace. https://www.greenpeace.org/usa/global-warming/climate-deniers/koch-industries/. Accessed 16.1.21.

30. Patterson, J., 2010. 'Your Take—Climate Change Is a Civil Rights Issue.' *The Root*. https://www.theroot.com/your-take-climate-change-is-a-civil-rights-issue-1790879295. Accessed 18.11.20.

31. Atkin, E., 14.12.20. 'The stealth climate villains of 2020.' *HEATED*. https://heated.world/p/the-stealth-climate-villains-of-2020. Accessed 16.1.21.

32. Duffin, E., 15.9.20. 'Gender distribution of billionaires around the world.' *Statista*. https://www.statista.com/statistics/778577/billionaires-gender-distribution/#:~:text=Gender%20distribution%20of%20billionaires%20worldwide%202019&text=This%20statistic%20shows%20the%20gender,world's%202%2C825%20billionaires%20were%20women. Accessed 16.11.20.

33. For a daily update on 'real-time' billionaires, check out the *Forbes* website, which helpfully lists today's 'winners and losers'. When I last looked, Warren Buffet had gained $1 billion over the past 24 hours, while Elon Musk (my heart bleeds) had mislaid $919 million. The thirteen people topping that day's list were all men. https://www.forbes.com/real-time-billionaires/#6f47e8ae3d78. Accessed 4.1.21.

34. 'Time to Care', 19.1.20. Oxfam. https://www.oxfamamerica.org/explore/research-publications/time-care/. Accessed 16.11.20.

35. Chandler, D., 16.4.2008. 'Leaving our mark'. *TechTalk*, 52(23).

36. Bhushan, C., 2018. 'A Commentary on the Consumption of Rich Indians versus Rich (and Poor) Americans.' Centre for Science and Environment. https://www.cseindia.org/a-commentary-on-consumption-rich-indians-versus-rich-and-poor-americans-9019. Accessed 5.2.21.

37. Johnsson-Latham, G., 2007. 'A study on gender equality as a prerequisite for sustainable development.' Environment Advisory Council, Sweden; Johnsson-Latham, G., 2010. 'Why More Attention to Gender and Class Can Help Combat Climate Change and Poverty'. In: Dankelman, I., ed. *Gender and Climate Change: An Introduction*. London: Earthscan.

38. Cohen, M.G., 2014. 'Gendered Emissions: Counting Greenhouse Gas Emissions by Gender and Why it Matters.' In: Lipsig-Mummé, C. and McBride, S., eds, 2015. *Work in a Warming World*. Montreal: McGill-Queen's University Press.

39. Räty, R. and Carlsson-Kanyama, A., 2010. 'Energy consumption by gender in some European countries'. *Energy Policy*, 28.

40. 'The Carbon Inequality Era', op. cit.

41. Röhr, U., 26.5.20. 'Feminist Climate Conference Webinar', Green European Foundation.

42. Cohen, op. cit.

43. Alber, G. et al., 2017. 'Gender and urban climate change policy'. In: Buckingham, S. and Le Masson, V., eds. *Understanding Climate Change Through Gender Relations*. Abingdon, Oxon: Routledge.

44. Kaufman, M., 1.5.20. 'The carbon footprint sham'. *Mashable*. https://mashable.com/feature/carbon-footprint-pr-campaign-sham/?europe=true. Accessed 16.11.20. Shell tried to pull off a similar ploy when, in 2020, it posted a climate poll on Twitter asking, "What are you willing to change to help reduce emissions?" US Congresswoman Alexandria Ocasio-Cortez's reply—"I'm willing to hold you accountable for lying about climate change for 30 years when you secretly knew the entire time that

fossil fuels emissions would destroy our planet"—was liked 350,000 times within a day of being posted. Carrington, D., 3.11.20. 'Shell accused of gaslighting as Ocasio-Cortez sends tweet viral.' *The Guardian*. https:// www.theguardian.com/business/2020/nov/03/shells-climate-poll-on-twitter-backfires-spectacularly. Accessed 24.11.20.

45. Doyle, J., 2011. 'Where has all the oil gone? BP branding and the discursive elimination of climate change risk.' In: Heffernan, N. and Wragg, D., eds. *Culture, Environment and Ecopolitics*. Newcastle upon Tyne: Cambridge Scholars Publishing.

46. See for example Cherry, M. and Sneirson, J., 2011. 'Beyond Profit: Rethinking Corporate Social Responsibility and Greenwashing After the BP Oil Disaster.' *Tulane Law Review*, 85(4); Kusnetz, N., 16.7.20. 'What Does Net Zero Emissions Mean for Big Oil? Not What You'd Think.' *Inside Climate News*. https://insideclimatenews.org/news/15072020/oil-gas-climate-pledges-bp-shell-exxon. Accessed 23.11.20.

47. 'Bad Company: BP, human rights and corporate crimes', June 2017. Cultureunstained.org. https://cultureunstained.files.wordpress.com/2017/06/bad-company-bp-human-rights-and-corporate-crimes-culture-unstained-june-20171.pdf. Accessed 7.12.20.

48. 'Reimagining energy', n.d. BP. https://www.bp.com/en/global/corporate/news-and-insights/reimagining-energy.html. Accessed 16.11.20.

49. 'BPX Energy', n.d. BP. https://www.bp.com/en_us/united-states/home/who-we-are/what-we-do/upstream/bpx-energy.html. Accessed 23.11.20.

50. 'Corporate Carbon Policy Footprint—the 50 Most Influential', Oct. 2019. *InfluenceMap*. https://influencemap.org/report/Corporate-Climate-Policy-Footpint-2019-the-50-Most-Influential-7d09a06d9c4e602a3d2f5c1ae13301b8. Accessed 16.11.20. In 2020, BP announced that it would slash its oil and gas production and invest in renewables, a response both to years of protester pressure and also to the relative high cost of fossil fuel extraction compared with renewable energy. Climate campaigner Bill McKibben tweeted, "Far from perfect, but far from normal."

51. MacGregor, S., 2010. 'Gender and Climate Change: From Impacts to Discourses,' op. cit. The NPR series *Throughline*, in a fascinating podcast called 'The Litter Myth', 5.9.19, traced the 1970s creation of a similar "Keep America Beautiful" campaign, which shifted the blame for litter away from the companies producing single-use packaging, and onto Americans themselves. The campaign shamed ordinary people for thoughtlessly shucking away their rubbish and in the process bringing a tear to the eye of a Native

American man (in reality a Sicilian). https://www.npr.org/2019/09/04/757539617/the-litter-myth. Accessed 16.1.21.

52. Weller, I., 2017. 'Gender Dimensions of Sustainable Consumption'. In: MacGregor, S., ed. *Routledge Handbook of Gender and Environment*. Abingdon, Oxon: Routledge.

53. Hitczenko, M., 2016. 'The influence of gender and income on the household division of financial responsibility.' Working Papers No. 16–20, Federal Bank of Boston.

54. Isaacs, N., 2018., pp. 51, 52, 53. *Every Woman's Guide to Saving the Planet*. Sydney, NSW: Harper Collins.

55. E.g. see Childs, M., 13.2.20. 'Does carbon offsetting work?' Friends of the Earth. https://friendsoftheearth.uk/climate-change/does-carbon-offsetting-work. Accessed 20.11.20.

56. O'Malley, K., 7.6.19. 'How to shop sustainably in 7 simple ways, according to an eco-friendly fashion campaigner'. *The Independent*.

57. Copperman, D., 19.6.19. 'How & Where to Shop Sustainably in London.' *Eco-Age*. https://eco-age.com/magazine/how-where-shop-sustainably-london/. Accessed 9.2.21.

58. Randall, Ro., 30.7.12. 'Feminism and behaviour change: do current demands for environmental behaviour change disadvantage women?' https://rorandall.org/2012/07/30/feminism-and-behaviour-change-do-current-demands-for-environmental-behaviour-change-disadvantage-women/. Accessed 20.11.20.

59. Cohen, 2014, op. cit.

60. Karpf, A., 12.12.03. 'Dairy Monsters.' *The Guardian*.

61. Philpott, T. and Lurie, J., 31.12.15. 'Here's the Real Problem With Almonds.' *The New Republic*. https://newrepublic.com/article/125450/heres-real-problem-almonds#:~:text=They%20certainly%20have%20used%20up,percent%20of%20the%20state's%20annual. Accessed 20.11.20.

62. Khakh, C., 9.12.19. 'An Exploration of Alternative Dairy—The Environmental and Economic Impacts of Oat, Almond and Soy Milks.' *The Cornell Daily Sun*. https://cornellsun.com/2019/12/09/an-exploration-of-alternative-dairy-the-environmental-and-economic-impacts-of-oat-almond-and-soy-milks/#:~:text=Thus%20far%2C%20oat%20milk%20does,compared%20to%20soy%20and%20almond.&text=Furthermore%2C%20oats%20also%20use%2080,soy%20milk%20or%20dairy%20milk. Accessed 20.11.20.

63. Chiorando, M., 4.9.20. 'Oatly Canceled? Plant-Based Brand Responds to Backlash Over Controversial Investor.' *Plant Based News*. https://plant-basednews.org/news/oatly-backlash-controversial-investor/. Accessed 20.11.20.

64. Watts, J. et al., 26.11.20. 'Chicken in British shops and restaurants linked to deforesting in Brazil.' *The Guardian*.

65. 'Measuring Poverty 2020', July 2020. Social Metrics Commission. https://socialmetricscommission.org.uk/wp-content/uploads/2020/06/Measuring-Poverty-2020-Web.pdf. Accessed 9.2.21.

66. Mikaela Loach on *Woman's Hour*, 25.11.20. BBC Radio 4.

67. O'Neill et al., 2010. 'Global demographic trends and future carbon emissions.' *Proceedings of the National Academy of Sciences of the United States*. 107(41).

68. E.g. Stephenson, J., 2010. 'Population dynamics and climate change: what are the links?' *Journal of Public Health*, 32(10).

69. 'Climate Change 2014 Synthesis Report Summary for Policymakers', 2014, p. 5. IPCC. https://www.ipcc.ch/site/assets/uploads/2018/02/AR5_SYR_FINAL_SPM.pdf. Accessed 21.11.20.

70. 'Human Health: Impacts, Adaptation and Co-Benefits', 2014. IPCC. https://www.ipcc.ch/site/assets/uploads/2018/02/WGIIAR5-Chap11_FINAL.pdf. Accessed 21.11.20.

71. 'Chapter 2: Mitigation pathways compatible with $1.5^0$C in the context of sustainable development'. IPCC. https://report.ipcc.ch/sr15/pdf/sr15_chapter2.pdf. Accessed 21.11.20.

72. Hawken, P., 2018. Drawdown. London: Penguin.

73. Evans, H., 17.6.19. 'Want to Save the Planet? Invest in Family Planning'. Population Connection. https://www.populationconnection.org/climate-change-family-planning/. Accessed 21.11.20.

74. Interview with BBC Breakfast, 28.9.20. https://www.bbc.co.uk/news/av/science-environment-54319449. Accessed 21.11.20.

75. Manavis, S., 3.11.20. 'David Attenborough's claim that humans have overrun the planet is his most popular comment.' *New Statesman*. https://www.newstatesman.com/politics/environment/2020/11/david-attenbor-ough-s-claim-humans-have-overrun-planet-his-most-popular. Accessed 21.11.20.

76. Sasser, J., 2018. *On Infertile Ground*. New York: New York University Press.

77. Schneider-Mayerson, M. and Ling Leong, K., Nov. 2020. 'Eco-reproductive concerns in the age of climate change.' *Climatic Change*, 163.

78. Sasser, op. cit.

79. Gladstone, M., 11.9.19. 'Decades after forced sterilization, Native American women in the US still face rejection and retraumatization in healthcare.' *Lady Science*. https://www.ladyscience.com/features/forced-sterilization-native-american-women-face-rejection-retraumatization-in-healthcare. Accessed 23.11.20.

80. Rao, A., 9.9.19. 'Indigenous Women in Canada Are Still Being Sterilized Without Their Consent.' *Vice*. https://www.vice.com/en/article/9keaev/indigenous-women-in-canada-are-still-being-sterilized-without-their-consent. Accessed 23.11.20.

81. Dickerson, C. et al., 29.9.20. 'Immigrants Say They Were Pressurised Into Unneeded Surgeries.' https://www.nytimes.com/2020/09/29/us/ice-hysterectomies-surgeries-georgia.html. Accessed 23.11.20.

82. Sasser, op. cit.

83. Kwauk, C., and Braga, A., 27.9.17. '3 Ways to link girls' education actors to climate change.' Brookings Institution. https://www.brookings.edu/blog/education-plus-development/2017/09/27/3-ways-to-link-girls-education-actors-to-climate-action/?utm_medium=social&utm_source=facebook&utm_campaign=global. Accessed 23.11.20.

84. Senby, D., 28.9.17. 'Want to Stop Climate Change? Put More Girls in School, New Study Says.' *Global Citizen*. https://www.globalcitizen.org/en/content/girls-education-emergencies-climate-change/. Accessed 23.11.20.

85. Kwauk and Braga, op. cit.

86. Bhatia, R. et al., April 2019. 'A feminist exploration of "populationism": engaging contemporary forms of population control.' *Gender, Place and Culture*, 27(1).

87. Bowles, N., 18.3.19. 'Replacement Theory, a Racist, Sexist Doctrine Spread in Far Right Circles.' *The New York Times*. https://www.nytimes.com/2019/03/18/technology/replacement-theory.html. Accessed 23.11.20.

88. Aton, A., 5.8.19. 'El Paso Shooting.' *E&E News*. https://www.eenews.net/stories/1060857195. Accessed 23.11.20.

89. Hartmann, B., 8.10.20. 'Rebooting the Scarcity Scare: Population, Conflict and Climate Change', paper given at 'Confronting the Climate Crisis: Pathways to Just and Sustainable Futures' webinar. Consortium of Gender, Security and Human Rights. https://genderandsecurity.org/events-news/confronting-climate-crisis-feminist-pathways-just-and-sustainable-futures.

90. Monbiot, G., 25.2.2009. 'Cutting consumption is more important than

limiting population.' *The Guardian*. https://www.theguardian.com/environment/georgemonbiot/2009/feb/25/population-emissions-monbiot. Accessed 23.11.20.

91. Episode 2, 'The White Man Stole the Weather', *Mothers of Invention* podcast. https://www.mothersofinvention.online/thewhitemanstoletheweather. Accessed 23.11.20.

## 4. CULTURAL CREEDS: ECO-FEMINISM AND PETRO-MASCULINITY

1. Resolution adopted by the UN General Assembly, 22.4.09. http://undocs.org/A/RES/63/278. Accessed 27.11.20. The 2015 Paris Agreement was more qualified in its use of the term, noting that biodiversity was "recognised by some cultures as Mother Earth": *Paris Agreement*, 2015. UNFCCC. https://unfccc.int/sites/default/files/english_paris_agreement.pdf. Accessed 19.12.20.

2. Ortner, S., 1974. 'Is female to male as nature is to culture?'. In: Rosaldo, M., and Lamphere, L., eds. *Woman, Culture, and Society*. Stanford, CA: Stanford University Press.

3. Merchant, C., 'Preface: 1990', p.xvi. In: *The Death of Nature*. London: HarperCollins.

4. Ibid., p. 3.

5. Bacon, F., quoted in ibid., p. 171.

6. Ibid.

7. Johnson, A., and Wilkinson, K., 2020, p.xviii. *All We Can Save*. New York: One World.

8. E.g. Bolen J., 2005. *Urgent Message from Mother*. Boston, MA: Conari Press.

9. Plumwood, V., 2003, p. 9. *Feminism and the Mastery of Nature*. Abingdon, Oxon: Routledge.

10. McSmith, A., 12.4.12. 'The woman who brought up Margaret Thatcher.' *The Independent*. https://www.independent.co.uk/news/uk/politics/woman-who-brought-margaret-thatcher-8570609.html. Accessed 28.11.20.

11. Plumwood, op. cit., p. 20.

12. Mies, M., and Shiva, V., 2014, p. 19. *Ecofeminism*. London: Zed Books.

13. Gaard, G., 1993, p. 301. *Ecofeminism: women, animals, nature*. Philadelphia, PA: Temple University Press.

14. Finney, C., 2014. *Black Faces, White Spaces*. Chapel Hill, NC: University of North Carolina Press.

15. Lanham, J.D., 2017. *The Home Place: Memoirs of a Colored Man's Love Affair with Nature*. Minneapolis, MI: Milkweed Editions.

16. James, S., 1985, quoted in Salleh, A., 2017. *Ecofeminism as Politics*. London: Zed Books..

17. Mathews, F., 2017. 'The dilemma of dualism.' In: MacGregor, 2017, op. cit.

18. Salleh, op. cit., p. 137.

19. Plumwood, op. cit., p. 39.

20. MacGregor, S. and Seymour, N., 2017. 'Introduction.' In: MacGregor, S. and Seymour, N., eds. *Men and Nature: Hegemonic Masculinities and Environmental Change*. RCC Perspectives.

21. Kronsell, A., 2017. 'The contribution of feminist perspectives to climate governance.' In: Buckingham, S. and Le Masson, V. *Understanding Climate Change Through Gender Relations*. Abingdon, Oxon: Routledge.

22. Connell, R., 2017. 'Foreword: Masculinities in the Sociocene.' In: MacGregor, S. and Seymour, N., op. cit.

23. Daggett, C., 2018. 'Petro-masculinity: Fossil Fuels and Authoritarian Desire.' *Millennium*, 47(1).

24. Brum, E., 6.7.19. 'The Amazon is a Woman.' *Atmos*. https://atmos.earth/amazon-rainforest-indigenous-activism-history/. Accessed 30.11.20.

25. Rearick, Z., 15.10.20. 'Masculinity is the unspoken undercurrent in Trumpism and the fracking debate.' *The Philadelphia Inquirer*. https://www.inquirer.com/opinion/commentary/fracking-pennsylvania-trump-gender-roles-masculinity-20201015.html. Accessed 5.12.20.

26. Ibid.

27. Daggett, op. cit.

28. Alaimo, S., 27.10.16. 'Climate change, carbon-heavy masculinity, and the politics of exposure.' University of Minnesota Press blog. https://uminnpressblog.com/2016/10/27/climate-change-carbon-heavy-masculinity-and-the-politics-of-exposure/. Accessed 1.12.20.

29. Adams, C., 2015, p. 186. *The Sexual Politics of Meat*. London: Bloomsbury Academic.

30. Rozin, P. et al., 2012. 'Is Meat Male? A Quantitative Multimethod Framework to Establish Metaphoric Relationships.' *Journal of Consumer Research*, 39(3).

31. '7 Reasons why meat is bad for the planet'. Greenpeace. https://www.greenpeace.org.uk/news/why-meat-is-bad-for-the-environment/. Accessed 1.12.20.

32. Twist, M-A., n.d. 'You are what you eat: Why do male consumers avoid

vegetarian options?' The University of Chicago Press. https://press.uchi-cago.edu/pressReleases/2012/May/JCR_1205_MeatMen.html?next&placeutm_source=bottom_floater. Accessed 1.12.20.

33. Brough, A. et al., 2016. 'Is Eco-Friendly Unmanly? The Green Feminine Stereotype and Its Effect on Sustainable Consumption.' *Journal of Consumer Research*. 43.

34. Brough, A. and Wilkie, J., 26.12.2017. 'Men Resist Green Behaviour as Unmanly.' *Scientific American*. https://www.scientificamerican.com/arti-cle/men-resist-green-behavior-as-unmanly/. Accessed 1.12.20.

35. McCright, A., and Dunlap, R., 2011. 'Cool dudes: the denial of climate change among conservative white males in the United States.' *Global Environmental Change*, 21(4). A Norwegian study came up with similar findings: Krange et al., 2019. 'Cool dudes in Norway: climate change denial among conservative men.' *Environmental Sociology*, 5(1).

36. Anshelm, J. and Hultman, M., 2014. 'A green fatwā? Climate change as a threat to the masculinity of industrial modernity.' *NORMA: International Journal for Masculinity Studies*, 9(2).

37. Nagel, J., 2016. *Gender and Climate Change*. New York: Routledge. See also Oreskes, N. and Conway, E., 2011. *Merchants of Doubt*. London: Bloomsbury; 'Koch: Industries: Secretly Funding the Climate Denial Machine.' Greenpeace USA. https://www.greenpeace.org/usa/global-warming/climate-deniers/koch-industries/. Accessed 4.12.20; Leonard, C., 2019. *Kochland*. New York: Simon and Schuster.

38. Karpf, A., 4.12.17. 'How best to silence the powerless? Play the victim.' *The Guardian*.

39. Seager, J., 7.10.20. 'Petro-Bromance: Masculinity Driving the Climate Crisis.' Presentation at 'Confronting the Climate Crisis: Feminist Pathways to Just and Sustainable Futures'. The Consortium on Gender, Security and Human Rights.

40. Karpf, A., 31.1.12. 'Green jobs: a utopia we nearly had.' *The Guardian*; Wainwright, H. and Elliott, D., 2018. *The Lucas Plan*. Nottingham: Spokesman.

41. Wansink, 2006, cited in Rozin, op. cit.

42. Connell, R.W., 1995. *Masculinities*. Cambridge: Polity Press.

43. Hultman, M. and Pulé, P., 2018. *Ecological Masculinities*. Abingdon, Oxon: Routledge.

44. Haraway, D., 2003. *The Companion Species Manifesto: Dogs, People and Significant Otherness*. Chicago, IL: Prickly Paradigm Press.

45. Alaimo, S., 2000. *Undomesticated Ground: Recasting Nature as Feminist Space*. Ithaca, NY: Cornell University Press.

46. Pease, B., 2016, p. 30, 'Masculinism, climate change and "man-made" disasters.' In: E. Enarson and B. Pease, eds., *Men, Masculinities and Disaster*. Abingdon, Oxon: Routledge.

47. Lorde, A., 2019. *Sister Outsider*. London: Penguin.

## 5. WHERE ARE ALL THE WOMEN?

1. Wahlström, M. et al., eds., 2019. 'Protests for a future.' Protest Institute. https://protestinstitut.eu/wp-content/uploads/2019/07/20190709_Protest-for-a-future_GCS-Descriptive-Report.pdf. Accessed 12.12.20.

2. 'What Do the Statistics on UNFCCC Women's Participation Tell Us?' 12.5.19. WEDO. https://wedo.org/what-do-the-statistics-on-womens-participation-tell-us/. Accessed 15.12.20.

3. 'Pocket Guide to Gender Equality Under the UNFCCC', 2020. Oxford Climate Policy. https://wedo.org/2020-pocket-guide-to-gender-equality-under-the-unfccc/. Accessed 17.1.21.

4. 'Women's Participation in the UNFCCC', Jan. 2020. WEDO. https://wedo.org/wp-content/uploads/2020/01/Factsheet-UNFCCC-Progress-Achieving-Gender-Balance-2019.pdf. Accessed 17.1.21.

5. 'Conference of the Parties: Gender composition,' 19.9.19. Report by the Secretariat. UNFCCC. https://unfccc.int/sites/default/files/resource/CP2019_09E.pdf. Accessed 15.12.20.

6. 'Pocket Guide to Gender Equality Under the UNFCCC', op. cit.

7. Gay-Antaki, M. and Liverman, D., 2018. 'Climate for women in climate science: Women scientists and the Intergovernmental Panel on Climate Change.' *PNAS*, 115(9). https://www.pnas.org/content/115/9/2060#:~:text=Over%20time%2C%20we%20show%20that,the%20most%20recent%20assessment%20reports. Accessed 15.12.20.

8. 'Women's Participation in Global Environmental Decision Making.' In: 'Pocket Guide to Gender Equality Under the UNFCCC', op. cit.

9. 'Gender Climate Tracker', n.d. https://genderclimatetracker.org/. Accessed 17.1.21.

10. Tanyag, M. and True, J., 16.12.19. 'Climate conferences are male, pale and stale—it's time to bring in women.' *The Conversation*. https://theconversation.com/climate-conferences-are-male-pale-and-stale-its-time-to-bring-in-women-128060. Accessed 15.12.20.

11. Gay-Antaki and Liverman, op. cit.

12. Selm, K. et al., 2019. 'Educational Attainment predicts negative perceptions women have of their own climate change knowledge.' *PLOS One*, 14(1).

13. McCright, A., 2010. 'The Effects of Gender on Climate Change Knowledge and Concern in the American Public.' *Population and Environment*, 32(1).

14. Grunspan, D. et al., 2016. 'Males Under-Estimate Academic Performance of Their Female Peers in Undergraduate Biology Classrooms.' *PLOS One*, 11(2).

15. 'Science and Engineering Indicators 2018.' National Science Foundation. https://nsf.gov/statistics/2018/nsb20181/digest/sections/u-s-s-e-workforce-trends-and-composition. Accessed 15.12.20.

16. '2019 Workforce Statistics—One million women in STEM in the UK', 2019. Wise Women. https://www.wisecampaign.org.uk/statistics/2019-workforce-statistics-one-million-women-in-stem-in-the-uk/. Accessed 9.2.21.

17. 'Women, Gender Equality and the Energy Transition in the EU,' May 2019. European Parliament. https://www.europarl.europa.eu/RegData/etudes/STUD/2019/608867/IPOL_STU(2019)608867_EN.pdf. Accessed 16.12.20.

18. Matheson, J., 11.7.19. 'Women in Social Science: The Personal and the Statistical.' Campaign for Social Science. https://campaignforsocialscience. org.uk/news/women-in-social-science-the-personal-and-the-statistical/#:~:text=It%20reflects%20the%20wider%20picture,and%20just%2021%25%20in%202001. Accessed 9.2.21.

19. Perry, G., 8.10.14. 'Grayson Perry: The rise and fall of Default Man.' *New Statesman*. https://www.newstatesman.com/culture/2014/10/grayson-perry-rise-and-fall-default-man. Accessed 9.2.21.

20. Haraway, D., 1988. 'Situated Knowledges: The Science Question in Feminism and the Privilege of Partial Perspective.' *Feminist Studies*, 14(3).

21. *The Paris Agreement*, 2015. UNFCCC. https://unfccc.int/sites/default/files/english_paris_agreement.pdf. Accessed 19.12.20.

22. Morrow, K., 2017. 'Changing the Climate of Participation.' In: MacGregor, S., ed. 2017. *Routledge Handbook of Gender and Environment*. Abingdon, Oxon: Routledge; Terry, G., 2009. 'No climate justice without gender justice: an overview of the issues.' *Gender and Development*, 17(1).

23. 'Draft decision CP.20L Lima work programme on gender', n.d. UNFCCC. https://unfccc.int/files/meetings/lima_dec_2014/decisions/application/pdf/auv_cop20_gender.pdf. Accessed 19.12.20.

24. Di Chiro, G., 2017. 'Welcome to the White (M)Anthropocene.' In: MacGregor, S., ed., 2017, op. cit.

25. Holland, O., 2.9.19. 'Scientists and designers are proposing radical ways

to "refreeze" the Arctic.' CNN Style. https://edition.cnn.com/style/article/refreeze-arctic-design-scn/index.html. Accessed 9.2.21.

26. Simon, M., 5.10.18. 'We're Destroying the Sea—But It Could Save Us From Ourselves.' *WIRED*. https://www.wired.com/story/the-sea-could-save-us-from-ourselves/. Accessed 18.12.20.

27. Gorvett, Z., 26.4.16. 'Our rapidly warming world could cause serious problems for civilisation in decades to come. But could a giant space umbrella help cool down our planet? BBC Future investigates.' BBC. https://www.bbc.com/future/article/20160425-how-a-giant-space-umbrella-could-stop-global-warming. Accessed 18.12.20.

28. Sax, S., 18.12.19. 'Geoengineering's Gender Problem Could Put the Planet at Risk.' *WIRED*. https://www.wired.com/story/geoengineerings-gender-problem-could-put-the-planet-at-risk/. Accessed 18.12.20.

29. 'Hands Off Mother Earth! Manifesto Against Geoengineering', Oct. 2018. *Geoengineering Monitor*. https://www.geoengineeringmonitor.org/2018/10/hands-off-mother-earth-manifesto-against-geoengineering/. Accessed 18.1.21.

30. Marshall, B.K. et al., 2006. 'Environmental Risk Perceptions and the White Male Effect: Pollution Concerns among Deep South Coastal Residents.' *Journal of Applied Sociology*, 23(2).

31. Ellison, K., 28.3.18. 'Why Climate Change Sceptics Are Backing Geoengineering'. *WIRED*. https://www.wired.com/story/why-climate-change-skeptics-are-backing-geoengineering/. Accessed 18.12.20.

32. Seager, J., 2009. 'Death By Degrees: Taking a Feminist Hard Look at the $2^0$C Climate Policy.' *Kvinder, Køn og Foraksning*, 3–4.

33. Ibid.

34. Nagel, J., 2016. *Gender and Climate Change*. New York: Routledge.

35. Ratcliffe, R., 12.10.18. 'Prince William accused of "white saviour" mentality in Africa wildlife film.' *The Guardian*. https://www.theguardian.com/global-development/2018/oct/12/prince-william-accused-of-white-saviour-mentality-over-wildlife-conservation-video-tanzania. Accessed 21.12.20; Mbara, J. and Ogada, M., 2016. *The Big Conservation Lie*. Lens & Pen Publishing.

36. '"The source of the danger is black people"—Why is racism normalized in conservation?', n.d. *Survival International*. https://www.survivalinternational.org/articles/racism-in-conservation. Accessed 21.12.20.

37. 'The Big Green Lie', 2020. Survival International https://www.survivalinternational.org/campaigns/biggreenlie. Accessed 21.12.20.

38. 'No REDD Papers, vol. 1', November 2011. Global Alliance Against REDD+. http://no-redd.com/no-redd-papers/. Accessed 22.12.20.

39. 'Indigenous Women and REDD: Making Their Voice Heard', 2014. Asia Indigenous People's Pact. https://www.iwgia.org/images/publications/0697_Indigenous_omen_and_REDD_EB.pdf. Accessed 22.12.20.

40. 'Gender and REDD+ Policy Brief', 2017. UNDP. https://www.undp.org/content/undp/en/home/librarypage/womens-empowerment/gender-and-REDD.html. Accessed 22.12.20.

41. Tovar-Restrepo, M., 2017. 'Planning for climate change: REDD+SES as gender-responsive environmental action.' In: MacGregor, S. *Routledge Handbook of Gender and Environment*. Abingdon, Oxon: Routledge.

42. Larson, A. et al., 2018. 'Gender lessons for climate initiatives: A comparative study of REDD+ impact on subjective wellbeing.' *World Development*, 108.

43. Larson, A. and Evans, K., 18.4.18. 'In REDD+ villages, women say their wellbeing has declined.' *Forest News*. https://forestsnews.cifor.org/55753/in-redd-villages-women-say-their-wellbeing-has-declined?fnl=. Accessed 22.12.20.

44. Jones, V., 17.5.07. 'Vanity Fair: The Unbearable Whiteness of Green.' *HuffPost*. https://www.huffpost.com/entry/vanity-fair-the-unbearabl_b_48766?guccounter=1&guce_referrer=aHR0cHM6Ly93d3cuZ29vZ2xlLmNvbS88&guce_referrer_sig=AQAAAAuJJ3CwPcHs_cAXJBhjgSCIpLCE9xhat3mC4v0jUSWHb6momFWycvYGRVh6wNGI2ceFCkWsA819Y5yPCVZI5eton8Vbx5I1UVGXGkPQQNBby11qjb9UeasD6LtPJ9fa9aE4Hm6gyWf5IzcpK-F7Hxv-jhzNLANcHMMQhtSVNpYJ. Accessed 20.12.20.

45. Evelyn, K., 29.1.20. '"Like I wasn't there": climate activist Vanessa Nakate on being erased from a movement.' *The Guardian*. https://www.theguardian.com/world/2020/jan/29/vanessa-nakate-interview-climate-activism-cropped-photo-davos. Accessed 20.12.20.

46. 'Statement on systemic and pervasive racism within the environmental field,' 2020. *Sierra Club*. https://www.sierraclub.org/sites/www.sierraclub.org/files/uploads-wysiwig/Statement%20on%20systemic%20and%20pervasive%20racism%20within%20the%20environmental%20field.pdf. Accessed 21.12.20.

47. Norrie, R., March 2017. 'The Two Sides of Diversity.' Policy Exchange. https://policyexchange.org.uk/publication/the-two-sides-of-diversity/. Accessed 21.12.20.

48. Taylor, D., 2014. 'The State of Diversity in Environmental Organizations.' *Green 2.0*. http://vaipl.org/wp-content/uploads/2014/10/Executive Summary-Diverse-Green.pdf. Accessed 21.12.20.

49. '2020 NGO and Foundation Transparency Report Card', *Green 2.0*. https://diversegreen.org/transparency-cards/2020-ngo-foundation-report/. Accessed 17.1.21.

50. Ochefu, C., 4.10.20. 'I May Destroy You: lessons for environmentalism.' *It's Freezing in LA!* https://www.itsfreezinginla.co.uk/post/i-may-destroy-you#:~:text=This%20year%2C%20Michaela%20Coel's%20I,the%20show%20have%20been%20overlooked. Accessed 22.12.20.

51. Ibid.

52. Pearson, A., et al., 2017. 'Race, Class, Gender and Climate Change Communication.' *Oxford Research Encyclopedia of Climate Science*. Oxford: OUP; Ballew, M. et al., 2020. 'Which racial/ethnic groups care most about climate change?' New Haven, CT: Yale Program on Climate Change Communication.

53. Pearson, A. et al., 2018. 'Diverse Segments of the US public underestimate the environmental concerns of minority and low-income Americans.' *PNAS*, 115(49).

54. 'Statement on Extinction Rebellion's relationship with the police', 1.8.20. Extinction Rebellion. https://extinctionrebellion.uk/2020/07/01/statement-on-extinction-rebellions-relationship-with-the-police/. Accessed 22.12.20.

55. Hallam, R., 2019. 'Common Sense for the 21st Century.' Carmarthenshire: Common Sense for the 21st Century.

56. Dembicki, G., 28.4.20. 'A Debate Over Racism Has Split One of the World's Most Famous Climate Groups.' *Vice*. https://www.vice.com/en/article/jgey8k/a-debate-over-racism-has-split-one-of-the-worlds-most-famous-climate-groups. Accessed 22.12.20.

57. Ford, Z., 29.10.12. 'Anti-Gay Preacher Blames Hurricane Sandy on Homosexuality and Marriage Equality.' *Think Progress*. https://archive.thinkprogress.org/anti-gay-preacher-blames-hurricane-sandy-on-homosexuality-and-marriage-equality-fa202cecf4ac/. Accessed 22.12.20.

58. Tashman, B., 29.6.11. 'Joyner: Hurricane Katrina was God's Judgment for Homosexuality.' *Right Wing Watch*. https://www.rightwingwatch.org/post/joyner-hurricane-katrina-was-gods-judgment-for-homosexuality/. Accessed 23.12.20.

59. Gaard, G., 2019. 'Out of the closets and into the climate! Queer feminist

climate justice.' In: Bhavnani, K. et al. *Climate Futures*. London: Zed Books.

60. 'LGBT Americans Think, Act, Vote More Green than Others', 26.11.10. *Business Wire*. https://www.businesswire.com/news/home/20091026 005727/en/LGBT-Americans-Act-Vote-Green. Accessed 2.12.20.

61. Seymour, N., 2013. *Strange Futures: Futurity, Empathy and the Queer Ecological Imagination*. Chicago, IL: University of Illinois Press.

62. Seymour, N., 2017. 'Transgender Environments'; Butler, C., 2017. 'A fruitless endeavour: confronting the heteronormativity of environmentalism.' Both in: MacGregor, S., ed. *Routledge Handbook of Gender and Environment*. Abingdon, Oxon: Routledge.

63. Seymour, 2013, op. cit.; Bagemihl, B., 2000. *Biological Exuberance: Animal Homosexuality and Natural Diversity*. New York: St Martin's Press.

64. Mortimer-Sandilands, C. and Erickson, B., 2010. *Queer Ecologies: Sex, Nature, Politics, Desire*. Bloomington, IN: Indiana University Press.

65. Spence, M., 2000. *Dispossessing the Wilderness: Indian Removal and the Making of the National Parks*. New York: OUP USA.

66. DeLuca, K. and Demo, A., 2001. 'Imagining Nature and Erasing Race and Class.' *Environmental History*, 6(4).

67. Wolbring, G., 2009. 'A Culture of Neglect: Climate Discourse and Disabled People.' *M/C Journal*, 12(4).

68. Ibid.

69. Bell, S. et al., 2020. 'Seeking a disability lens within climate change migration discourses, policies and practices.' *Disability and Society*, 35(4).

70. 'Disability and Climate Resilience: A Literature Review', April 2017. Leonard Cheshire Disability.

71. 'Analytical Study on the promotion and protection of the rights of persons with disabilities in the context of climate change. United Nations. https://reliefweb.int/sites/reliefweb.int/files/resources/A_HRC_44_ 30_E.pdf. Accessed 23.12.20.

72. Gaskin, C. et al., 2017. 'Factors Associated with Climate Change Vulnerability and the Adaptive Capacity of People with Disability: A Systematic Review.' *Weather, Climate and Society*, 9(4).

73. 'Disability and Climate Resilience: A Literature Review', op. cit.

74. Lee, H., et al., 26.3.20. 'Disability Inclusion Helpdesk Query No. 30.' Social Development Direct. https://www.sddirect.org.uk/media/2058/ disability-inclusion-helpdesk-query-30-climate-resilience.pdf. Accessed 23.12.20.

75. 'UN survey shows needs of persons with disabilities largely ignored during disasters', 2013. https://news.un.org/en/story/2013/10/452852-un-survey-shows-needs-persons-disabilities-largely-ignored-during-disasters. Accessed 23.12.20.

76. Karpf, A., 1988. *Doctoring the Media: The Reporting of Health and Medicine*. Abingdon, Oxon: Routledge.

77. Twigg, J. et al., July 2018. 'Disability inclusion and disaster risk reduction: overcoming barriers to progress.' Overseas Development Institute Briefing Note. https://www.odi.org/publications/11166-disability-inclusion-and-disaster-risk-reduction-overcoming-barriers-progress. Accessed 28.12.20.

78. Lorde, A., 2019. *Sister Outsider*. London: Penguin.

79. Lee et al., op. cit.

80. Wright, E., 19.2.20. 'Climate Change, Disability, and Eco-Ablism: why we need to be inclusive to save the planet.' *Uxdesign*. https://uxdesign.cc/climate-change-disability-and-eco-ableism-why-we-need-to-be-inclusive-when-trying-to-save-the-88bb61e82e4e. Accessed 23.12.20.

81. Twigg et al., op. cit.

82. Lee et al., op. cit.

6. ECO-WARRIORS AND CLIMATE CHAMPIONS: WOMEN AND GIRLS TAKING ACTION

1. Brum, E., 28.4.20. 'The Amazon is a Woman.' *Atmos*. https://atmos.earth/amazon-rainforest-indigenous-activism-history/. Accessed 3.1.21.

2. Branford, S. and Tedre, N., 5.8.14. 'Amazon tribe fights Brazil dam project.' BBC. https://www.bbc.co.uk/news/world-latin-america-27834240. Accessed 3.1.21.

3. Watts, J., 21.12.19. '"The forest is shedding tears": the women defending their Amazon homeland.' *The Observer*.

4. Ensler, E., 10.8.20. '"The Amazon is the entry door of the world": why Brazil's biodiversity crisis affects us all.' *The Guardian*. https://www.theguardian.com/environment/2020/aug/10/the-amazon-is-the-vagina-of-the-world-why-women-are-key-to-saving-brazils-forests-aoe. Accessed 4.1.21.

5. '"Our territory, our body, our spirit": Indigenous women unite in historic march in Brazil', 14.8.19. *Amazon Frontlines*. https://www.amazonfrontlines.org/chronicles/indigenous-women-march-brazil/. Accessed 4.1.21.

6. Anderson, M., 1.8.19. '8 reasons this landmark ruling in Ecuador signals hope in the struggle to save the Amazon rainforest.' *Amazon Frontlines*. https://www.amazonfrontlines.org/chronicles/8-reasons-waorani-victory/. Accessed 4.1.21.

7. Baragwanath, K. and Bayi, E., 2020. 'Collective property rights reduce deforestation in the Brazilian Amazon.' *PNAS*, 117(34).

8. Nepstad, D. et al., 2006. 'Inhibition of Amazon Deforestation and Fire by Parks and Indigenous Lands.' *Conservation Biology*, 20(1).

9. Goldberg, E., 23.7.20. 'How Covid-19 Made it Easier to Talk About Climate Change.' *The New York Times*. https://www.nytimes.com/2020/07/24/us/climate-change-green-new-deal-covid-coronavirus.html. Accessed 4.1.21.

10. 'Black and Green Ambassadors', n.d. Bristol Green Capital Partnership. https://bristolgreencapital.org/project_cat/blackandgreenambassadors/. Accessed 4.1.21.

11. Laville, S., 16.12.20. 'Ella Kissi-Debrah: how a mother's fight for justice may help prevent other air pollution deaths.' *The Guardian*. https://www.theguardian.com/environment/2020/dec/16/ella-kissi-debrah-mother-fight-justice-air-pollution-death. Accessed 4.1.21.

12. Laughland, O. and Lartey, J., 6.5.20. 'One town's battle for clean air.' *The Guardian*.

13. 'Women of Cancer Alley: Film Series'. https://www.youtube.com/watch?v=fButa8WgAnk. Accessed 4.1.21.

14. 'Flint water crisis: ex-governor and eight others charged after new inquiry,' 15.1.21. *The Guardian*. https://www.theguardian.com/us-news/2021/jan/14/flint-water-crisis-charges-rick-snyder-nick-lyon-eden-wells. Accessed 18.1.21.

15. 'LeeAnne Walters', 2018. The Goldman Environmental Prize. https://www.goldmanprize.org/recipient/leeanne-walters/. Accessed 18.1.21.

16. Author interview, Kathrin Gutmann, via Zoom, 3.11.20.

17. 'Ende Gelände 2021', n.d. Ende Gelände. https://www.ende-gelaende.org/unsere-barrieren-durchfliessen-inklusion/. Accessed 7.1.21.

18. Lucas, C., 29.11.19. 'Joining Climate Strikers in Brighton'. https://www.carolinelucas.com/latest/joining-climate-strikers-in-brighton. Accessed 18.1.21.

19. Lucas, C., 2018, pp. 117, 118. In: Friends of the Earth and C40 Cities, eds, *Why Women Will Save the Planet*. London: Zed Books.

20. Harvey, F., 20.2.21. 'Margaret Atwood: women will bear the brunt of dystopian climate future.' *The Guardian*. https://www.theguardian.com/environment/2018/may/31/margaret-atwood-women-will-bear-brunt-of-dystopian-climate-future. Accessed 5.1.21.

21. Gomez, J., 20.2.20. 'Margaret Atwood: "The people who supress women

also pretend there is no climate crisis". France 24. https://amp.france24.com/en/culture/20200220-encore-margaret-atwood-on-women-s-rights-and-the-climate-crisis. Accessed 5.1.21.

22. See website: https://firedrillfridays.com/. Accessed 5.1.21.

23. 'Jane Fonda: "I'm willing to step in to the fire"', 29.11.20. BBC News. https://www.bbc.co.uk/news/av/world-us-canada-55109882. Accessed 5.1.21.

24. See Higgins's website: https://pollyhiggins.com/. Accessed 5.1.21.

25. Monbiot, G., 28.3.19. 'The destruction of the Earth is a crime. It should be prosecuted.' *The Guardian*.

26. 'AG Healey Amends Lawsuit Against Exxon Adding New Significant Facts about Company's Continued Deception', 5.6.20. Office of Attorney General Maura Healey, Massachusetts government. https://www.mass.gov/news/ag-healey-amends-lawsuit-against-exxon-adding-new-significant-facts-about-companys-continued. Accessed 9.1.21.

27. Kaminski, I., 21.12.19. 'Court ruling boosts fight to curb carbon emissions.' *The Guardian*.

28. 'Dutch Climate Case Urgenda: The Verdict #aftermovie', 27.6.15. https://www.youtube.com/watch?v=T6RhH09cVLc. Accessed 7.1.21.

29. de Wit, E. and Seneviratne, S., Dec. 2020. 'Climate change litigation update.' Norton Rose Fulbright. https://www.nortonrosefulbright.com/en/knowledge/publications/0c9b154a/climate-change-litigation-update. Accessed 9.2.21.

30. Van der Voo, L., 5.6.19. 'Test cases: Climate activists take on the state across the globe.' *The Guardian*.

31. Schwartz, J., 17.1.20. 'Court Quashes Youth Climate Case Against Government.' *The New York Times*. Accessed 7.1.21.

32. Standaert, M., 19.7.20. 'China's first climate striker: give it up or you can't go back to school.' *The Guardian*. https://www.theguardian.com/world/2020/jul/20/chinas-first-climate-striker-cant-return-to-school. Accessed 11.1.21.

33. Margolin, J., 19.12.18. 'Don't underestimate 17-year-old climate change activist Jamie Saraí Margolin—and don't call her "sweetie".' *Assembly*, Malala Fund. https://assembly.malala.org/stories/jamie-margolin-zero-hour. Accessed 11.1.21.

34. Author interview, Maria Belen, Quito, 20.9.19.

35. 'Watch: Child Activists Confront Sen. Dianne Feinstein On Climate Change', 25.2.19. NBC News. https://www.youtube.com/watch?v=lu-VzZ45MwI. Accessed 11.1.21.

36. Prakash, V. and Girgenti, G., 2020. *Winning the Green New Deal*. New York: Simon & Schuster.

37. 'Watch: Child Activists Confront Sen. Dianne Feinstein', op. cit.

38. Margolin, op. cit.

39. Prakash and Girgenti, op. cit.

40. '"WE CALL BS" Emma Gonzales', 18.2.18. https://www.youtube.com/watch?v=5gbVkQ5C8tQ. Accessed 12.1.21.

41. Unigwe, C., 5.10.19. 'Beyond the west, there are many Gretas.' *The Guardian*.

42. For an interesting discussion of the symbolic role of the child, see Edelman, L., 2004. *No Future: Queer Theory and the Death Drive*. Durham, NC: Duke University Press.

43. Thunberg, G. and others, 10.1.20. 'At Davos we will tell world leaders to abandon the fossil fuel economy.' *The Guardian*. https://www.theguardian.com/commentisfree/2020/jan/10/greta-thunberg-davos-tycoons-fossil-fuels-dismantle-climate-crisis. Accessed 10.2.21.

44. Karpf, A., 18.1.20. 'Don't let prejudice against older people contaminate the climate movement.' *The Guardian*. https://www.theguardian.com/commentisfree/2020/jan/18/ageism-climate-movement-generation-stereotypes. Accessed 12.1.21.

45. Trendell, A., 16.12.19. 'Billie Eilish: "Greta Thunberg is paving the way. Hopefully the old people start listening to us so we don't all die."' *NME*. https://www.nme.com/news/music/billie-eilish-greta-thunberg-is-paving-the-way-hopefully-the-old-people-start-listening-to-us-so-we-dont-all-die-2588145. Accessed 12.1.21.

46. Thunberg, G. et al., 23.5.19. 'Young people have led the climate strikes. Now we need adults to join us too.' *The Guardian*.

47. 'Grace Yang', 2019. Meddling Kids Movement. https://www.meddlingkidsmovement.com/climate-justice. Accessed 12.1.21.

48. 'India climate activist Licypriya Kangujam on why she took a stand', 6.2.20. BBC. https://www.bbc.co.uk/news/world-asia-india-51399721. Accessed 12.1.21.

49. Author interview, Licypriya Kangujam, via Zoom, 5.10.20.

50. Crippa, M. et al., 2020. 'Fossil CO2 emissions of all world countries, 2020 report'. European Commission Joint Research Centre. https://edgar.jrc.ec.europa.eu/overview.php?v=booklet2020. Accessed 12.1.21. (Europe figure represents the UK plus the EU.)

51. Malik Chua, J., 18.12.19. 'Is it even possible to be a sustainable influencer?'

*Fashionista.* https://fashionista.com/2019/12/sustainable-fashion-influencers-instagram. Accessed 12.1.21.

52. Feller, M., 23.1.20. 'Can Instagram Influencers Help Save the Planet?' *Elle.* https://www.elle.com/culture/career-politics/a30629637/sustainable-influencers-instagram-climate-crisis/. Accessed 12.1.21.

53. 'TikTok by the Numbers: Stats, Demographics & Fun Facts', 6.1.21. Omnicore. https://www.omnicoreagency.com/tiktok-statistics/. Accessed 13.1.21.

## 7.  ENGENDERING CLIMATE SOLUTIONS

1. 'Impact story: Hilaria', n.d. Solar Sister. https://solarsister.org/impact-story/hilaria/. Accessed 21.1.21.

2. 'Gwyneth Paltrow's Goop pays $145,000 in vaginal egg lawsuit', 5.9.18. BBC. https://www.bbc.co.uk/news/world-us-canada-45426332. Accessed 4.2.21.

3. Cornwall, A., 2018. 'Beyond "Empowerment Lite": Women's Empowerment, Neoliberal Development and Global Justice.' *Cadernos Padu*, 52.

4. Westholm, L. and Arora-Jonsson, S., 2018. 'What room for politics and change in global climate governance? Addressing gender in co-benefits and safeguards.' *Environmental Politics*, 27(5).

5. Arora-Jonsson, A., 2017. 'Gender and Environmental Policy'. In: MacGregor, S., ed., 2017. *Routledge Handbook of Gender and Environment.* Abingdon, Oxon: Routledge.

6. Cornwall, 2018, op. cit.

7. Warhurst, A., 9.4.09. '"Girl Effect" Could Lift the Global Economy'. *Bloomberg.* https://www.bloomberg.com/news/articles/2009-04-08/girl-effect-could-lift-the-global-economybusinessweek-business-news-stock-market-and-financial-advice. Accessed 23.1.21.

8. 'Nike Foundation launches new girleffect.org', 11.12.12. NIKE News. https://news.nike.com/news/nike-foundation-launches-new-girleffectorg. Accessed 24.1.21.

9. Crenna-Jennings, W., 2021. 'Young people's mental and emotional health.' Education Policy Institute. https://epi.org.uk/wp-content/uploads/2021/01/EPI-PT_Young-people%E2%80%99s-wellbeing_Jan2021.pdf. Accessed 4.2.21.

10. 'Young people's well-being in the UK: 2020', 2.10.20. Office for National Statistics. https://www.ons.gov.uk/peoplepopulationandcommunity/wellbeing/bulletins/youngpeopleswellbeingintheuk/2020. Accessed 4.2.21.

11. 'Coronavirus and the impact on students in higher education in England', 2021. Office for National Statistics. https://www.ons.gov.uk/peoplepopulationandcommunity/educationandchildcare/articles/coronavirusandtheimpactonstudentsinhighereducationinenglandseptembertodecember2020/2020-12-21#personal-well-being-loneliness-and-mental-health. Accessed 4.2.21.

12. Roberts, K., 23.7.10. 'Save a Girl, Save the World.' Oprah.com. http://www.oprah.com/world/psi-interviews-jennifer-buffett-and-maria-eitel/all. Accessed 23.1.21.

13. Hengeveld, M., 20.7.15. 'Nike's girl effect.' Al Jazeera America. http://america.aljazeera.com/opinions/2015/7/nikes-girl-effect.html. Accessed 23.1.21.

14. 'Innovation Station: Women's Weather Watch, Fiji', 28.1.19. FemLINK Pacific & ActionAid Australia. https://actionaid.org.au/articles/innovation-station-womens-weather-watch-fiji/. Accessed 21.1.21; Shetty, G., n.d. 'Natural Disasters and Empowered Fijian Women.' The Borgen Project. https://borgenproject.org/natural-disasters-and-empowered-fijian-women/#:~:text=The%20Women's%20Weather%20Watch%20Program,-The%20Women's%20Weather&text=The%20base%20is%20in%20Fiji,prepare%20them%20for%20the%20worst. Accessed 24.1.21.

15. 'Water and women's rights in Ethiopia: Fatuma's story', 6.6.16. CARE International. https://www.careinternational.org.uk/stories/water-and-womens-rights-ethiopia-fatumas-story. Accessed 22.1.21.

16. 'Scaling Adoption of Clean Cooking Solutions through Women's Empowerment', n.d. Global Alliance for Clean Cookstoves. https://www.cleancookingalliance.org/resources_files/scaling-adoption-womens-empowerment.pdf. Accessed 22.1.21.

17. 'Women introduce new climate-adapted fishing technique on Lake Togo and gain foot in a male dominated sector', n.d. Women & Gender Constituency. https://womengenderclimate.org/gjc_solutions/women-introduce-new-climate-adapted-fishing-technique-on-lake-togo-and-gain-foot-in-a-male-dominated-sector/. Accessed 21.1.21.

18. 'Case Study: Innovative rainwater harvesting empowers women in Gujarat, India', May 2020. https://cdkn.org/wp-content/uploads/2020/06/Bhungroo-Case-Study-2.pdf. Accessed 21.1.21; 'Bhungroo: Five Year Goals', n.d. Bhungroo, Naireeta Services. https://www.naireetaservices.com/. Accessed 8.2.21.

19. Mehta, A., 17.4.18. 'Gender gap in land ownership.' National Council of

Applied Economic Research. https://www.ncaer.org/news_details. php?nID=252&nID=252. Accessed 17.4.15.

20. 'Case Study', op. cit.

21. Mitra, A., 30.4.93. 'Chipko: an unfinished mission.' *DownToEarth*. https://www.downtoearth.org.in/coverage/chipko-an-unfinished-mission-30883. Accessed 22.1.21.

22. Joyeux, B. and Shiva, V., 28.11.16. 'Sowing the Seeds of Resistance.' *Green European Journal*, 14. https://www.greeneuropeanjournal.eu/sowing-the-seeds-of-resistance/. Accessed 22.1.21; 'Navdanya's Organizational Over View', n.d. Navdanya. http://www.navdanya.org/site/component/content/article?id=621. Accessed 22.1.21.

23. Shiva, V., 12.11.13. 'Seed Monopolies, GMOs and Farmer Suicides in India—a response to Nature.' *Navdanya's Diary*. http://www.navdanya.org/blog/?p=744. Accessed 8.2.21.

24. Shiva, S., 1999. 'Monocultures, Monopolies, Myths and the Masculinization of Agriculture.' *Development*, 42(2).

25. Friends of the Earth, op. cit.

26. Aguilar, L., et al., 2015. 'Roots for the Future: The landscape and way forward on gender and climate change.' Global Gender and Climate Alliance. https://portals.iucn.org/union/sites/union/files/doc/roots-for-the-future-en.pdf. Accessed 21.1.21.

27. 'Enhanced Lima work programme on gender and its gender action plan', 12.12.19. UNFCCC, COP25. https://unfccc.int/sites/default/files/resource/cp2019_L03E.pdf. Accessed 22.1.21.

28. Bohland, P., 8.1.20. 'Women's Groups Applaud Gender Action Plan Following COP 25'. Inter Press Service. https://reliefweb.int/report/world/women-s-groups-applaud-gender-action-plan-following-cop-25. Accessed 22.1.21.

29. 'C40 Cities: Why Cities?', n.d. C40 Cities. https://www.c40.org/why_cities#:~:text=Cities-consume-over-two-thirds,levels-and-powerful-coastal-storms. Accessed 8.2.21.

30. '20 Women Mayors of C40 Cities Reveal the Growing Power of the Women4Climate Movement', 14.6.18. C40 Cities. https://www.c40.org/press_releases/20-women-mayors-of-c40-cities-reveal-the-growing-power-of-the-women4climate-movement#:~:text=20%20Women-Mayors-of-C40,Power-of-the-Women4Climate-Movement. Accessed 9.2.21.

31. 'DC Green Bank', 3.4.17. District of Columbia Department of Energy & Environment. https://doee.dc.gov/greenbank. Accessed 8.2.21.

32. Elliott, T., 25.11.19. 'Montreal Is Making Huge Investments In Housing & Green Space, Here's What To Expect.' *MTLBlog*. https://www.mtlblog.com/en-ca/news/montreal/mayor-plante-announces-huge-investments-in-housing-and-green-space-heres-what-to-expect. Accessed 9.1.21.

33. Hannam, P., 25.6.19. 'City of Sydney officially declares "climate emergency".' *The Sydney Morning Herald*, https://www.smh.com.au/environment/climate-change/city-of-sydney-officially-declares-climate-emergency-20190625-p520zd.html. Accessed 9.1.21.

34. Blanchar, C., 16.1.20. 'Barcelona announces €563 million plan to reduce greenhouse gases.' *El País*. https://english.elpais.com/elpais/2020/01/16/inenglish/1579177477_798192.html. Accessed 9.1.21.

35. Burgen, S., 12.11.20. 'Barcelona starts 10-year plan to reclaim its streets from motor traffic.' *The Guardian*.

36. Rowling, M., 16.1.20. '"This is not a drill": Barcelona declares a climate emergency.' *The Independent*. https://www.independent.co.uk/news/world/europe/barcelona-climate-emergency-ada-colau-spain-a9286756.html. Accessed 9.1.21.

37. 'Why does Barcelona need a Climate Plan?', n.d. Barcelona for Climate. https://www.barcelona.cat/barcelona-pel-clima/en/climate-plan/why-does-barcelona-need-climate-plan. Accessed 9.1.21.

38. Guillot, L., 18.2.20. 'How France's youngest green mayor wants to transform her city.' *Politico*. https://www.politico.eu/article/france-youngest-green-mayor-leonore-moncondhuy/. Accessed 9.1.21.

39. Nossiter, A., 5.10.19. 'The Greening of Paris Makes Its Mayor More Than a Few Enemies.' *The New York Times*. https://www.nytimes.com/2019/10/05/world/europe/paris-anne-hildago-green-city-climate-change.html. Accessed 9.1.21.

40. Carvajal, K.G. & Alam, M.M., 24.1.18. 'Transport is not gender-neutral'. World Bank blog. https://blogs.worldbank.org/transport/transport-not-gender-neutral. Accessed 4.2.21.

41. 'Public Transport and Gender', 2018. Women's Budget Group. https://wbg.org.uk/wp-content/uploads/2018/10/Transport-October-2018-w-cover.pdf. Accessed 4.2.21.

42. O'Sullivan, F., 18.2.20. 'Paris Mayor: It's Time for a "15-Minute City".' *Bloomberg City Lab*. https://www.bloomberg.com/news/articles/2020-02-18/paris-mayor-pledges-a-greener-15-minute-city. Accessed 9.1.21.

43. See, for instance: Zaretsky, E., 1976. *Capitalism, the Family and Personal Life*. London: Pluto Press; Greed, C., 1994. *Women and Planning*.

Abingdon, Oxon: Routledge; Hanson, S. and Pratt, G., 1995. *Gender, Work, and Space*. Abingdon, Oxon: Routledge.

44. Belaich, C., 21.2.20. 'Dominique Bertinotti: à Paris, "il faut montrer ce qu'est une ville écolo"'. *Libération*.

45. Roberts, H., 9.11.20. 'Virginia Raggi prepares for Act II as Rome's mayor.' *Politico*. https://www.politico.eu/article/virginia-raggi-rome-mayor-prepares-act-2/. Accessed 10.1.21; Giuffrida, A., 4.11.18. 'Rubbish, potholes, rats—as the Eternal City crumbles, the far right promises salvation.' *The Observer*.

46. Garrigou, A-S., 29.11.20. 'A new vision to Sierra Leone, an interview with Mayor of Freetown Yvonne Aki-Sawyerr.' Anne-Sophie Garrigou blog. https://www.annesophiegarrigou.com/blog/a-new-vision-to-sierra-leone-an-interview-with-mayor-of-freetown-yvonne-aki-sawyerr. Accessed 9.1.21.

47. Perrone, A., 4.6.19. 'Finland vows to become carbon neutral by 2035.' *The Independent*. https://www.independent.co.uk/news/world/europe/finland-carbon-neutral-fossil-fuels-climate-change-global-warming-a8943886.html. Accessed 10.1.21.

48. Henley, J., 27.6.19. 'New Danish leader pledges 70% cut to carbon emissions by 2030.' *The Observer*.

49. Norgaard, K. and York, R., 2005. 'Gender Equality and State Environmentalism.' *Gender and Society*, 19(4).

50. Nugent, C. and Shandra, J., June 2009. 'State Environmental Protection Efforts, Women's Status and World Politics.' *Organization and Environment* 22(2).

51. Ergas, C. and York, R., 2012. 'Women's status and carbon dioxide emissions: A quantitative cross-national analysis.' *Social Science Research*, 41.

52. Liao, L. et al., 2015. 'Gender diversity, board independence, environmental committee and greenhouse gas disclosure.' *The British Accounting Review*, 47.

53. Mavisakalyan, A. and Tarverdi, Y., 2019. 'Gender and climate change: Do female parliamentarians make a difference?' *European Journal of Political Economy*, 56.

54. Norgaard and York, op. cit.

55. 'The Nordics: Major net exporter of fossil fuels', 6.7.12. Nordic Energy Research. https://www.nordicenergy.org/figure/major-net-exporter-of-fossil-fuels/#:~:text=Norway%20is%20the%20world's%205th,power%20plants%20without%20CCS%20technology. Accessed 10.1.21.

56. Xiao, C. and McCright, A., 2017. 'Gender Differences in Environmental Concern.' In: MacGregor, S., ed., 2017. *Routledge Handbook of Gender and Environment*. Abingdon, Oxon: Routledge.

57. Norgaard and York, op. cit.

58. Ergas and York, op. cit.

59. 'Joel Pett: The Cartoon seen "round the world"', 18.3.12. *Lexington Herald Leader*. https://www.kentucky.com/opinion/op-ed/article44162106. html. Accessed 10.1.21.

## 8. A GREEN NEW DEAL FOR WOMEN

1. 'H.Res.109—Recognizing the duty of the Federal Government to create a Green New Deal', 7.2.19. 116th US Congress, 1st Session, House of Representatives. https://www.congress.gov/bill/116th-congress/house-resolution/109/text. Accessed 27.1.21.

2. Rupar, A., 2.3.19. 'CPAC speakers keep saying Democrats want to ban cows and legalize infanticide. They don't.' *Vox*. https://www.vox.com/2019/3/2/18246812/cpac-2019-themes-cows-infanticide-don-jr-pence-meadows. Accessed 27.1.21.

3. Ardagna, A., 14.3.19. 'GOP lawmaker: Green New Deal is tantamount to genocide.' *Politico*. https://www.politico.com/story/2019/03/14/green-new-deal-genocide-1270839. Accessed 27.1.21.

4. Bendix, A., 6.4.19. 'Trump knocks Green New Deal, calling Alexandria Ocasio-Cortez a "wonderful young bartender".' *Business Insider*. https://www.businessinsider.com/trump-alexandria-ocasio-cortez-bartender-2019-4?r=US&IR=T. Accessed 27.1.21.

5. Caygle, H. et al., 7.2.18. '"Too hot to handle": Pelosi predicts GOP won't trigger another shutdown.' *Politico*. https://www.politico.com/story/2019/02/07/pelosi-trump-government-shutdown-1154355. Accessed 27.1.21.

6. 'Alexandria Ocasio-Cortez Arrives at Sit-In at Pelosi Office', 14.11.18. Storyful. https://finance.yahoo.com/video/alexandria-ocasio-cortez-arrives-sit-000830808.html?guccounter=1&guce_referrer=aHR0cHM6Ly93d3cuZ29vZ2xlLmNvbS8&guce_referrer_sig=AQAAADTCgzUp8LmQ79kpkQtWtIwx7a5fhrnxirrNFtsNBr7Zs3d-xTo8rcmMXchPCkBNigBeiUod-CM1KK5Qdp9Cl4CIpzoGVi5El2x4iUcsv67LIac-MAzkqrtidJGzh4ITZLy3qCQxgeskPpuGZUi4YcwmOETbJsfO6bmQuWeHyHWKt. Accessed 27.1.21.

7. Relman, E. and Hickey, W., 14.2.19. 'More than 80% of Americans support almost all of the key ideas in Alexandria Ocasio-Cortez's Green New Deal.'

*Business Insider*. https://www.businessinsider.com/alexandria-ocasio-cortez-green-new-deal-support-among-americans-poll-2019–2?r=US&IR=T. Accessed 27.1.21.

8. 'Annex to the Communication on the European Green New Deal', 11.12.19. European Commission. https://eur-lex.europa.eu/legal-content/EN/TXT/?qid=1596443911913&uri=CELEX:52019DC0640#document2. Accessed 27.1.21.

9. 'A Green New Deal', July 2008. Green New Deal Group & New Economics Foundation. https://neweconomics.org/uploads/files/8f737ea195fe56db2f_xbm6ihwb1.pdf. Accessed 27.1.21.

10. See Green New Deal UK website: https://www.greennewdealuk.org/. Accessed 27.1.21.

11. 'Ten Proposals for a Green Reset in Coventry', 12.5.20. Coventry for a Green New Deal. https://coventrygnd.wordpress.com/2020/05/12/10-accelerate-scale-up-and-democratise-the-councils-climate-change-strategy/. Accessed 27.1.21; 'PLAN25: becoming carbon neutral', n.d. Goldsmiths, University of London. https://www.gold.ac.uk/media/docs/about/green-new-deal/PLAN25-Carbon-Reducion-Plan.pdf. Accessed 27.1.21.

12. 'H.Res.109', op. cit.

13. Chomsky, N. and Pollin, R., 2020. *Climate Crisis and the Green New Deal*. London: Verso.

14. Kappert, I., 13.7.20. 'The European Green Deal and Gender Diversity'. Heinrich Böll Stiftung. https://eu.boell.org/en/2020/07/13/european-green-deal-and-gender-diversity. Accessed 27.1.21.

15. Aronoff, K. et al., 2019. *A Planet to Win: Why We Need a Green New Deal*. London: Verso.

16. 'Green New Deal', n.d. UK Student Climate Network. https://d1h1wq-tygap0e8.cloudfront.net/uploads/2019/08/GNDDoc.pdf. Accessed 27.1.21.

17. 'If Not Now, When?', 2019. Green Party manifesto, 2019. https://www.greenparty.org.uk/assets/files/Elections/Green%20Party%20Manifesto%202019.pdf. Accessed 27.1.21.

18. 'Labour commits to decarbonisation by 2030 with Green New Deal', 24.9.19. Labour For A Green New Deal. https://www.labourgnd.uk/news/2019/9/24/labour-backs-gnd. Accessed 9.2.21.

19. 'A Feminist Agenda for a Green New Deal', 20.9.19. The Feminist Agenda for a Green New Deal. http://feministgreennewdeal.com/wp-content/

uploads/2019/09/Feminist-GND-Kickstart-note-Final-Draft-9.20.2019. pdf. Accessed 27.1.21.

20. 'Achieving Net-Zero', Feb. 2020. CBI. https://www.cbi.org.uk/media/ 5579/cbi-green-recovery-roadmap.pdf. Accessed 28.1.21.

21. Hepburn, C. et al., 2020. 'Will COVID-19 fiscal recovery packages accelerate or retard progress on climate change?' *Oxford Review of Economic Politics*, 36(S1).

22. '"Build build build": Prime Minister announces New Deal for Britain', 30.6.20. Prime Minister's Office, 10 Downing Street. https://www.gov. uk/government/news/build-build-build-prime-minister-announces-new-deal-for-britain. Accessed 28.1.21.

23. Littig, B., 2017. 'Good green jobs for whom? A feminist critique of the green economy.' In: MacGregor, S., ed. *Routledge Handbook of Gender and Environment*. Abingdon, Oxon: Routledge.

24. 'The Green New Deal', n.d. Bernie Sanders website. https://berniesanders. com/issues/green-new-deal/. Accessed 29.1.21.

25. Wintermayr, I., 27.2.12. 'How can women benefit from green jobs? An ILO approach.' European Parliament, Women's and Gender Equality Committee. https://www.europarl.europa.eu/document/activities/cont /201203/20120301ATT39684/20120301ATT39684EN.pdf. Accessed 27.1.21.

26. Cohen, M. and MacGregor, S., 2020. 'Towards a Feminist Green New Deal for the UK.' Women's Environmental Network. https://www.wen. org.uk/2020/05/19/femgreennewdeal/. Accessed 28.1.21.

27. De Henau, J. and Himmelweit, S., 2020. 'A Care-Led Recovery from Coronavirus.' Women's Budget Group. https://wbg.org.uk/wp-content/ uploads/2020/06/Care-led-recovery-final.pdf. Accessed 28.1.21.

28. Weintrobe, S., 10.9.15. 'The new imagination in a culture of uncare.' http:// www.sallyweintrobe.com/10-sept-2015-the-new-imagination-in-a-culture-of-uncare/. Accessed 28.1.21; Weintrobe, S., 2021. *Psychological Roots of the Climate Crisis: Neoliberal Exceptionalism and the Climate of Uncare*. New York: Bloomsbury Academic.

· 29. 'Creating a Caring Economy: A Call to Action', 2020. Women's Budget Group. https://wbg.org.uk/commission/. Accessed 28.1.21.

30. I discuss this in more detail in Karpf, A., 2014. *How to Age*. London: Pan Macmillan.

31. 'Mental health at work', 2017. Centre for Mental Health. https://www. centreformentalhealth.org.uk/sites/default/files/2018-09/Centrefor

MentalHealth_Mental_health_problems_in_the_workplace.pdf. Accessed 4.2.21; 'Mental health and employers', 2020. Deloitte. https://www2.deloitte.com/content/dam/Deloitte/uk/Documents/consultancy/deloitte-uk-mental-health-and-employers.pdf. Accessed 4.2.21.

32. 'Creating a Caring Economy', op. cit.

33. Ibid.

34. MacGregor, S., 7.10.20. 'Confronting the Climate Crisis: Feminist Pathways to Just and Sustainable Futures'. Online webinar. The Consortium on Gender, Security and Human Rights.

35. Titmuss, R., 1970. *The Gift Relationship*. London: Allen & Unwin.

36. 'Goldsmith Street', 11.4.18. JCT. https://corporate.jctltd.co.uk/gold-smith-street/#:~:text=Goldsmith%20Street%20delivers%20105%20 homes,is%20both%20competitive%20and%20economical. Accessed 28.1.21.

37. 'Creating a Caring Economy', op. cit.

38. Waring, M., 1988. *If Women Counted*. New York: Harper & Row. New edition published as Waring, M., 1999. *Counting for Nothing*. Toronto: University of Toronto Press.

39. Waring, M., 1999, op. cit.

40. Elliott, L., 18.1.21. 'Bobby Kennedy was right: GDP is a poor measure of a nation's real health.' *The Guardian*.

41. Quoted in ibid.

42. Meadows, D. et al., 1972. *The Limits to Growth*. Available online via the Donella Meadows Collection, Dartmouth College: https://collections.dartmouth.edu/teitexts/meadows/diplomatic/meadows_ltg-diplomatic.html. Accessed 30.1.21.

43. Meadows, D.H. et al., 1972. 'The Limits to Growth: A Report to The Club of Rome.' https://web.ics.purdue.edu/~wggray/Teaching/His300/Illus-trations/Limits-to-Growth.pdf. Accessed 30.1.21.

44. Meadows, D. et al., 2004. 'A Synopsis: *Limits to Growth: The 30-Year Update*.' The Donella Meadows Project Academy for Systems Change. http://donellameadows.org/archives/a-synopsis-limits-to-growth-the-30-year-update/. Accessed 30.1.21.

45. Hickel, J. and Kallis, G., 2019. 'Is Green Growth Possible?' *New Political Economy*, 25(4).

46. Higgins, E. '"How Dare You!": Greta Thunberg Rages at "Fairytales of Eternal Economic Growth" at UN Climate Summit', 23.9.19. Common Dreams. https://www.commondreams.org/news/2019/09/23/how-dare-

you-greta-thunberg-rages-fairytales-eternal-economic-growth-un-climate. Accessed 28.1.21.

47. Asara, V. et al., 2015. 'Socially sustainable degrowth as a social-ecological transformation: repoliticizing sustainability.' *Sustainability Science*, 10.

48. Karpf, A., 7.9.14. 'Wait a second—that upgrade high won't last.' *The Guardian*.

49. Soper, K., 2020. *Post-Growth Living: For an Alternative Hedonism*. London: Verso.

50. See for instance Dengler, C. and Seebacher, L., March 2019. 'What About the Global South? Towards a Feminist Decolonial Degrowth Approach.' *Ecological Economics*, 157.

51. Raworth, K., 2017. *Doughnut Economics*. London: Random House Business Books.

52. Pettifor, A., 2019. *The Case for the Green New Deal*. London: Verso.

53. Ibid., p. 77.

54. Aldrick, P., 30.11.20. 'BBC "misled viewers" on scale of national debt.' *The Times*. https://www.thetimes.co.uk/article/bbc-misled-viewers-on-scale-of-national-debt-ckvkcwc7j. Accessed 20.1.21.

55. Rehman, A., 4.5.19. 'The "green new deal" supported by Ocasio-Cortez and Corbyn is just a new form of colonialism.' *The Independent*. https://www.independent.co.uk/voices/green-new-deal-alexandria-ocasio-cortez-corbyn-colonialism-climate-change-a8899876.html. Accessed 30.1.21.

56. Ibid.

57. Knack, R.E., May 2005. 'Pay As You Park'. *Planning* magazine, available online at: http://shoup.bol.ucla.edu/PayAsYouPark.htm. Accessed 30.1.21.

58. Plumer, B. 'Cars take up too much space in cities. New technology could change that.' *Vox*. https://www.vox.com/a/new-economy-future/cars-cities-technologies. Accessed 30.1.21.

59. 'The Occupy movements have dramatized questions about public space: Who owns it? And who can use it?', 10.10.12. LSE blog. https://blogs.lse.ac.uk/politicsandpolicy/legacy-of-occupy-sennett/. Accessed 30.1.21.

60. Althoff, T. et al., 2017. 'Large-scale physical activity data reveal worldwide activity inequality.' *Nature*, 547.

61. Lack, E., 29.7.20. 'Is Luxembourg's free public transport one to replicate or avoid?' *The New European*. https://www.theneweuropean.co.uk/brexit-news/emma-luck-luxembourg-first-country-to-introduce-free-public-transport-88454. Accessed 31.1.21; Barry, E., 14.1.20. 'Should Public

Transit Be Free? More Cities Say, Why Not?' *The New York Times*. https://www.nytimes.com/2020/01/14/us/free-public-transit.html. Accessed 31.1.21; 'Why this German city plans to make public transport free', 18.6.19. *The Local*. https://www.thelocal.de/20190618/why-this-german-city-plans-to-make-public-transport-free. 31.1.21.

62. 'Public Transport and Gender', 2018. Women's Budget Group. https://wbg.org.uk/wp-content/uploads/2018/10/Transport-October-2018-w-cover.pdf. Accessed 31.1.21.

63. Harrouk, C., 25.12.19. 'What Can Cities Imagined by Women Look Like? The Case of Barcelona'. *ArchDaily*. https://www.archdaily.com/927948/how-can-cities-imagined-by-women-look-like-the-case-of-barcelona. Accessed 4.2.21.

64. Waite, R. and Buxton, P., 13.6.18. 'AJ100: women now make up a third of architects at UK's largest practices'. *Architects' Journal*. https://www.architectsjournal.co.uk/news/aj100-women-now-make-up-a-third-of-architects-at-uks-largest-practices#:~:text=The%20106%20AJ100%20practices%20now,architects%20was%2027%20per%20cent. Accessed 4.2.21.

65. 'The cost of living alone', 4.4.19. Office for National Statistics. https://www.ons.gov.uk/peoplepopulationandcommunity/birthsdeathsandmarriages/families/articles/thecostoflivingalone/2019-0404#:~:text=Living%20alone%20set%20to%20increase&text=By%202039%2C%20the%20number%20of,rise%20to%2010.7%20million2.&text=While%20the%20number%20of%20people,53%25%20over%20the%20same%20period. Accessed 4.2.21.

66. 'Tackle loneliness this Christmas: 6 ways you can help', n.d. Benenden Health. https://www.benenden.co.uk/be-healthy/lifestyle/tackle-loneliness-this-christmas-six-ways-you-can-help-today/?utm_source=pr&utm_medium=social&utm_campaign=social&utm_content=loneliness_older_generation. Accessed 30.1.21; Stepler, R., 18.2.16. 'Smaller Share of Women Ages 65 and Older Are Living Alone.' Pew Research Center. https://www.pewsocialtrends.org/2016/02/18/1-gender-gap-in-share-of-older-adults-living-alone-narrows/. Accessed 30.1.21.

67. Hayden, D., 1996. *The Grand Domestic Revolution*. Cambridge, MA: MIT Press.

68. Monbiot, G., 19.9.19. 'For the sake of the life on Earth, we must put a limit on wealth.' *The Guardian*.

69. See, for instance, Federici, S., 2018. *Re-Enchanting the World: Feminism*

*and the Politics of the Commons*. Oakland, CA: Pm Press; Clement, F. et al., 2019. 'Feminist political ecologies of the commons and commoning'. *International Journal of the Commons*, 13(1).

70. Karpf, A., 8.3.20. 'We all benefit from a more gender-equal society. Even men.' *The Guardian*. https://www.theguardian.com/commentisfree/2020/mar/08/gender-equal-international-womens-day-men. Accessed 10.1.21.

71. 'The health and wellbeing of men in the WHO European Region: better health through a gender approach', 2018. WHO. https://www.euro.who.int/__data/assets/pdf_file/0007/380716/mhr-report-eng.pdf?ua=1. Accessed 10.1.21.

72. Audette, P. et al., 2019. '(E)Quality of Life: A Cross-National Analysis of the Effect of Gender Equality on Life Satisfaction.' *Journal of Happiness Studies*, 20.

73. Maume, D., et al., 2018. 'Gender Equality and Restless Sleep Among Partnered Europeans.' *Journal of Marriage and Equality*, 80.

74. Holter, Ø., 2014. '"What's in it for Men?": Old Question, New Data.' *Men and Masculinities*, 17(5).

75. Torsheim, T. et al., 2006. 'Cross-national variation of gender differences in adolescent subjective health in Europe and North America.' *Social Science and Medicine*, 62.

76. De Looze, M. et al., 2019. 'Country-Level Gender Equality and Adolescents' Contraceptive Use in Europe, Canada and Israel: Findings from 33 Countries.' *Perspectives on Sexual Reproduction and Health*, 51(1).

77. Rudman, L. and Phelan, J., 2007. 'The Interpersonal Power of Feminism: Is Feminism Good for Romantic Relationships?' *Sex Roles*, 57.

78. 'Life expectancy in Iceland is one of the highest in Europe', 29.6.20. Statistics Iceland. https://statice.is/publications/news-archive/births-and-deaths/deaths-in-2019/#:~:text=In%202019%2C%20the%20life%20expectancy,population%20age%2Dspecific%20mortality%20rates. Accessed 10.1.21.

79. 'The Global Gender Gap Report', 2020. World Economic Forum. http://www3.weforum.org/docs/WEF_GGGR_2020.pdf. Accessed 8.2.21.

80. Karpf, A., 2.11.02. 'A chain reaction.' *The Guardian*. https://www.the-guardian.com/theguardian/2002/nov/02/weekend7.weekend2. Accessed 4.2.21.

81. All suggestions being taken seriously by the new Centre for Climate Repair at Cambridge University. Pearce, F., 29.5.19. 'Geoengineer the Planet? More Scientists Now Say It Must Be an Option.' *Yale Environment 360*.

https://e360.yale.edu/features/geoengineer-the-planet-more-scientists-now-say-it-must-be-an-option. Accessed 30.1.21.

CONCLUSION

1. 'Special Report: Global Warming 1.5°C', 2018. IPCC. https://www.ipcc.ch/sr15/chapter/spm/. Accessed 3.2.21.

2. 'About: What Is Dark Optimism?', n.d. Dark Optimism. https://www.darkoptimism.org/about/. Accessed 2.2.21.

3. Andrew, A. et al., 27.5.20. 'How are mothers and fathers balancing work and family under lockdown?' Institute of Fiscal Studies. https://www.ifs.org.uk/uploads/BN290-Mothers-and-fathers-balancing-work-and-life-under-lockdown.pdf. Accessed 31.1.21.

4. Sharp, C. et al., Sept. 2020. 'Schools' responses to Covid-19: The challenges facing schools and pupils in September 2020'. Slough: National Foundation for Educational Research. https://www.nfer.ac.uk/media/4119/schools_responses_to_covid_19_the_challenges_facing_schools_and_pupils_in_september_2020.pdf. Accessed 5.2.21.

5. Oxfam, Jan. 2021. 'The Inequality Virus: Bringing together a world torn apart by coronavirus through a fair, just and sustainable economy.' https://oxfamilibrary.openrepository.com/bitstream/handle/10546/621149/bp-the-inequality-virus-250121-en.pdf. Accessed 1.2.21.

6. Ambrose, J., 20.7.20. 'Carbon savings from Covid-19 lockdown halve within weeks.' *The Guardian*.

7. Watts, J., 10.11.20. 'Many plan to fly and drive more than previously after pandemic.' *The Guardian*.

8. 'Report on Motoring 2020: Driving through the pandemic', 2020. RAC. https://www.rac.co.uk/drive/features/report-on-motoring-2020/. Accessed 3.2.21.

9. Harvey, F., 9.11.21. 'Revealed: coronavirus recovery plans threaten global climate rescue hopes.' *The Guardian*. https://www.theguardian.com/environment/2020/nov/09/revealed-covid-recovery-plans-threaten-global-climate-hopes. Accessed 31.1.21.

10. '£27 billion roads investment to support 64,000 jobs', 21.8.20. Highways England. https://www.gov.uk/government/news/27billion-roads-investment-to-support-64000-jobs. Accessed 9.2.21.

11. Carrington, D., 22.1.21. 'Move to stop UK building Europe's biggest gas-fired power plant fails.' *The Guardian*.

12. Collins, C., 26.1.21. 'Updates: Billionaire Wealth, U.S. Job Losses and

Pandemic Profiteers.' Inequality.org. https://inequality.org/great-divide/updates-billionaire-pandemic/. Accessed 9.2.21.

13. Collins, C. et al., 23.4.20. 'Billionaire Bonanza 2020.' Institute for Policy Studies. https://ips-dc.org/wp-content/uploads/2020/04/Billionaire-Bonanza-2020.pdf. Accessed 1.2.21.

14. 'Riding the storm', 2020. UBS. https://www.ubs.com/content/dam/static/noindex/wealth-management/ubs-billionaires-report-2020-spread.pdf. Accessed 3.2.21; Neate, R., 7.10.20. 'Billionaires' wealth rises to $10.2 trillion amid Covid crisis.' *The Guardian*. https://www.theguardian.com/business/2020/oct/07/covid-19-crisis-boosts-the-fortunes-of-worlds-billionaires.

15. 'The Inequality Virus', op. cit. My emphasis.

16. Taylor, A. and Paquette, D., 26.1.21. 'Only one of the world's 29 poorest counties has started coronavirus vaccination.' *The Washington Post*. https://www.washingtonpost.com/world/2021/01/26/guinea-covid-vaccinations-poor-countries/. Accessed 1.2.21.

17. Perry, F., 30.4.20. 'How cities are clamping down on cars.' BBC. https://www.bbc.com/future/article/20200429-are-we-witnessing-the-death-of-the-car. Accessed 2.2.21.

18. Laker, L., 21.4.20. 'Milan announces ambitious scheme to reduce car use after lockdown.' *The Guardian*. https://www.theguardian.com/world/2020/apr/21/milan-seeks-to-prevent-post-crisis-return-of-traffic-pollution. Accessed 9.2.21.

19. 'The Inequality Virus', op. cit.

20. 'Climate Chronology', 2019. University of Maine. https://umaine.edu/soe/wp-content/uploads/sites/199/2019/07/Climate-Chronology-February-2019.pdf. Accessed. 3.2.21.

21. Roy, A., 3.4.20. 'The pandemic is a portal.' *Financial Times*. https://www.ft.com/content/10d8f5e8-74eb-11ea-95fe-fcd274e920ca. Accessed 1.2.21.

22. 'ExxonMobil announces emission reduction plans; expects to meet 2020 goals', 14.12.20. ExxonMobil. https://corporate.exxonmobil.com/News/Newsroom/News-releases/2020/1214_ExxonMobil-announces-2025-emissions-reductions_expects-to-meet-2020-plan#:~:text=ExxonMobil-announces-emission-reduction-plans%3B-expects-to-meet-2020-goals,-share-share&text=ExxonMobil-plans-to-reduce-the,2025%2C-compared-to-2016-levels. Accessed 8.2.21.

23. Atkin, E., 15.12.20. 'Exxon's climate plan doesn't actually commit to reducing emissions.' *HEATED*. https://heated.world/p/exxons-climate-plan-doesnt-actually. Accessed 1.2.21.

24. Crowley, K. and Rathi, A., 5.10.20. 'Exxon's Plan for Surging Carbon Emissions Revealed in Leaked Documents.' *Bloomberg Green*. https://www.bloomberg.com/news/articles/2020-10-05/exxon-carbon-emissions-and-climate-leaked-plans-reveal-rising-co2-output. Accessed 1.2.21.

25. Lo, J., 21.10.20. 'Peru and Switzerland sign "world first" carbon offset deal under the Paris Agreement.' *Climate Home News*. https://www.climatechangenews.com/2020/10/21/peru-switzerland-sign-world-first-carbon-offset-deal-paris-agreement/. Accessed 2.2.21.

26. Rérolle, R., 4.11.18. '"Gilets jaunes": "Les élites parlent de fin du monde, quand nous, on parle de fin du mois".' *Le Monde*. https://www.lemonde.fr/politique/article/2018/11/24/gilets-jaunes-les-elites-parlent-de-fin-du-monde-quand-nous-on-parle-de-fin-du-mois_5387968_823448.html. Accessed 2.2.21.

27. 'No Better Time for Climate Reparations', 24.1.21. *Hot Take* podcast. https://realhottake.substack.com/p/no-better-time-for-climate-reparations-b84. Accessed 2.2.21.

28. 'Biden Bolsters DOJ Focus on Environmental Justice, Climate (3)', 27.1.21. *Bloomberg Law*. https://news.bloomberglaw.com/environment-and-energy/biden-bolsters-doj-focus-on-environmental-justice-climate. Accessed 2.2.21.

29. Atkin, E., 21.2.21. 'The conservative climate fear-mongering begins.' *HEATED*. https://heated.world/p/the-conservative-climate-fear-mongering. Accessed 2.2.21.

30. Margolin, J., 2020. *Youth to Power*. New York: Hachette.

31. Prakash, V. and Girenti, G., 2020. *Winning the Green New Deal*. New York: Simon and Schuster.

# BIBLIOGRAPHY

Abdo, M. et al., 2019. 'Impact of Wildfire Smoke on Adverse Pregnancy Outcomes in Colorado, 2007–2015.' *International Journal of Environmental Research and Public Health*, 16(19).

Acha, M., 2019. 'Climate justice must be anti-patriarchal, or it will not be systemic.' In: K-K. Bhavnani et al., eds. *Climate Futures*. London: Zed.

Adams, C., 2015. *The Sexual Politics of Meat*. London: Bloomsbury Academic.

Aguilar, L. et al., 2015. 'Roots for the Future: The landscape and way forward on gender and climate change.' *Global Gender and Climate Alliance*.

Alaimo, S., 2000. *Undomesticated Ground: Recasting Nature as Feminist Space*. Ithaca, NY: Cornell University Press.

———, 27.10.16. 'Climate change, carbon-heavy masculinity, and the politics of exposure.' University of Minnesota Press blog.

Alber, G. et al., 2017. 'Gender and urban climate change policy.' In: S. Buckingham and V. Le Masson, eds. *Understanding Climate Change Through Gender Relations*. Abingdon, Oxon: Routledge.

Althoff, T. et al., 2017. 'Large-scale physical activity data reveal worldwide activity inequality.' *Nature*, 547.

American College of Obstetricians and Gynaecologists, 2013. *Exposure to Toxic Environmental Agents, 2013*.

Amnesty International, 2016. *Canada: Out of Sight, Out of Mind: Gender, Indigenous Rights and Energy Development in Northeast British Columbia*.

Andrew, A. et al., 27.5.20. 'How are mothers and fathers balancing work and family under lockdown?' Institute of Fiscal Studies.

Anshelm, J. and Hultman, M., 2014. 'A green fatwā? Climate change as a threat to the masculinity of industrial modernity.' *NORMA: International Journal for Masculinity Studies*, 9(2).

Aronoff, K. et al., 2019. *A Planet to Win*. London: Verso.

# BIBLIOGRAPHY

Arora-Jonsson, A., 2017. 'Gender and Environmental Policy'. In: S. MacGregor, ed. *Routledge Handbook of Gender and Environment*. Abingdon, Oxon: Routledge.

Arora-Jonsson, S., 2011. 'Virtue and vulnerability: Discourses on women, gender and climate change.' *Global Environmental Change*, 21(2).

Asia Indigenous People's Pact, 2014. *Indigenous Women and REDD: Making Their Voice Heard*.

Atkin, E., 15.12.20. 'Exxon's climate plan doesn't actually commit to reducing emissions.' *Heated.world*.

———, 21.2.21. 'The conservative climate fear-mongering begins.' *Heated. world*.

Audette, P. et al., 2019. '(E)Quality of Life: A Cross-National Analysis of the Effect of Gender Equality on Life Satisfaction.' *Journal of Happiness Studies*, 20.

Austin, D., 2016. 'Hyper-masculinity and disaster.' In: E. Enarson and B. Pease, eds. *Men, Masculinities and Disaster*. Abingdon, Oxon: Routledge.

Bagemihl, B., 2000. *Biological Exuberance: Animal Homosexuality and Natural Diversity*. New York: St Martin's.

Ballew, M. et al., 2020. 'Which racial/ethnic groups care most about climate change?' New Haven, CT: Yale Program on Climate Change Communication.

Baragwanath, K. and Bayi, E., 2020. 'Collective property rights reduce deforestation in the Brazilian Amazon.' *PNAS*, 117(34).

Basel Action Network, 2019. *Holes in the Circular Economy*.

Bell, S. et al., 2020. 'Seeking a disability lens within climate change migration discourses, policies and practices.' *Disability and Society*, 35(4).

Bem, S., 2008. *The Lenses of Gender: Transforming the Debate on Sexual Inequality*. New Haven, CT: Yale University Press.

Béné, C. and Merten, S., 2008. 'Women and Fish-for-Sex: Transactional Sex, HIV/AIDS and Gender in African Fisheries.' *World Development*, 36(5).

Bhatia, R. et al., April 2019. 'A feminist exploration of "populationism": engaging contemporary forms of population control.' *Gender, Place and Culture*, 27(1).

Bhavnani, K-K. et al., eds, 2019. *Climate Futures*. London: Zed.

Bhushan, C., 2018. 'A Commentary on the Consumption of Rich Indians versus Rich (and Poor) Americans.' Centre for Science and Environment.

Black, G., 30.7.13. 'Your Clothes Were Made by a Bangladeshi Climate Refugee.' *Mother Jones*.

# BIBLIOGRAPHY

Bowles, N., 18.3.19. 'Replacement Theory, a Racist, Sexist Doctrine Spread in Far Right Circles.' *The New York Times*.

Brides of the Sun, n.d. *An Investigation into How Climate Change is Creating a Generation of Child Brides*.

Brody, A. et al., March 2008. 'Gender and climate change: mapping the link-ages.' *BRIDGE*, Institute of Development Studies, Sussex for DFID.

Brough, A. et al., 2016. 'Is Eco-Friendly Unmanly? The Green Feminine Stereotype and Its Effect on Sustainable Consumption.' *Journal of Consumer Research*, 43.

Brough, A. and Wilkie, J., 26.12.17. 'Men Resist Green Behaviour as Unmanly.' *Scientific American*.

Brown, O., 2008. 'Migration and Climate Change.' International Organization for Migration.

Buckingham, S. and Le Masson, V., eds, 2017. *Understanding Climate Change Through Gender Relations*. Abingdon, Oxon: Routledge.

Butler, C., 2017. 'A fruitless endeavour: confronting the heteronormativity of environmentalism.' In: S. MacGregor, ed. *Routledge Handbook of Gender and Environment*. Abingdon, Oxon: Routledge.

Byanyima, W., 18.12.15. 'What to do about climate change? Ask women—they have the most to lose.' *The New Humanitarian*.

Carbon Disclosure Project, 2017. *The Carbon Majors Database*.

Care International, 2016. *Water and women's rights in Ethiopia: Fatuma's story*.

Carmichael, S. and Hamilton, C., 1992. *Black Power: The Politics of Liberation in America*. New York: Vintage.

Castañeda Camey, I. et al., 2020. 'Gender-based violence and environment linkages: the violence of inequality.' IUCN.

Catalyst, 2019. *Women in Energy—Gas, Mining and Oil: Quick Take*.

Chandler, D., 16.4.08. 'Leaving our mark.' *TechTalk*, 52(23).

Cherry, M. and Sneirson, J., 2011. 'Beyond Profit: Rethinking Corporate Social Responsibility and Greenwashing After the BP Oil Disaster.' *Tulane Law Review*, 85(4).

Childs, M., 13.2.20. 'Does carbon offsetting work?' Friends of the Earth.

Chomsky, N. and Pollin, R., 2020. *Climate Crisis and the Green New Deal*. London: Verso.

Clement, F. et al., 2019. 'Feminist political ecologies of the commons and communing.' *International Journal of the Commons*, 13(1).

Cohen, M.G., 2015. 'Gendered Emissions: Counting Greenhouse Gas Emissions by Gender and Why it Matters.' In: C. Lipsig-Mummé and

S. McBride, eds. *Work in a Warming World*. Montreal: McGill-Queen's University Press.

Cohen, M. and MacGregor, S., 2020. 'Towards a Feminist Green New Deal for the UK.' Women's Environmental Network.

Connell, R.W., 1995. *Masculinities*. Cambridge: Polity.

Connell, R., 2017. 'Foreword: Masculinities in the Sociocene.' In: S. MacGregor and N. Seymour, eds. *Men and Nature: Hegemonic Masculinities and Environmental Change*. RCC Perspectives.

Cornwall, A., 30.11.11. 'Current challenges for women's rights and development.' Womankind.org.

———, 2018. 'Beyond "Empowerment Lite": Women's Empowerment, Neoliberal Development and Global Justice.' *Cadernos Padu*, 52.

——— and Rivas, A-M., 2015. 'From "Gender Equality and Women's Empowerment" to Global Justice: Reclaiming a Transformative Agenda for Gender and Development.' *Third World Quarterly*, 36(2).

Crowley, K. and Rathi, A., 5.10.20. 'Exxon's Plan for Surging Carbon Emissions Revealed in Leaked Documents.' *Bloomberg Green*.

Daggett, C., 2018. 'Petro-masculinity: Fossil Fuels and Authoritarian Desire.' *Millennium*, 47(1).

Dankelman, I., ed., 2010. *Gender and Climate Change: An Introduction*. London: Earthscan.

De Henau, J. and Himmelweit, S., 2020. 'A Care-Led Recovery from Coronavirus.' Women's Budget Group.

De Looze, M. et al., 2019. 'Country-Level Gender Equality and Adolescents' Contraceptive Use in Europe, Canada and Israel: Findings from 33 Countries.' *Perspectives on Sexual Reproduction and Health*, 51(1).

DeLuca, K. and Demo, A., 2001. 'Imagining Nature and Erasing Race and Class.' *Environmental History*, 6(4).

Dengler, C. and Seebacher, L., 2019. 'What About the Global South? Towards a Feminist Decolonial Degrowth Approach.' *Ecological Economics*, 157 (March).

Di Chiro, G., 2017. 'Welcome to the White (M)Anthropocene.' In: S. MacGregor, ed., 2017. *Routledge Handbook of Gender and Environment*. Abingdon, Oxon: Routledge.

Dogra, N., 2014. *Representations of Global Poverty*. London: I.B. Tauris.

Doyle, J., 2011. 'Where has all the oil gone? BP branding and the discursive elimination of climate change risk.' In: N. Heffernan and D. Wragg, eds. *Culture, Environment and Ecopolitics*. Newcastle: Cambridge Scholars.

# BIBLIOGRAPHY

Draper, R., Feb. 2019. 'This metal is powering today's technology—at what price?' *National Geographic*.

Duffin, E., 15.9.20. 'Gender distribution of billionaires around the world.' *Statista*.

Dwyer, E. and Woolf, L., 2018. *Down by the River*. Oxfam Research Reports.

Edelman, L., 2004. *No Future: Queer Theory and the Death Drive*. Durham, NC: Duke University Press.

Elliott, L., 18.1.21. 'Bobby Kennedy was right: GDP is a poor measure of a nation's real health.' *The Guardian*.

Elwell-Sutton, T., 20.5.20. 'Emerging Findings on the impact of COVID-19 on black and minority ethnic people.' The Health Foundation.

Enarson, E. and Pease, B., eds, 2016. *Men, Masculinities and Disaster*. Abingdon, Oxon: Routledge.

Environmental Justice Association, 2021. *Climate Displacement in Bangladesh*.

Ergas, C. and York, R., 2012. 'Women's status and carbon dioxide emissions: A quantitative cross-national analysis.' *Social Science Research*, 41.

Ervin, J., 2018. 'In defence of nature: women at the forefront.' United Nations Development Programme blog.

European Parliament, 2019. *Women, Gender Equality and the Energy Transition in the EU*.

FAO, 2011. *The Role of Women in Agriculture*. ESA Working Paper No. 11–02.

Federici, S., 2018. *Re-Enchanting the World: Feminism and the Politics of the Commons*. Oakland, CA: Pm Press.

Feller, M., 23.1.20. 'Can Instagram Influencers Help Save the Planet?' *Elle*.

Finney, C., 2014. *Black Faces, White Spaces*. Chapel Hill, NC: University of North Carolina Press.

Forests and Finances, 2020. *Is Your Money Destroying Rainforests or Violating Rights?*

Forti, V. et al., 2020. 'The Global E-waste Monitor'. United Nationals University.

Frank, C. and Guesnet, L., 2009. '"We were promised development and all we got is misery"—The Influence of Petroleum on Conflict Dynamics in Chad.' Brief 41, Bonn International Center for Conversion.

Friends of the Earth, 2015. *Why Women Will Save the Planet*. London: Zed.

Fullerton, Duncan G. et al., 2008. 'Indoor air pollution from biomass fuel smoke is a major health concern in the developing world.' *Transactions of the Royal Society of Tropical Medicine and Hygiene*, 102(9).

Gaard, G., 1993. *Ecofeminism: women, animals, nature*. Philadelphia, PA: Temple University Press, p. 301.

———, 2019. 'Out of the closets and into the climate! Queer feminist climate justice.' In: K-K. Bhavnani et al., eds. *Climate Futures*. London: Zed.

Gaskin, C. et al., 2017. 'Factors Associated with Climate Change Vulnerability and the Adaptive Capacity of People with Disability: A Systematic Review.' *Weather, Climate and Society*, 9(4).

Gay-Antaki, M. and Liverman, D., 2018. 'Climate for women in climate science: Women scientists and the Intergovernmental Panel on Climate Change.' *PNAS*, 115(9).

Geere, J. et al., 2018. 'Carrying water may be a major contributor to disability from musculoskeletal disorders in low income countries: a cross-sectional survey in South Africa, Ghana and Vietnam.' *Journal of Global Health*, 8(1).

Georgetown Institute for Women, Peace and Security, 2015. *Women and Climate Change*.

Gerrard, M., 2018. 'Climate Change and Human Trafficking After the Paris Agreement.' *University of Miami Law Review*, 72(2).

Global Alliance Against REDD+, 2011. *No REDD Papers, vol. 1*.

Global Alliance for Clean Cookstoves, 2014. *Gender and Livelihoods Impacts of Clean Cookstoves South Asia Study*.

Gössling, S., and Humpe, A., 2020. 'The global scale, distribution and growth of aviation: Implications for climate change.' *Global Environmental Change*, 65.

Greed, C., 1994. *Women and Planning*. Abingdon, Oxon: Routledge.

Green 2.0, 2020. *2020 NGO and Foundation Transparency Report Card*.

Grunspan, D. et al., 2016. 'Males Under-Estimate Academic Performance of Their Female Peers in Undergraduate Biology Classrooms.' *PLOS One*, 11(2).

Hanson, S. and Pratt, G., 1995. *Gender, Work, and Space*. Abingdon, Oxon: Routledge.

Haraway, D., 1988. 'Situated Knowledges: The Science Question in Feminism and the Privilege of Partial Perspective.' *Feminist Studies*, 14(3).

———, 2003. *The Companion Species Manifesto: Dogs, People and Significant Otherness*. Chicago, IL: Prickly Paradigm.

Hart, C. and Smith, G., 2013. *Scaling Adoption of Clean Cooking Solutions through Women's Empowerment*. Gender Alliance for Clean Cookstoves.

Hartmann, B., 8.10.20. 'Confronting the Climate Crisis: Pathways to Just and Sustainable Futures.' Webinar, Consortium of Gender, Security and Human Rights.

# BIBLIOGRAPHY

Hayden, D., 1996. *The Grand Domestic Revolution*. Cambridge, MA: MIT Press.

Haynes, A., 2017. 'Everyday life in rural Bangladesh'. In: S. Buckingham and V. Le Masson, eds, *Understanding Climate Change Through Gender Relations*. Abingdon, Oxon: Routledge.

Heacock, H. et al., 2016. 'E-waste and Harm to Vulnerable Populations: A Growing Global Problem.' *Environmental Health Perspectives*. May 2016, 124(5).

Health Effects Institute, 2020. *State of Global Air*.

Heede, R., 2019. 'Carbon Majors.' Climate Accountability Institute.

Hengeveld, M., 20.7.15. 'Nike's girl effect.' *Al Jazeera America*.

Hepburn, C. et al., 2020. 'Will COVID-19 fiscal recovery packages accelerate or retard progress on climate change?' *Oxford Review of Economic Politics*, 36(S1).

Hickel, J. and Kallis, G., 2019. 'Is Green Growth Possible?' *New Political Economy*, 25(4).

Holter, Ø., 2014. '"What's in it for Men?": Old Question, New Data.' *Men and Masculinities*, 17(5).

Houghton, R., 2009. '"Everything Became a Struggle, Absolute Struggle": Post-flood Increases in Domestic Violence in New Zealand.' In: E. Enarson and P. Dhar Chakrabarti, eds. *Women, Gender and Disaster*. Sage: New Delhi, pp. 99–111.

Hultman, M. and Pulé, P., 2018. *Ecological Masculinities*. Abingdon, Oxon: Routledge.

Human Rights Watch, 2015. *Marry Before Your House is Swept Away: Child Marriage in Bangladesh*.

InfluenceMap, 2019. *Corporate Carbon Policy Footprint—the 50 Most Influential*.

———, 2019. *Asset Management and Climate Change*.

Institute for Policy Studies, 2020. *Billionaire Bonanza 2020*.

Internal Displacement Monitoring Centre, 2020. *Women and Girls in Internal Displacement*.

International Labour Organization, 2015. *The Impact of Livelihood Recovery Initiatives in Reducing Vulnerability to Human Trafficking and Illegal Recruitment: Lessons from Typhoon Haiyan*.

IPCC, 2014. *Climate Change 2014 Synthesis Report Summary for Policymakers*.

———, 2014. *Human Health: Impacts, Adaptation and Co-Benefits*.

———, 2018. *Special Report: Global Warming 1.5°C*.

# BIBLIOGRAPHY

———, 2019. *Climate Change and Land*.

Jian, M., 2014. *The Dark Road*. London: Vintage.

Johnson, A., and Wilkinson, K., 2020. *All We Can Save*. New York: One World.

Johnsson-Latham, G., 2007. 'A study on gender equality as a prerequisite for sustainable development.' Environment Advisory Council, Sweden.

———, G., 2010. 'Why More Attention to Gender and Class Can Help Combat Climate Change and Poverty'. In: I. Dankelman, ed. *Gender and Climate Change: An Introduction*. London: Earthscan.

Jones, G.W., 2005. 'The "Flight from Marriage" in South-East and East Asia.' *Journal of Comparative Family Studies*, 36(1).

Joyeux, B. and Shiva, V., 28.11.16. 'Sowing the Seeds of Resistance.' *Green European Journal*.

Kajumba, T., 2018. 'How climate change impacts have challenged men's masculinity.' Kajumbatracy.blogspot.com.

Kalei Kanuha, V., 2002. 'Colonization and Violence against Women.' Asia Pacific Institute on Gender-Based Violence.

Kappert, I., 13.7.20. 'The European Green Deal and Gender Diversity.' Heinrich Böll Stiftung.

Karpf, A., 1988. *Doctoring the Media: The Reporting of Health and Medicine*. Abingdon, Oxon: Routledge.

———, 2.11.02. 'A chain reaction.' *The Guardian*.

———, 12.12.03. 'Dairy Monsters.' *The Guardian*.

———, 31.1.12. 'Green jobs: a utopia we nearly had.' *The Guardian*.

———, 2014. *How to Age*. London: Pan Macmillan.

———, 7.9.14. 'Wait a second—that upgrade high won't last.' *The Guardian*.

———, 4.12.17. 'How best to silence the powerless? Play the victim.' *The Guardian*.

———, 18.1.20. 'Don't let prejudice against older people contaminate the climate movement.' *The Guardian*.

———, 8.3.20. 'We all benefit from a more gender-equal society. Even men.' *The Guardian*.

Kaufman, M., 1.5.20. 'The carbon footprint sham'. *Mashable*.

Keller, R., 2015. *Fatal Isolation: The Devastating Paris Heatwave of 2003*. Chicago, IL: University of Chicago Press.

Kenner, D., 2019. *Carbon Inequality: The Role of the Richest in Climate Change*. Abingdon, Oxon: Routledge.

Kommenda, N., 19.7.19. 'How your flight emits as much CO2 as many people do in a year.' *The Guardian*.

# BIBLIOGRAPHY

Krange et al., 2019. 'Cool dudes in Norway: climate change denial among conservative men.' *Environmental Sociology*, 5(1).

Kronsell, A., 2017. 'The contribution of feminist perspectives to climate governance.' In: S. Buckingham and V. Le Masson. *Understanding Climate Change Through Gender Relations*. Abingdon, Oxon: Routledge.

Larson, A. et al., 2018. 'Gender lessons for climate initiatives: A comparative study of REDD+ impact on subjective wellbeing.' *World Development*, 108.

Larson, A. and Evans, K., 18.4.18. 'In REDD+ villages, women say their wellbeing has declined.' *Forest News*.

Le Masson, V. et al., 2016. 'Disasters and violence against women and girls.' Overseas Development Institute.

Lee, H., et al., 26.3.20. 'Disability Inclusion Helpdesk Query No. 30.' *Social Development Direct*.

Leonard, C., 2019. *Kochland*. New York: Simon and Schuster.

Leonard Cheshire Disability, 2017. *Disability and Climate Resilience: A Literature Review*.

Lewis, J. et al., 2017. 'Mining and Environmental Health Disparities in Native American Communities.' *Current Environmental Health Reports*, 4(2).

Liao, L. et al., 2015. 'Gender diversity, board independence, environmental committee and greenhouse gas disclosure.' *The British Accounting Review*, 47.

Littig, B., 2017. 'Good green jobs for whom? A feminist critique of the green economy.' In: S. MacGregor, ed. *Routledge Handbook of Gender and Environment*. Abingdon, Oxon: Routledge.

Lorde, A., 2019. *Sister Outsider*. London: Penguin.

Luft, R., 2008. 'Looking for Common Ground: Relief Work in Post-Katrina New Orleans as an American Parable of Race and Gender Violence'. *Feminist Formations*, 20(3).

MacGregor, S., 2010. 'Gender and climate change: from impacts to discourses.' *Journal of the Indian Ocean Region*, 6(2).

——, 2017a. *Routledge Handbook of Gender and Environment*. London: Routledge.

——, 2017b. 'Moving beyond impacts'. In: S. Buckingham and V. Le Masson, eds. *Understanding Climate Change through Gender Relations*. Abingdon, Oxon: Routledge.

——, 2019. 'Zooming in, calling out: (m)anthropogenic climate change through the lens of gender.' In: K-K. Bhavnani et al., eds. *Climate Futures*. London: Zed.

——, 2020. 'Confronting the Climate Crisis: Feminist Pathways to Just and

Sustainable Futures.' Webinar, The Consortium on Gender, Security and Human Rights.

—— and Seymour, N., 2017. 'Introduction.' In: S. MacGregor and N. Seymour, eds. *Men and Nature: Hegemonic Masculinities and Environmental Change*. RCC Perspectives.

—— and Seymour, N., eds, 2017. *Men and Nature: Hegemonic Masculinities and Environmental Change*. RCC Perspectives.

Malik Chua, J., 18.12.19. 'Is it even possible to be a sustainable influencer?' *Fashionista*.

Margolin, J., 2020. *Youth to Power*. New York: Hachette.

Marshall, B.K. et al., 2006. 'Environmental Risk Perceptions and the White Male Effect: Pollution Concerns among Deep South Coastal Residents.' *Journal of Applied Sociology*, 23(2).

Maslog, C., 8.1.15. 'Asia-Pacific Analysis: Asia's Invisible Women Farmers.' *SciDevNet*.

Mathews, F., 2017. 'The dilemma of dualism.' In: S. MacGregor, ed. *Routledge Handbook of Gender and Environment*. Abingdon, Oxon: Routledge.

Maume, D. et al., 2018. 'Gender Equality and Restless Sleep Among Partnered Europeans.' *Journal of Marriage and Equality*, 80.

Mavisakalyan, A. and Tarverdi, Y., 2019. 'Gender and climate change: Do female parliamentarians make a difference?' *European Journal of Political Economy*, 56.

Mbara, J. and Ogada, M., 2016. *The Big Conservation Lie*. Springfield, MO: Lens & Pen.

McAllister, L., 2020. 'Women, E-Waste and Technological Solutions.' Paper presented at 'Confronting the Climate Crisis: Feminist Pathways to Just and Sustainable Futures' webinar, The Consortium on Gender, Security and Human Rights.

McAllister, L. et al., 2014. 'Women, E-Waste, and Technological Solutions to Climate Change.' *Health and Human Rights Journal*, 16(1).

McCright, A., 2010. 'The Effects of Gender on Climate Change Knowledge and Concern in the American Public.' *Population and Environment*, 32(1).

—— and Dunlap, R., 2011. 'Cool dudes: the denial of climate change among conservative white males in the United States.' *Global Environmental Change*, 21(4).

McKinney, L. and Fulkerson, G., 2015. 'Gender Equality and Climate Justice: A Cross-National Analysis.' *Social Justice Research*, 28(3).

Meadows, D. et al., 1972. *The Limits to Growth*. Falls Church, VA: Potamac Associates.

# BIBLIOGRAPHY

Merchant, C., 1990. *The Death of Nature*. London: HarperCollins.

Mies, M. and Shiva, V., 2014. *Ecofeminism*. London: Zed, 18th edn.

Milam, L., 1975. *Sex and Broadcasting*. Berkeley, CA: Dildo Press, p. 351.

Mitra, A., 30.4.93. 'Chipko: an unfinished mission.' *DownToEarth*.

Mollett, S., 2017. 'Gender's critical edge'. In: S. MacGregor, ed. *Routledge Handbook of Gender and Environment*. Abingdon, Oxon: Routledge.

Monbiot, G., 25.2.09. 'Cutting consumption is more important than limiting population.' *The Guardian*.

———, 28.3.19. 'The destruction of the Earth is a crime. It should be prosecuted.' *The Guardian*.

———, 19.9.19. 'For the sake of the life on Earth, we must put a limit on wealth.' *The Guardian*.

Moore-Nall, A., 2015. 'The Legacy of Uranium Development on or near Indian Reservations and Health Implications Rekindling Public Awareness.' *Geosciences*, 5(1).

Morrow, K., 2017. 'Changing the Climate of Participation.' In: S. MacGregor, ed. *Routledge Handbook of Gender and Environment*. Abingdon, Oxon: Routledge.

Mortimer-Sandilands, C. and Erickson, B., 2010. *Queer Ecologies: Sex, Nature, Politics, Desire*. Bloomington, IN: Indiana University Press.

NAACP, 2016. *Coal-Blooded: Putting Profits Before People*.

Nagel, J., 2016. *Gender and Climate Change*. New York: Routledge.

Negi, B. et al., 2010. 'Climate Change and Women's Voices From India.' In: I. Dankelman, ed. *Gender and Climate Change: An Introduction*. London: Earthscan.

Nepstad, D. et al., 2006. 'Inhibition of Amazon Deforestation and Fire by Parks and Indigenous Lands.' *Conservation Biology*, 20(1).

Netflix, 2020. *David Attenborough: A Life on Our Planet*.

Norgaard, K. and York, R., 2005. 'Gender Equality and State Environmentalism.' *Gender and Society*, 19(4).

Norwegian Refugee Council, 2020. *Global Report on Internal Displacement*.

Nugent, C. and Shandra, J., June 2009. 'State Environmental Protection Efforts, Women's Status and World Politics.' *Organization and Environment* 22(2).

Ochefu, C., 4.10.20. 'I May Destroy You: lessons for environmentalism.' *It's Freezing in LA!* magazine.

Okanle, O. et al., 2017. 'Gender Paradoxes and Agricultural Monopoly in Nigeria: Implications for Policy and Food (In)Security in Africa.' *Gender and Behaviour*, 15(3).

# BIBLIOGRAPHY

O'Neill et al., 2010. 'Global demographic trends and future carbon emissions.' *Proceedings of the National Academy of Sciences of the United States*. 107(41).

Oreskes, N. and Conway, E., 2011. *Merchants of Doubt*. London: Bloomsbury.

Ortner, S., 1974. 'Is female to male as nature is to culture?' In: M. Rosaldo and L. Lamphere, eds. *Woman, Culture, and Society*. Stanford, CA: Stanford University Press.

O'Sullivan, F., 18.2.20. 'Paris Mayor: It's Time for a "15-Minute City".' *Bloomberg City Lab*.

Oxfam, 2005. *The Tsunami's Impact on Women*.

———, 2016. *Lake Chad's Unseen Crisis*.

———, 2020. *The Carbon Inequality Era*.

———, 2020b. *Time to Care*.

———, 2020c. 'Average Brit will emit more by January 12 than residents of seven African countries do in a year.'

———, 2021. *The Inequality Virus*.

Oxfam America, Winter 2008/9. *Climate Change and Women*.

Oxford Climate Policy, 2020. *Pocket Guide to Gender Equality Under the UNFCCC*.

Parkinson, D., and Zara, C., 2013. 'The hidden disaster: domestic violence in the aftermath of natural disaster.' *Australian Journal of Emergency Management*, 8(2).

Patterson, J., 2010. 'Your Take—Climate Change Is a Civil Rights Issue.' *The Root*.

Pearce, F., 29.5.19. 'Geoengineer the Planet? More Scientists Now Say It Must Be an Option.' *Yale Environment 360* magazine.

Pearson. A., et al., 2017. 'Race, Class, Gender and Climate Change Communication.' *Oxford Research Encyclopedia of Climate Science*. Oxford: OUP.

——— et al., 2018. 'Diverse Segments of the US public underestimate the environmental concerns of minority and low-income Americans.' *PNAS*, 115(49).

Pease, B., 2016. 'Masculinism, climate change and "man-made" disasters.' In: E. Enarson and B. Pease, eds., *Men, Masculinities and Disaster*. London: Routledge, p. 30.

Pettifor, A., 2019. *The Case for the Green New Deal*. London: Verso.

Plumwood, V., 2003. *Feminism and the Mastery of Nature*. Abingdon, Oxon: Routledge.

Randall, R., 30.7.12. 'Feminism and behaviour change: do current demands for environmental behaviour change disadvantage women?' rorandall.org.

# BIBLIOGRAPHY

Räty, R., and Carlsson-Kanyama, A., 2010. 'Energy consumption by gender in some European countries.' *Energy Policy*, 28.

Raworth, K., 20.10.14. 'Must the Anthropocene be a Manthropocene?' *The Guardian*.

——, 2017. *Doughnut Economics*. London: Random House Business.

Rearick, Z., 15.10.20. 'Masculinity is the unspoken undercurrent in Trumpism and the fracking debate.' *The Philadelphia Inquirer*.

Red Pepper, 3.5.19. 'An Open Letter to Extinction Rebellion.'

Rehman, A., 4.5.19. 'The "green new deal" supported by Ocasio-Cortez and Corbyn is just a new form of colonialism.' *The Independent*.

Relief Web, 2020. *Evicted by Climate Change: Confronting the Gendered Impacts of Climate-Induced Displacement*.

Resurrección, B., 2013. 'Persistent women and environment linkages in climate change and sustainable development agendas.' *Women's Studies International Forum*, 40(Sept–Oct).

Ribot, J. 2017. 'Vulnerability does not Fall from the Sky: Addressing a Risk Conundrum'. In: R. Kasperson et al., eds. *Risk Conundrums: Solving Unsolvable Problems*. London: Earthscan.

Ritchie, H., 2018. 'Global Inequalities in CO2 emissions.' *Our World in Data*.

Robinson, E. and Robbins, R.C., 1968. 'Sources, abundance, and fate of gaseous atmospheric pollutants. Final report and supplement.' Menlo Park, CA: Stanford Research Institute.

Robinson, M., 2018. *Climate Justice*. London: Bloomsbury.

Röhr, 2011. *Beyond Women and Girls' Vulnerability: a debate on gender, climate change and disaster risk reduction*. Brighton: Institute of Disaster Studies.

Röhr, U., 26.5.20. 'Feminist Climate Conference.' Webinar, Green European Foundation.

Rothe, D., 2017. 'Gendering Resilience: Myths and Stereotypes in the Discourse of Climate-induced Migration.' *Global Policy*, 8(1).

Rozin, P. et al., 2012. 'Is Meat Male? A Quantitative Multimethod Framework to Establish Metaphoric Relationships.' *Journal of Consumer Research*, 39(3).

Roy, A., 3.4.20. 'The pandemic is a portal.' *Financial Times*.

Rudman, L. and Phelan, J., 2007. 'The Interpersonal Power of Feminism: Is Feminism Good for Romantic Relationships?' *Sex Roles*, 57.

Salleh, A., 2017. *Ecofeminism as Politics*. London: Zed.

Sasser, J., 2018. *On Infertile Ground*. New York: New York University Press.

# BIBLIOGRAPHY

Save the Children, 2020. *The Global Girlhood Report, 2020.*

Schneider-Mayerson, M. and Ling Leong, K., Nov. 2020. 'Eco-reproductive concerns in the age of climate change.' *Climatic Change*, 163.

Schumacher, J. et al., 2010. 'Intimate partner violence and Hurricane Katrina: predictors and associated mental health outcomes.' *Violence and Victims*, 25(5).

Seager, J., 2009. 'Death By Degrees: Taking a Feminist Hard Look at the 2°C Climate Policy.' *Kvinder, Køn og Foraksning*, 3–4.

———, 2014. 'Disasters are gendered: what's new.' In: Z. Zommers and A. Singh, eds. *Reducing Disaster: Early Warning Systems for Climate Change.* New York: Springer, pp. 265–82.

———, 2020. 'Petro-Bromance: Masculinity Driving the Climate Crisis.' Presentation at 'Confronting the Climate Crisis: Feminist Pathways to Just and Sustainable Futures' webinar, The Consortium on Gender, Security and Human Rights.

Selm, K. et al., 2019. 'Educational Attainment predicts negative perceptions women have of their own climate change knowledge.' *PLOS One*, 14(1).

Seymour, N., 2013. *Strange Futures: Futurity, Empathy and the Queer Ecological Imagination.* Chicago, IL: University of Illinois Press.

———, 2017. 'Transgender Environments.' In: S. MacGregor, ed. *Routledge Handbook of Gender and Environment.* Abingdon, Oxon: Routledge.

Shiva, S., 1999. 'Monocultures, Monopolies, Myths and the Masculinization of Agriculture.' *Development*, 42(2).

Shiva, V., 12.11.13. 'Seed Monopolies, GMOs and Farmer Suicides in India—a response to Nature.' *Navdanya's Diary.*

Soper, K., 2020. *Post-Growth Living: For an Alternative Hedonism.* London: Verso.

Sotero, M., 2006. 'A Conceptual Model of Historical Trauma: Implications for Public Health Practice and Research.' *Journal of Health Disparities Research and Practice*, 1(1).

Spence, M., 2000. *Dispossessing the Wilderness: Indian Removal and the Making of the National Parks.* New York: OUP.

Taylor, D., 2014. 'The State of Diversity in Environmental Organizations.' *Green 2.0.*

Terry, G., 2009. 'No climate justice without gender justice: an overview of the issues.' *Gender and Development*, 17(1).

Thomas, E., 2017. *Domestic Violence and Sexual Assault in the Pacific Islander Community.* Asian/Pacific Islander Domestic Violence Research Project.

# BIBLIOGRAPHY

Thunberg, G. et al., 23.5.19. 'Young people have led the climate strikes. Now we need adults to join us too.' *The Guardian*.

Thuringer, C., 2016. 'Left Out and Behind: Fully Incorporating Gender into the Climate Discourse.' *New Security Beat*.

Titmuss, R., 1970. *The Gift Relationship*. London: Allen & Unwin.

Torsheim, T. et al., 2006. 'Cross-national variation of gender differences in adolescent subjective health in Europe and North America.' *Social Science and Medicine*, 62.

Tovar-Restrepo, M., 2017. 'Planning for climate change: REDD+SES as gender-responsive environmental action.' In: S. MacGregor, ed. *Routledge Handbook of Gender and Environment*. Abingdon, Oxon: Routledge.

Twigg, J. et al., July 2018. 'Disability inclusion and disaster risk reduction: overcoming barriers to progress.' Overseas Development Institute.

UN Women, 2013. *Climate Change, Disasters and Gender-Based Violence in the Pacific*.

UNDP, 2013. *Gender and Disaster Risk Reduction*.

———, 2016. *Gender and Sustainable Energy*.

———, 2017. *Gender and REDD+ Policy Brief*.

———, 2019. *Promoting Gender-Responsive Approaches to Natural Resource Management for Peace in North Kordofan, Sudan*.

UNFCCC, 2015. *The Paris Agreement*.

Unigwe, C., 5.10.19. 'Beyond the west, there are many Gretas.' *The Guardian*.

Union of Concerned Scientists, 2020. *Each Country's Share of CO2 Emissions*.

United Nations, 2020. *Analytical study on the promotion and protection of the rights of persons with disabilities in the context of climate change*.

University of Maine, 2019. *Climate Chronology*.

van Oldenborgh, G. et al., 2020. 'Attribution of Australian bushfire risk to anthropogenic climate change.' *Natural Hazards and Earth Sciences*, 69.

Wahlström, M. et al., eds, 2019. 'Protests for a future.' *Protest Institute*.

Wainaina, B., 2019. 'How to Write About Africa.' *Granta*, 92.

Wainwright, H. and Elliott, D., 2018. *The Lucas Plan*. Nottingham: Spokesman.

Wallace-Wells, D., 2019. *The Uninhabitable Earth*. London: Penguin.

Waring, M., 1988. *If Women Counted*. New York: Harper & Row.

———, 1999. *Counting for Nothing*. Toronto: University of Toronto Press.

Washington, H., 19.5.20. 'How environmental racism is fuelling the coronavirus pandemic.' Nature.com.

Weintrobe, S., 10.9.15. 'The new imagination in a culture of uncare.' Sallyweintrobe.com blog.

# BIBLIOGRAPHY

————, 2021. *Psychological Roots of the Climate Crisis: Neoliberal Exceptionalism and the Climate of Uncare*. New York: Bloomsbury Academic.

Weller, I., 2017. 'Gender dimensions of consumption.' In: S. MacGregor, ed. *Routledge Handbook of Gender and Environment*. Abingdon, Oxon: Routledge.

Westholm, L. and Arora-Jonsson, S., 2018. 'What room for politics and change in global climate governance? Addressing gender in co-benefits and safeguards.' *Environmental Politics*, 27(5).

Whittaker et al., 2015. 'Gendered responses to the 2009 Black Saturday bushfires in Victoria, Australia.' *Geographical Research*, 54(2).

WHO, 2014. 'Burden of Disease from Household Air Pollution for 2012.'

————, 2018. *The health and wellbeing of men in the WHO European Region: better health through a gender approach*.

Wintermayr, I., 2012. 'How can women benefit from green jobs? An ILO approach.' European Parliament.

Wolbring, G., 2009. 'A Culture of Neglect: Climate Discourse and Disabled People.' *M/C Journal*, 12(4).

Women's Budget Group, 2018. *Public Transport and Gender*.

————, 2020. *Creating a Caring Economy*.

World Economic Forum, 2020. *The Global Gender Gap Report*.

Wright, E., 19.2.20. 'Climate Change, Disability, and Eco-Ablism: why we need to be inclusive to save the planet.' *Uxdesign*.

Xiao, C. and McCright, A., 2017. 'Gender Differences in Environmental Concern.' In: S. MacGregor, ed. *Routledge Handbook of Gender and Environment*. Abingdon, Oxon: Routledge.

Zaretsky, E., 1976. *Capitalism, the Family and Personal Life*. London: Pluto.

# INDEX